EMILY PATTERSON

OTHER BOOKS
BY LISA ANNE SMITH

Vancouver Is Ashes:
The Great Fire of 1886 (2014)

Our Friend Joe:
The Joe Fortes Story (2012)

Travels with St. Roch:
A Book for Kids (2001)

Emily Patterson

THE HEROIC LIFE OF A
MILLTOWN NURSE

LISA ANNE SMITH

RONSDALE PRESS

EMILY PATTERSON
Copyright © 2017 Lisa Anne Smith

RONSDALE PRESS
3350 West 21st Avenue, Vancouver, B.C. Canada V6S 1G7
www.ronsdalepress.com

Typesetting: Julie Cochrane, in Granjon 11.5 pt on 15
Cover Design: Julie Cochrane
Cover Photo: Emily Patterson, c. 1880. Courtesy City of Vancouver Archives: P131.
    Photo: John M. White
Paper: Ancient Forest Friendly 55 lb. Enviro Book Antique White (FSC),
    100% post-consumer waste, totally chlorine-free and acid-free.

Ronsdale Press wishes to thank the following for their support of its publishing program: the Canada Council for the Arts, the Government of Canada, the British Columbia Arts Council, and the Province of British Columbia through the British Columbia Book Publishing Tax Credit program.

Library and Archives Canada Cataloguing in Publication

Smith, Lisa, 1959–, author
    Emily Patterson: the heroic life of a milltown nurse / Lisa Anne Smith.—First edition.

Includes bibliographical references and index.
Issued in print and electronic formats.
ISBN 978-1-55380-505-2 (softcover)
ISBN 978-1-55380-506-9 (ebook) / ISBN 978-1-55380-507-6 (pdf)

    1. Patterson, Emily, 1836-1909. 2. Nurses—British Columbia—Vancouver—Biography. 3. Vancouver (B.C.)—Biography. 4. Vancouver (B.C.)—History. I. Title.

RT37.P38S65 2017   610.73092   C2017-903922-9   C2017-903923-7

At Ronsdale Press we are committed to protecting the environment. To this end we are working with Canopy and printers to phase out our use of paper produced from ancient forests. This book is one step towards that goal.

Printed in Canada by Marquis Book Printing, Quebec

for Doug, Hillary and Bobby—
wishing you good health
and much happiness

CONTENTS

LIST OF ILLUSTRATIONS

The Midwife

"Emily, you will be frightened. I think it wise for you to go to your neighbour's house tonight." The midwife, an elderly woman rather stooped for her years, placed a full kettle of water upon the kitchen wood stove as she spoke. A nearby kerosene lantern softly illuminated her most prominent features—deep-set wrinkles and grey hair pulled back into a bun so taut it appeared to have been glued into place. Generally of a cheerful disposition, her expression was more serious than usual this evening. "Your mother's waters have broken and her baby is ready to be born."

Ten-year-old Emily, who had hovered nearby each time the midwife came calling, adamantly shook her head and insisted that she be allowed to stay.

"I want to help," she said with determination.

"Your mother will feel great pain while she works to give birth. You will find it upsetting."

"I will not," Emily assured her.

The midwife sighed. She had been making regular visits to the Thornton household for the past several weeks, just one in her lengthy list of homes with expectant mothers. She was perpetually weary after spending so many hours overseeing the delivery of babies—often in the dead of night—and she was too tired to argue.

"Very well," she responded, "you may stay. But be mindful that you do not get underfoot, for this delivery may take some time. I presume that your hands are well washed?"

Nodding that they were, Emily followed the midwife upstairs to her parents' bedroom, where Lucy Thornton lay upon a thick, straw-filled mattress that had recently been covered with newspaper and several additional layers of cotton ticking. By the light of the lantern, Emily could see that her mother's face was tight, her teeth gritted, eyes glazed. Seemingly oblivious to anyone else being in the room, she breathed heavily, sweat glistening on her forehead. Noticing a bowl of water and a small cloth by the bedside, Emily dipped the cloth into the water and gently dabbed her mother's brow.

"Look at the flowers I picked for you this morning, Mama," she said, pointing to a bright bouquet of daisies on the bureau. "Aren't they just lovely?"

The midwife glanced at her pocket watch. "You are doing well, Lucy. It won't be long now."

During the next hour, Emily looked on with growing apprehension as her mother's pain steadily increased.

"Is Mama all right?" she asked the midwife somewhat timidly.

"Of course she is." The midwife's voice had a warning tone.

Emily could feel her own inner turmoil rushing to the surface, but she knew that if she betrayed any fears she would be asked to leave. Well aware that childbirth was universally feared among mothers-to-be, the midwife kept up a steady stream of encouraging words. It was common knowledge that numerous complications could arise during labour, and there was never a guarantee that mother or baby would survive the ordeal. Keeping one hand over Lucy's abdomen, she held a pocket watch in the other to monitor the strength and timing of her contractions. Lucy's breath was now coming in short gasps.

"See that knotted bedsheet over there?" the midwife said to Emily, pointing to a sheet that had been draped over a nearby chair. "I want you to tie it firmly on the end of the bedpost and give the knotted end to your mother."

Emily did as she was told. As she looked on, her mother took hold of the knot and began to pull on it for all her worth. Minutes later, the midwife reported that baby's head was beginning to emerge. She put down the pocket watch and picked up a roll of clean cotton wadding.

"We must keep gentle control of the baby's head so that your mother does not tear," she explained to Emily. "Breathe and push, Lucy. Breathe and push."

"How much longer?" Lucy gasped.

"You're doing fine. Push, Mama," Emily urged, unconsciously repeating the midwife's commands. "Keep going!"

As Lucy gave one last guttural cry of pain, the midwife gently guided the baby the rest of the way out. Then, much to Emily's horror, she dangled it aloft by the feet and gave it a firm smack on the buttocks.

"What are you doing?" Emily exclaimed, as a crescendo of howls filled the bedroom.

"Helping baby to breathe," the midwife replied with the barest hint of a satisfied smile.

Her blow had produced the desired effect, for the baby continued to cry lustily, drawing great gasps of life-giving oxygen from the outside world. The midwife cheerfully announced that it was a girl.

"It's a girl, Mama!" Emily exclaimed in delight. "It's Josephine!" Josephine was a name that the Thorntons had decided upon weeks in advance.

"Would you like to cut the umbilical cord?" the midwife asked, drawing a pair of sterile scissors from a pot of water simmering on the hearth.

"Will that hurt Mama . . . or Josephine?" Emily asked tentatively.

"Of course not, the umbilical has no nerves, but I can do it if you wish."

Emily resolutely shook her head and took hold of the scissors. She carefully made the cut, noting how easy it was. While tiny Josephine Thornton continued to cry, the midwife wrapped her in soft clean sheeting and laid her in the bed alongside a tired but now beaming Lucy.

"We must keep mother and baby warm," she reminded Emily. "This fire will need regular replenishment."

"I'll make sure of that," Emily answered firmly.

The midwife smiled. "You did a good job, Emily," she said. "I believe that someday you will make a fine midwife yourself."

Emily gazed at baby Josephine, so impossibly tiny—her skin the colour of rose pink—already a thick growth of dark hair matted against her head. As the midwife had warned, the delivery of a baby was an unnerving experience, but Emily felt proud and exhilarated to have taken part in it. She had yearned to have a sibling again. For so many years she had waited and she now believed that there could not be a happier, prouder sister in all of Lincoln County—perhaps even the entire state of Maine—than Emily Susan Branscombe.

CHAPTER 1

Nurse in Training

Emily's birth was not unlike that of Josephine's. The daughter of John and Lucy Branscombe, she had been born at home in Bath, Lincoln County, Maine, on July 22, 1836, with a midwife in attendance. Lucy Branscombe, also a Bath native, was an industrious and hardworking housewife of staunchly Christian principles, where helpfulness and obedience were not only expected but demanded. Clad in her freshly laundered pinafore and high leather boots, Emily would help with the most mundane of household chores—from sweeping the hearth to scrubbing the soil off newly dug potatoes. By the young age of three, she was already tasked with carrying small parcels as she dutifully followed her mother and baby brother John in his perambulator about the Front Street marketplace.

But on May 19, 1840, Emily's well-ordered world was shattered when her father, John Branscombe, died at the age of twenty-eight. Death was an unfamiliar concept for a little girl not quite four years of age. All Emily knew was that she and her grieving mother, clad in black, had to make a lengthy walk behind a slow-moving cart to the Maple Grove Cemetery on Bath's outskirts, where they would watch the wooden box that contained John Branscombe's mortal remains lower slowly into the ground. She had gently been told that Papa "was safe in heaven," but that did not seem to remedy the empty feeling that lingered in her heart. Death would visit the Branscombes yet again on March 3, 1842, this time for Emily's brother John. By then, Emily had begun to understand that death was to be expected—a grim reaper, whose random choice of victims spared no boundaries or sympathies. Headstones throughout the cemetery told the story—weather-beaten monuments etched with the names of Bath citizens from all walks of life. Some individuals had been blessed with well-advanced years, while others were not far out of childhood. Then there were those tiny souls who had barely left their mother's wombs—their graves often guarded by angels of stone, gently gazing down.

Lucy Branscombe married the town blacksmith, Joshua Thornton, on May 12, 1842, little more than two months after the death of her son. However uncertain she was about having a new father, Emily knew that her mother had been sad and lonely, and she hoped that this second marriage would rekindle her happiness. The Thorntons lived in a house on the corner of South and Washington Street, within easy walking distance of the town centre and riverfront. Most advantageous was the close proximity of the South Grammar School—a mere one-block walk from her home. Emily excelled at her studies, taking particular interest in science and geography. She was a voracious reader, stealing away as time allowed to whatever remote corner of the Thornton household she could find to immerse herself in a book.

Emily longed for another sibling to ease the sorrow of losing her

Emily's birth record

brother but would have to wait several years before the arrival of her half-sister Josephine in 1846. Josephine's birth was followed by that of Joshua Junior in 1848 and John, named in honour of Emily's dearly departed father and brother, in 1850. Emily had been present at every delivery, gaining more knowledge in the skills of midwifery while assisting in whatever way she was able. She learned about the "absolute necessity" of handwashing to avoid infections like the dreaded puerperal fever, how horrific complications could occur by improperly administering ergot of rye to hasten contractions, how postpartum hemorrhage could result if the placenta had not been fully expelled from the uterus. Emily asked questions and even wrote detailed notes on everything that she observed, to peruse repeatedly in her spare time. As she grew older, all manner of medically related topics became her fascination. She would learn the rudimentary skills of dealing with a fracture or bringing down a fever. She would rush to the scene with clean water and bandaging if Joshua skinned his knee or John needed an oatmeal poultice after his latest encounter with poison ivy. Her ministrations did not go unnoticed by her mother.

"You have the makings of being our new Granny Lombard!" Lucy told her with a smile.

"I do wish that I could have known her!" Emily replied.

Sarah "Granny" Lombard was legendary among old-timers of Bath—a woman who had served both as midwife and doctor in the town and the surrounding area through much of the eighteenth and early nineteenth century. Sarah had been on call day or night, sometimes riding on horseback for miles along narrow, thickly forested bridal paths when word came that her services were required. Emily often found herself imagining what it would have been like to be the brave and heroic Sarah, to tend to patients' wants and needs and feel the immense satisfaction of making them better.

➤✦

By the time she reached her early twenties, Emily had grown into an attractive young woman who enjoyed Bath's society life, dances and parties, but she also took pleasure in solitude or the company of a few close friends. She did not partake of alcohol—her Christian upbringing having instilled her with a firm belief in abstinence—a stance widely embraced across the entire state of Maine. The Thorntons, like many others, were ardent supporters of the "Maine Law"—an 1851 state-wide prohibition on the manufacture and sale of liquor, which had been the longtime vision of Neal Dow, mayor of Bath's neighbouring city Portland. Dow's argument was that rampant consumption of alcohol was having a detrimental effect on the state of Maine's industry and productivity. The only way to reverse the alarming trend was through strict government control. Yet despite the prohibition, there were still those few individuals who managed to flout the law of the land. Whenever Emily came across these "wayward souls," as her mother called them, she would more often than not smile at their flirtations, while inwardly reminding herself never to fall prey to such bravado. Over time she came to notice that men off the ships, newly landed from places afar, were particularly notorious for their drinking habits. One summer morning, an encounter with one such "wayward soul" would mark a dramatic turning point in her life.

It was a beautiful day. Having finished her regular round of morning chores, Emily decided that she would put on one of her finer dresses and stroll into town for a cup of tea and a good read of a new medical book. She had long finished her childhood schooling years but yearned to begin studies in the field of nursing. Word from overseas told of a remarkable English woman by the name of Florence Nightingale who had administered care to soldiers wounded on the battlefields of Crimea. Florence Nightingale had taken her training in Germany, and while Emily had little hope of travelling that great a distance, another medical institution much closer at hand had caught her attention: the Geneva Medical College of New York. Founded in 1834, Geneva Medical College had seen a number of graduate physicians, and in 1849, one of those graduates happened to be Dr. Elizabeth Blackwell—the first female doctor in the United States. While no school dedicated to the field of nursing existed in the country at present, Emily could not help being inspired and optimistic thanks to the groundbreaking career path of Dr. Blackwell of the Geneva Medical College.

A youthful Emily, c. 1857.

The Kennebec River sparkled invitingly in the morning sun as Emily strolled down Front Street towards the centre of town. Bath was a thriving port and industrial hub for the construction of wooden sailing vessels on the Kennebec, and Front Street was a-bustle with mariners coming and going. Fishmongers, blacksmiths, grocers, bakers, wheel-wrights and other business folk plied their trades alongside tall schoo-ners, square-rigged brigantines and sleek clippers drifting idly at an-chor in the Kennebec docklands. Great stacks of cut lumber—pine, maple, beech, elm and the much prized oak—lay in waiting for production at shipbuilding facilities up and downriver. As always, Emily found herself enjoying the pungent smell of the wood. It had been floated downriver from the profusion of vast, verdant forests throughout the rain-lashed state of Maine. The wood was Bath's lifeblood, providing a wealth of raw materials for the shipbuilding industry.

An hour later as Emily sat alone reading and enjoying her tea in the Sagadahock House hotel lobby, a rough-looking man sidled up to her in hopes of making her acquaintance. He smelled of rum—still readily available if one knew where to look—and he clearly had not had a change of clothes in recent times.

"Would you like some company, m'lady?"

Emily was absorbed in her studies and did not want to be interrupted.

"Not today, thank you," she replied casually, barely glancing up from her book. "I'm waiting for someone."

"Well, someone as attractive as you shouldn't have to wait alone," he chortled, pulling up a chair opposite.

"Do *not* sit down. That chair is spoken for." Emily's firm voice and firmer glare made the man hesitate. In the same moment, another man approached from a nearby table, having heard the exchange.

"That's enough of that, Wilkins. Back to the ship where you belong, or you'll be in the brig!"

Wilkins sheepishly left the tea room and the second man smiled at Emily.

"Apologies for that behaviour, miss. He's been at sea too long, I'm afraid."

"I could have handled that situation myself, you know," Emily retorted, eager to return to her reading.

"A little waif like yourself? I'm not so sure."

"You underestimate me, sir. For what I may lack in stature, I more than make up for judging sobriety. Your Wilkins was so drunk that if the situation warranted, I believe I could have pushed him to the floor with a tip of the finger."

The man laughed. "You are a good judge of sobriety," he agreed. "Now would that judgment permit me to join you at this table for a cup of tea and a bit of civilized conversation, or is that book of yours too riveting to put aside for a half hour?"

For the first time, Emily took a closer look at the gentleman standing before her. He was of average height, perhaps ten years her senior, tidily dressed, with a trimmed beard. He smelled faintly of sea spray and pipe tobacco, and his eyes spoke somewhat of sadness. Despite her continued mild annoyance over the unexpected interruptions, Emily could not deny the pleasurable sense of being flattered.

"Very well," she sighed, closing her book. "You may join me . . . but bear in mind that I must be leaving soon."

CHAPTER 2

A Captain's Wife

A few months after their chance encounter in the Sagadahock House tea room, Emily Branscombe and Captain John Peabody Patterson were engaged to be married. Like any typical mother, Lucy Thornton fretted over the well-being of her daughter. Emily tried to allay her fears, gently explaining that Captain Patterson was a respectable and trustworthy gentleman, of "good country stock," well-bred and hard-working. Born about 1826 in New Hampshire to John and Cordelia Patterson, he was the eldest of thirteen siblings and had been raised in Pittston—a farming community some twenty miles north of Bath on the Kennebec. At an early age, young John had gone to sea, gradually working his way up the ranks and eventually attaining his captaincy. He had travelled all over the world's trade routes, shipping lumber and ivory and, for a time, had been commissioned to the slave trade, transporting Negro slaves to New Orleans.

"The slave trade!" Lucy had exclaimed.

"He hated it," Emily quickly interjected. "He had no part in the treatment of the slaves . . . he'd simply been hired to transport them, and he definitely didn't like what he saw. He said it was terrible."

"As a sea captain, he should have taken it upon himself to refuse the transport of human cargo."

Emily decided that she would not pursue the matter, tactfully going on to describe how her future husband had taken training in carpentry with hopes to settle to a more domesticated life. He had married a woman named Maria, who gave birth to his son, Edward Everett Patterson, in Lynn, Massachusetts. But then Maria had died and John Patterson had found himself alone with a young boy and nowhere to turn but back to his family in Pittston. Leaving Edward to be looked after by his parents and siblings, he returned to the sea, working the lucrative mail run up and down the eastern seaboard. But he grieved for Maria and sorely missed Edward, not having any real sense of future purpose—until the point when he met Emily.

"After we're married he'll take Edward and me to China!" Emily said, her eyes shining.

"Emily," her mother sighed. "You're so young . . . barely finished school. You had hopes to become a nurse."

"I'll be fine, Mama. And I *will* be a nurse . . . to John and Edward. They need me and I know that this is right for me."

Emily and John were married in New York City and set sail for China soon afterward. In the months that followed, Emily adapted well to her role as captain's wife and stepmother to young Edward. As she expected, seasickness had troubled her at times and there were days when she longed to step ashore at the nearest port—any port. There was little that one could do to alleviate the miserable condition in rough seas, but following her husband's advice, she found some degree of relief by seating herself mid-ship and taking in long steady breaths of fresh air. Then there were the halcyon days when tropical sunshine and steady breezes combined for ideal sailing and the crewmen would point out dolphins leaping in the ship's wake or a whale breaching on the distant horizon. Emily would assist Edward with his studies or immerse herself in yet more research of her own. John Patterson, keenly aware of his new wife's interest in health care, had purchased several books for her in New York, and she spent many a shipboard hour absorbed in works such as Charles Williams's *Principles of Medicine* and John Erichsen's *The Science and Art of Surgery*.

Recognizing that the crewmen had work of their own to carry on with, Emily seldom engaged in anything more than passing conversation with them. It was only when her husband happened to mention one young deckhand aboard that she thought it best to intervene.

"I'm worried about our man Burt Thomas," John told her one evening as they were finishing dinner in their forward cabin. "He's something of a simple chap but lately he seems to be quite listless . . . totally lacking in energy. Could you have a look at him?"

"Of course," Emily replied. "Bring him here."

John briefly left, returning with a young man who appeared to be little more than sixteen years of age. Emily immediately noted that his eyes were dark and sunken, his face as pallid as chalk. His blond hair was dry and scruffy, wisps of it dangling about his ears like corkscrews. Asking him to roll up his sleeves and trousers she found that his arms and legs were swollen and covered with red spots of variable size.

"Burt, would you open your mouth for me, please?" she asked gently.

Burt clamped his mouth shut and shook his head no vigorously.

"Do as you're told, Mr. Thomas," John said sternly.

Burt reluctantly opened his mouth. Emily had to quickly check herself to stifle a gasp. Several of the lad's teeth were showing signs of rot and his gums were oozing blood. Predictably his breath was foul. Emily looked knowingly from her husband to her patient.

"What we have here," she said, "is a case of scurvy."

"Scurvy!" John thundered. "How can that be? Scurvy has been preventable for years! We have a good variety of food stocks on board. How could this happen?"

"It can happen," Emily said, "if proper diet is not followed. Burt, what do you eat at mealtimes?"

"Porridge an' fish," he replied.

"Only porridge and fish day after day? No pickled cabbage . . . or dried apple and cranberry . . . or fried potato?"

He shook his head again, appearing defiant. "My teeth hurts every time I chew. So I only eat food I don't hafta chew."

Emily and her husband exchanged significant glances.

"Well, what about lime water?" Emily asked. "Do you ever drink lime water?"

"Tastes bad! I don't like it!"

"Can you show me the teeth that hurt?"

"I don't wanna get 'em pulled!" Burt said shrilly, tears starting to brim in his eyes. "It hurts gettin' a tooth pulled!"

"But young man," John said with a warning tone, "if you don't get this dealt with you will become very sick indeed."

After briefly putting her index finger to her lips—a simple motion that Emily often used to encourage her outspoken husband to calm down—she went to a nearby cupboard and lifted out a wooden box. Digging amidst the straw inside she produced a glass bottle marked "Chloroform" and a cylindrical vessel with a hose and face mask attached.

"Burt," she said gently, "of course you are scared. A toothache hurts. I have some things here that will help you feel much better and you will feel very little pain while we get rid of those troublesome teeth."

Burt looked doubtful but agreed to sit in a chair. Upon her query as to which teeth hurt, he pointed out two upper molars.

"Yes, those look sore indeed," she told him. She could easily see that Burt must have been in considerable pain for days. The molars were eroded with decay. She opened a bottle of chloroform and poured a fine stream of the colourless liquid into the vessel.

"Now Burt," she continued. "When I put this mask over your mouth and nose I want you to breathe deep and slow. You will start to feel relaxed and maybe even a little sleepy."

Emily had deliberately kept hidden a small pair of metal forceps while she performed the sedation. However fearful he was, Burt was cooperating. As the chloroform took effect, his head drooped and his jaw slackened. Quick as a flash she removed the mask and positioned the forceps around the first tooth. Stiffening her slender frame, hands firmly clamped against the metal tool, she gave a sharp twist to the right and left, followed by a hard yank. Burt moaned as she successfully extracted the first tooth but remained somewhat oblivious as she relocated the forceps for the second tooth. Two more twists, another hard yank and both of the rotten teeth were out.

"Well done, Burt!" she praised. "It's all over!"

If Burt had heard her he gave little indication as he continued to moan. Blood was flowing freely from the extraction points and Emily deftly staunched them with thick wads of cotton. John dutifully stood by during the entire operation ready to provide assistance if needed and was once again grateful that she didn't request it. He had watched his wife perform a tooth pulling before and confessed that he was always rendered "weak at the knees" by the process. As Burt slowly regained his awareness, Emily encouraged him to take hold of the cotton wadding and press it down firmly on the sockets.

"To make the blood clot," she told him. "I will give you more wadding so that you can do it yourself until the bleeding stops. Then we'll have you rinse with salty water."

Her final course of treatment was to supply her patient with a small bottle of "Oil of Cloves," to be used if other teeth began to ache.

"Now that solves one problem but the other is up to you," she said firmly. "Starting today I want you to eat apples and cranberries with all of your meals. We'll ask the cook to soften them up for you in some hot water. Will you do that for us?"

Nodding that he would, Burt eased out of the chair, clutching his wads of cotton.

"I'll want to keep a check on you, Burt," she added as he slunk away.

"Scurvy!" John muttered, shaking his head. "How ridiculous is that?"

"I suppose I had better keep a closer eye on your crewmen," Emily replied with a smile. "If only he had sprinkled paprika on his fish at dinnertime he might have saved himself much grief."

"Paprika?" her husband asked.

"Yes," she replied with a smile. "Paprika is dried, ground red pepper. A scurvy fighter if there ever was one!"

＞＜

There had been much talk aboard ship of the unrest in Chinese ports due to the Opium War. In the early months of 1858, parts of the city of Canton were under siege and Captain Patterson had chosen to avoid calling there.

"What's opium, Emily?" Edward had wanted to know during one of their many study sessions together.

"Opium," Emily replied sternly, "is a substance derived from a poppy flower."

"Why do you sound so angry?" Edward asked, not exactly sure what "substance" and "derived" meant.

"I'm angry because I don't like the trouble that opium has caused here in China . . . all over the world, for that matter." Emily explained to her stepson that the violence happening in Canton all stemmed from the opium trade. It had been difficult to fathom that the innocent-looking milky resin that oozed from cuts made to unripe poppy seeds could cause nations to go to war. After being air-dried in open boxes, the resin turned into a granular substance called opium—a powerful drug which was useful in controlling pain when correctly prescribed by doctors. But opium was highly addictive and its abuse had run rampant in many parts of the world, including China. Prior to the 1830s, Canton had been the only Chinese port open to Western merchants. Chinese officials did not want Western ideas or influence corrupting their traditional beliefs. British and American merchants, desperately seeking to break down trade barriers, had decided to flood the Canton market with the one product that increasing numbers of Chinese citizens wanted—opium. By the late 1830s, a British physician practising in Canton estimated that twelve million Chinese people were addicted to opium.

"The Chinese emperor tried to stop opium from being brought into China," Emily explained to Edward, "but warships had come from Britain, France, Russia and our own country to fight for control of the ports."

"Who is winning?" Edward asked innocently, always fascinated when the subject of war came up.

"It's difficult to say if anybody wins when there is war and people are suffering, Edward," Emily sighed. "But the ports are reopening and it appears that China has lost the battle . . . so I suppose that we are winning."

><

By the summer of 1859, Emily, John and Edward were back in New York, where John made overtures to the lumber industry and Emily settled into planning for the arrival of her first child. After carefully weighing the teachings of her Christian upbringing against modern-day science, Emily had reluctantly decided to opt for the use of chloroform.

"It worked so well with Burt," she reasoned to her husband. "I'm certain that God never intended for us mothers-to-be to suffer needlessly."

The relatively new practice of using anaesthesia during childbirth was still something of a contentious choice for many women. There were those who felt that pain was a God-given directive, not to be interfered with. God's words were spoken in Genesis 3:16: ". . . in sorrow thou shalt bring forth children." Then there was the testimonial of Queen Victoria, notoriously fearful of labour, who had requested chloroform for the birth of her son Prince Leopold in 1853. Following the trouble-free delivery, she had described her experience in glowing terms: "That blessed chloroform . . . soothing, quieting and delightful beyond measure." While Emily would not quite be able to say that childbirth was "soothing and quieting," she and John were delighted to welcome their baby daughter, Abbie Lowell Patterson, into the world on October 14, 1859.

New York was a crowded metropolis of over eight hundred thousand inhabitants, almost half of whom had emigrated from foreign lands. The streets of Manhattan Island's central business district were jammed with pedestrian and vehicular traffic. Conditions were generally filthy—the odours of sewage, manure, coal fires and local butcheries permeated the air, and poverty amidst certain circles was unmistakable. New York was burgeoning with children. Census records taken a decade earlier showed that fully one third of the city's population was under the age of fifteen. Children who had lost their parents were sent to New York, as were children turned loose by parents unable or unwilling to fend for them. Children who had run away from drunkenness and physical abuse made their way to New York. Over the course of years, New York had inadvertently become a perceived safe haven for thousands of young people. Some would find their way to orphanages or be placed aboard one of the newly emerging "Orphan Trains" which transported them to adoptive homes in rural communities. Many would simply live on the streets, scratching out a meagre existence selling newspapers or matches or rags to stay alive.

The Pattersons travelled by train to Bath for a Christmas reunion and there was much to catch up on. Emily sat in the Thornton parlour, trying to relate the past few years of adventures—both high and low—to her mother.

"It's terrible, Mama. My heart breaks for them," she said, recalling the pathetic little New York waifs that she had seen and often treated for everything from influenza to frostbite.

Josephine, Joshua and John could be heard outside, laughingly throwing snowballs at each other.

"My heart breaks for us all," Lucy replied sombrely, placing a teacup down upon a wooden trolley. "There is talk of war and life is changing here in Bath . . . in all of Maine, for that matter. I fear that soon there will be more bloodshed."

Lucy Thornton was well justified with her concerns. A groundswell movement to abolish slavery was rapidly gaining momentum, with Northern states strongly in favour of abolition and Southern states strongly opposed. On October 16, 1859, abolitionist John Brown and a small band of men had attempted to capture a federal weapons arsenal at Harper's Ferry, Virginia—their plan being to arm as many slaves as possible with muskets so that they could mount a massive revolt. When some of Brown's men were killed, the raid was quickly subdued by local townspeople and the militia. Brown and four of his colleagues were hanged for treason on December 2. To Confederates in the Southern states, the events at Harper's Ferry added fuel to their desire to secede from the union and form a separate nation. To northern Unionists like Emily and John Patterson, John Brown was a martyr to the cause. Public sentiment ran high that his fight to end slavery would not be in vain.

Emily could see that her husband was restless. John Patterson sat up late many nights, deep in thought. She knew that his days facilitating the slave trade troubled him deeply, yet he had no desire to go to war over the issue. Nor did he wish to return to the long-haul days at sea.

"What are we going to do, John?" Emily asked him firmly one evening, not long into the New Year. She had asked him to take her to the Sagadahock House for tea, and she watched while he absently stirred his teaspoon in the steaming beverage, much preoccupied.

"John!" she repeated. "You've said very little for days. I'd like to know what you are thinking."

"I'm thinking this tearoom isn't as crowded as it used to be," John replied.

"There's more to it than that. Please talk to me about it."

John frowned and reluctantly submitted to Emily's inquiries, launching into a tirade of all his misgivings. He had wanted to settle down and build a home for Emily, Edward and Abbie. His plan all along had been to take up employment with the lumber industry—perhaps even establish his own sawmill. But Bath, like other Maine townships, had begun to experience an economic downturn. Rumblings of civil war in the South had resulted in a general shift in demand from wooden to metal-hulled ships. The glory days of Bath's wooden shipbuilding industry and Maine's lumber industry as a whole were on the wane.

"I'd like to go west," he said finally. "Word has it that there is good harvestable timber up around Washington Territory and lots of it. Wide, open country with plenty of game . . . tillable soil . . . just the right mix of sun and rainfall. . . . We could make our way to San Francisco, replenish our finances and continue on from there."

John looked at her squarely. "It would mean saying goodbye to your family and friends, perhaps for a very long time . . . perhaps forever."

"Perhaps not," she replied simply. "I've been raised to be optimistic and besides, it's the duty of a captain's wife to follow her husband, wherever he leads, don't you agree?"

CHAPTER 3

To the West

John and Emily discussed a number of options for their relocation westward. Connections could be made via the Portland & Kennebec Railway to Boston or New York, from whence they could embark on a steamer around Cape Horn. The time-honoured, southerly route around the bottom of South America—once an arduous, five- to seven-month journey by sail—had been shortened with the advent of steamships. Passenger vessels departed regularly from the Boston and New York dockyards. However, no amount of increased power by steam could compensate for the notorious weather conditions of the cape, and many ships continued to be lost, despite their technological advancements. Recalling her previous experiences with Cape Horn's ferocity while travelling to and from China, Emily had no particular desire to revisit the region.

A second option was to follow in the footsteps of those thousands of hardy souls from all walks of life who had chosen to make their way overland to the West. In earlier years, this legendary exodus meant enduring long months on the trail, courting inhospitable conditions ranging from dry desert plains to flash floods to bone-chilling cold in the snow-laden Sierra Nevadas. Thousands of lives had been claimed by cholera, typhoid, dysentery and tuberculosis. Heatstroke, tainted water and rattlesnake bites had also taken their grim toll. Hostilities with native tribes, while infrequent, had led to wariness and mistrust. By 1860, trail life still had its perils but substantial improvements were happening. It was now possible to travel from New York City to St. Joseph, Missouri, in the space of a week by a rail and riverboat network, effectively covering nearly half the distance to the West Coast.

Then there was the intriguing and relatively new third option for the Pattersons. On January 28, 1855, the first through train of the Panama Railway had made its forty-seven-mile journey over completed track from the Atlantic to the Pacific side of the Panama isthmus. The railway, painstakingly built over five years at an astronomical cost of eight million dollars, was a wondrous feat of engineering—enabling passengers to travel in comfort and style over a region that had once been mostly swampland and dense mangrove forest. The human cost had been much higher, with over twelve thousand workers succumbing to malaria and yellow fever in the mosquito-infested construction zones. Accessing the western side of North America via the Panama Railway was an expensive option with individual tickets priced at twenty-five dollars in gold, but the railway cut off many additional weeks of sea travel. In the end, John Patterson's proposal was a simple one.

"Fancy a journey by rail?" he asked.

Emily replied with a simple and emphatic, "Yes!"

John Patterson travelled to New York in advance to put some of the packed trunks into storage and to book passage with the shipping and Panama Railway agencies. Many members of the Thornton and Patterson families came to the Bath train station one early February morning to bid farewell to Emily and the children.

"I'm very proud of you!" Lucy told her daughter, as they exchanged final hugs of farewell. "You are strong and you will do just fine."

"I plan to, Mama," Emily said.

Within brief days, the Pattersons were onboard ship steaming southward for Aspinwall, the Atlantic terminus of the Panama Railway.

✢

Clutching Abbie in one arm and holding tightly to Edward's hand, Emily found herself surrounded by loud and persistent streets vendors as she followed her husband through the hot and crowded Aspinwall marketplace.

"Come my lub, buy dis bottle Jamaky rum, brot it from dar meself!"

"Here honey, hab one dese big pine-apples! Dey de best!"

The city of Aspinwall, if one could call it a city, had sprung up almost overnight on Manzanillo Island during the Panama Railway's construction. With the exception of Panama Railway employees, most of the local residents were Jamaicans, natives of mixed African ancestry or the indigenous Panamanians—dark of skin and often clad in the flimsiest of attire. Shops, groggeries, billiard halls and gambling dens competed for space along the main cobblestone thoroughfares. Living quarters ranged from whitewashed wooden hotels and cottages to simple clapboard shanties built atop pilings. Wooden plank sidewalks criss-crossed the neighbouring bog lands, which apparently served as refuse locations for all manner of decaying animal and vegetable matter. A noxious stench lingered in the air and Emily noticed several women passersby discreetly holding handkerchiefs to their noses. If both her hands hadn't been occupied, she would have done likewise. Aspinwall was a cesspool of filth.

"Some of those buildings were pre-assembled in Maine," John explained to Emily, "then disassembled and shipped here for rebuilding piece by piece. Quite ingenious, wouldn't you say?"

"Yes, quite!" Emily nodded, desperately trying to disguise her growing desire to retch.

The train ride across the Panama isthmus was much better. Foremost for Emily was the heady realization that over thirteen thousand nautical miles and months of travel by sea were being reduced to a mere six or seven hours. The passenger cars were somewhat rustic with their cane-bottomed seats and blinds in place of windows, but the fresh jungle air was glorious and the view changed with every turn along the circuitous route. Vegetation was luxuriant with dense masses of flowering and fruit-bearing trees and shrubs. Villagers in the whistle-stop communities of Gatun and Gorgona emerged from huts built of reed and palm thatch to hawk their wares of bread and eggs to passengers when the train arrived. Emily purchased a loaf of bread and broke off pieces for her family to munch as they continued their journey.

It was evening by the time the train arrived in Panama, but there was little to be seen of the legendary city at the crossroad between the Pacific and Atlantic oceans. Darkness came early in these parts and with Panama Bay being too shallow to accommodate large, ocean-going vessels, small steamers were employed to shuttle passengers from the railway terminus wharf to their pre-booked San Francisco-bound ships lying at anchor offshore. Emily watched with some degree of apprehension as the trunks containing all of her family's worldly possessions were craned aboard a luggage scow. The wharf was jammed with passengers from all walks of life—tail-coated businessmen with their elegantly dressed wives, youthful lads in coveralls and tarnished hobnail boots, wizened gold miners absently chewing tobacco, mothers desperately trying to keep together excited gaggles of children—all

Panama Railway Summit Station etching, 1855.

eagerly awaiting their turn to climb aboard the shuttle steamers. Emily could barely distinguish the many languages being spoken among the crowd—English, French, German, Spanish, Italian, Cantonese, all interspersed with an unintelligible babble of local dialect. It was plain to see that the Panama Railway had been a success story as far as collecting people from the four corners of the earth and swiftly dispatching them from ocean to ocean.

Three weeks after their departure from New York, the Pattersons arrived in San Francisco. Emily watched from the passenger deck in fascination while the cliff heads of the legendary Golden Gate entrance to San Francisco harbour gradually emerged through the morning mist. San Francisco in 1860 was a city still reeling from the after-effects of the California Gold Rush. The boom years of 1848 and 1849 had seen the city's population burgeon from fewer than one thousand inhabitants to over twenty-five thousand. Although the gold mines were long exhausted, their glittering yield continued to cast its indelible stamp upon the bayside metropolis. San Francisco was a boisterous, multi-ethnic city now of fifty-seven thousand—its expansive bay a major port of call where passengers often waited for days to be given clearance to disembark.

Edward was restless and fuming after their ship had laid at anchor for a third day, tantalizingly close to shore.

"When can we get off?"

"I'm sure it will be soon, Edward," Emily sighed, admittedly more than eager to descend the gangway and stand upon solid ground herself. The Pattersons had travelled Second Class on each leg of their sea-going journey. While not as filthy and crowded as the facilities in Steerage, those of Second Class were not much of an improvement—tight, compact cabins with narrow beds, a tiny wash basin and not much else. Meals served up in the dining room had been simple fare—hot porridge in the morning, followed by soups boiled up with dehydrated vegetables and salt beef, sea biscuits, hot coffee and tea. The one saving grace of waiting to disembark was that the Pattersons could venture up on deck and breathe deeply of the fresh harbour air—a welcome relief from the seemingly constant odour of smoke, vomit and urine which permeated quarters below.

On the morning of the fourth day, Emily awoke to the welcome sound of the ship's engines rumbling in preparation for docking. Within the hour, the Pattersons had disembarked into the busy streets of San Francisco's District 3—a northeast waterfront neighbourhood largely comprising dockyards, rooming houses and storage buildings. The first order of the day was to find temporary living quarters, as close to the docks as possible for easy transport of luggage. John Patterson went off alone and hurried back several minutes later, announcing that he had secured a room in a lodging house not too far away on Pacific Street. The next step was to hire a horse and dray to haul the weighty trunks up the road. Carrying the increasingly heavy Abbie in one arm, Emily was much relieved to learn that she would not have to climb the steep rise leading up the barren reaches of Telegraph Hill as she, John and Edward trudged behind the dray. John pointed out the wooden semaphore station which had been constructed upon its summit in 1850 to signal the identification of approaching ships to San Francisco residents. A massive Star-Spangled Banner rippled in the breeze atop the station's tall flagpole. The two adjoining wooden arms that could be swung into position to relay various messages in semaphore were no longer in use.

"The semaphore station became redundant only three years after it was built, with the invention of the electromagnetic telegraph," John explained.

"I would have liked to have seen it in operation," Emily remarked.

"That was the problem. In a thick fog, the arms could not be seen . . . and from what I have been told, the fog can get very thick at the harbour entrance."

It was hard for Emily to imagine that fog could ever exist on such a glorious spring day.

>‹

The Pattersons' Pacific Street lodging house was somewhat crowded, but a marked improvement from living quarters aboard ship. Over the ensuing days, Emily did her best to create a homelike atmosphere, lining up the trunks for use as tables and chairs and remaking the beds that had been provided with her own clean linens. There was a communal kitchen area with two large cast iron stoves, a massive pantry and several dining tables. Coal and ice were delivered daily and a wide selection of fresh fruits, vegetables and fish were readily available from nearby shops. For all intents and purposes, the lodging house seemed like a little piece of San Francisco paradise to Emily, but she was soon to learn that the location had its seamier side. Several blocks of Pacific Avenue and surrounding streets were home to San Francisco's notorious Barbary Coast—an enclave for prostitutes, criminals and all manner of illicit activity. Emily soon came to know her lodging-house neighbours, John and Rebecca Park, who were well familiar with the area's reputation. John Park was a San Francisco City Hall police officer, and it was not long before Rebecca would confide to Emily her underlying misgivings over her husband's profession.

"It's a city of vigilante justice!" she warned one day, as the two women sat drinking tea in the kitchen. "You must take care not to know too much or see too much. San Francisco has never been the same since the gold rush waned. Everyone is trying to make ends meet . . . any way they can!"

"I don't expect we're going to stay here very long," Emily replied. "My husband wants to continue north, as soon as our financial situation is healthy again."

As the women conversed, their teacups began to gently rattle upon the table and a low rumbling echoed through the room.

"Gracious, what is happening?" Emily exclaimed.

"That," chuckled Rebecca when the rattling subsided, "was just another of our small earthquakes. They happen often so you'd better get used to them."

San Francisco, as Emily learned from Rebecca, was delicately balanced over a geologically unsound foundation. Much of the city's original downtown core had been built above the reclaimed Yerba Buena

Cove marshlands. That fact, coupled with San Francisco's close proximity to the San Andreas Fault, resulted in alarmingly frequent earth
tremors which rattled windows and caused wooden structures to creak
and groan atop their earthen foundations.

"Well," Emily sighed, finishing her tea and lifting a stirring Abbie
out of her cot. "I can see that we shall have an interesting time here!"

Late one evening, Emily was preparing to settle herself in for bed when
she heard the unmistakable sound of gunfire. Several shots rang out in
the alley next to the lodging house, quickly followed by the thud of
running feet. The silence that followed was short-lived. A man's guttural cries of pain reverberated in the air. With her husband attending to
some business down on the docks, Emily knew that the advisable thing
to do would be to wait and let someone else deal with the situation. But
there was no audible sound of hallways doors opening or anyone making the effort to provide assistance. After checking to see that Edward
and Abbie had not been awoken by the noise, she hurried downstairs,
lantern in hand, to find two rough-looking men half carrying, half
dragging a third man with a bloodied leg into the ground-floor lobby.

"He's been shot!" one of them cried upon seeing Emily.

Emily glanced quickly about. The ground floor of the lodging house
was a quiet place after hours with little in the way of furnishings than a
long table which doubled as a desk, a single chair, a divan with two
velveteen pillows and an umbrella stand.

"Lay him down here," Emily directed, pointing to the table. "Then
one of you go and find a doctor."

The wounded man actually managed to ease himself upon the table.
Bidding him to lie still while the remaining man kept watch, Emily ran
upstairs, returning minutes later with her arms full of supplies hastily
gathered together in a bedsheet.

"What are your names?" she asked the victim's companion, at the
same time emptying the bedsheet of its contents onto the nearby divan.

"I'm Jim," he replied shakily. "This is . . . Pete."

"Good evening, gentlemen," she said courteously while proceeding to tear a sizeable strip off the bedsheet. "My name is Emily and I am a nurse."

Pete's trouser leg was so bloodied that it would be difficult to find the bullet's point of entry.

"I'm afraid we must remove these trousers, Pete."

Pete merely groaned in reply. Unfastening his suspenders and hauling down his trousers, Emily could now see a mass of ripped flesh at the side of his right thigh, bleeding freely.

"It appears that you have been grazed rather than hit directly," she told him. "That's very good news. Jim, I want you to take that pillow from the divan and position it beneath Pete's knee so that the wound is above his heart."

Jim seemed distracted but did as he was told. She next instructed him to give Pete two sips from a bottle of laudanum while she tied the torn strip of bedsheet a few inches above the wound. Laudanum, a mixture of opium and alcohol, was a powerful painkiller that she kept in regular supply. Skillfully she fashioned a tourniquet, twisting it about and securing it tightly with a wooden spoon.

"The tourniquet will help to control the bleeding," she explained as she tore off another strip of bedsheet, "but we don't want to leave it on too long. It will cut off circulation and I'm certain you would like to keep using that leg, wouldn't you, Pete!"

"Am I gonna lose it?" Pete asked, between gritted teeth.

"Of course not! Most gunshot wounds can be dealt with very readily if they have not hit an artery or organ. We'll patch this up as best we can and then have you seen by a doctor."

With a thick wad of sheeting she began to apply firm pressure upon the wound. After a few minutes she loosened the tourniquet and retied it to hold the pressure bandage in place. How long would it take for a doctor to arrive? Surely in a city the size of San Francisco there would be one close at hand, would there not? After waiting impatiently a while longer she decided she had best check on Edward and Abbie.

"Jim, you must keep pressure on that wound. I will be back shortly."

She fancied that she heard the men exchange a bit of hushed conversation as she left the room. Hurrying upstairs, she found that Abbie had awoken and was crying lustily.

"Oh, Abbie," Emily sighed, lifting her daughter from the cot. "This is not a good time!"

Twenty minutes later she ran back downstairs to find that the man she had sent off in search of a doctor had returned with a small express cart. He and Jim were in the process of hastily loading Pete aboard, taking little care with the injured leg.

"Where is the doctor?" Emily exclaimed.

Jim turned to her briefly with a quick tip of his hat. "Much obliged for the care, ma'am," he told her.

The men disappeared off into the night. Emily could only stare dumbfounded after them, acutely aware of the fact that the group had been up to something untoward. John Patterson came into the building shortly thereafter to find his dejected wife gathering up the remaining bloodied sheeting and pillow. The bottle of laudanum was not to be found.

"An unwise course of action for you, Emily," he said with a frown upon learning of the night's events. "I suspect that those men were criminals on the run, who could have caused you a lot of trouble."

Emily sighed in exasperation. "I suppose as soon as they learned it wasn't such a serious injury they were off."

The next morning John Patterson found the bullet in the alley and showed it to his wife. "A Minié," he said grimly. "A new kind of bullet, much more lethal than the old round musket ball. Pete, or whatever his real name was, should consider himself extremely fortunate that his attacker was a poor shot."

"He should consider himself extremely fortunate that I didn't kick his sorry backside to kingdom come," Emily muttered.

John Patterson had found employment aboard a steamship mail carrier and soon moved his family to a less volatile neighbourhood. By the close of 1861, Emily was well on in pregnancy with her second child. Up every morning before daybreak, she would empty coal clinkers from the ash box, stoke the cast iron cookstove to life, pump water for the kettle to make tea and fry up the remains of the previous day's porridge. Edward would be woken up, fed breakfast and sent off to school—his lunch of bread, cheese and a piece of fruit tidily packed into an empty lard pail. Rooms would be swept clean, chamber pots emptied into the outdoor privy, more water would be heated for Abbie to be bathed and dressed, and then there would be a walk to the local shops. En route, Emily would make a daily habit of visiting the post office for any news from Maine—urgently desired, for civil war was raging in the east.

As Emily's mother predicted, there had been bloodshed—and it was occurring on an increasingly alarming scale. No less than eleven states had seceded from the Union in the previous year and had formally declared themselves a separate country, the Confederate States of America, under command of President Jefferson Davis. On January 27, 1862, President Abraham Lincoln had issued General War Order Number One, ordering that "the 22nd day of February, 1862, be the day for a general movement of the land and naval forces of the United States against the insurgent forces." It was clear that certain adversaries were unwilling to wait. Between February 13 and 16, Union and Confederate forces waged a fierce battle at Fort Donelson, on the Tennessee River, resulting in over seventeen thousand casualties. While the state of Maine had yet to experience any of the violence, thousands of men were shipping south, leaving behind their families, farms and livelihoods.

Emily and John welcomed their second daughter, Rebecca Park Patterson, into the world on March 9, 1862. Emily had asked her former neighbour Rebecca Park to be her midwife—a task which Rebecca performed admirably—and to be her daughter's namesake.

"I would like her to grow up in a peaceful country," Emily said tiredly, as she watched Rebecca gently wrap her baby and lay her in the cradle. "Do you think there may be an attack on San Francisco?"

"They'd be foolish to even attempt it!" Rebecca retorted. "Fifty cannon have been installed at Fort Point, with more on order. The harbour entrance is very well fortified."

CHAPTER 4

Quarantine

A few weeks after the birth of Rebecca, John Patterson came home excitedly announcing that he had found a new job.

"I met a gentleman down by the docks, a Captain Edward Stamp by name. He was looking for men to employ at a new sawmill he's established up the coast . . . a place called Alberni. We had quite an interesting discussion about it, and he's offered me a position."

"Is that in Washington Territory?" Emily asked.

"No, further north, in the Crown Colony of Vancouver Island . . . far enough away that I'll be bringing you and the children with me."

Emily watched as her husband dug out a nautical map from the kitchen cupboard and spread it out on the dining table. He pointed out a long inlet which penetrated deep inland from the west coast of Vancouver Island.

"Alberni is here," he said, indicating the extreme eastern end of the inlet. "We travel north by steamer to Victoria, here at the southern end of Vancouver Island, take on additional supplies, and then continue to Alberni—about a further day's passage away."

"Is it a very large community?" Emily asked, noting that there was no mention of it on the map.

"I understand there's about two hundred people living there at present, not counting the Tseshaht of course."

"The Tseshaht?"

"Local Indian tribe. Friendly, I believe, but I guess we shall have to see. According to Stamp, word is spreading fast of the timber stock available . . . Douglas fir, red cedar . . . all fine quality, and there's a broad fertile valley well suited to farming. The summer before last he brought in fifty workers to construct a mill and townsite. I dare say it will not be long before Alberni's on the map."

"Well then," Emily said, with just the barest hint of reproach, "the children and I will agree to join you."

Emily had to acknowledge that a plan to relocate was long overdue, for life in San Francisco was not to her taste. It was busy, noisy and crime-ridden. Newspaper reports added to the gloom with confirmation that war continued to rage in the southeast. In early March, the Confederate ironclad vessel *Merrimack* sank two wooden Union ships and then battled the Union ironclad *Monitor* to a draw off Hampton Roads, Virginia. Seemingly overnight, the final curtain was being drawn on the glorious era of the wooden-hulled ships.

Although Emily was vaguely aware of Canadian localities such as Halifax and Quebec City on the eastern seaboard, the Pacific Northwest region may just as well have been located on the far side of the moon. During her schooling years in Maine, she had learned of early explorers who had encountered a vast wilderness of impassable ice as they sought the Holy Grail of Arctic navigation, the elusive Northwest Passage. Had not the vessels and crewmen of the Franklin Expedition vanished into oblivion during their 1845 voyage? Her husband assured her that Alberni was located "well to the south" of the Arctic.

Emily insisted that the Pattersons' journey northward would commence only after baby Beckie was a few months older and Edward had the opportunity to complete his year of school.

"I'm sure he'd do just as well with his studies at sea," John grumbled, as he reluctantly consented to the arrangement.

>‹

"So many people!"

Clutching Beckie tightly in her arms, Emily noted the fact aboard the SS *Pacific* as the vessel nosed its way out of San Francisco early one summer morning. Whatever merchandise and personal luggage did not fit in the hold was piled on deck, with passengers jockeying for position wherever they could find space.

"Over two hundred on board, so I've heard," John Patterson replied. "Only about thirty in First Class."

"It seems to me that this ship is a little too full for safety!" Emily frowned.

"Demand has been soaring with all the gold being discovered up north," her husband told her. "Huge profits to be made for everyone involved and the California Steam Navigation Company has been capitalizing, no doubt."

The California Steam Navigation Company had been servicing the San Francisco Bay Area and nearby rivers since 1854 and had built up a local monopoly on passenger and freight service. With the 1858 discovery of gold in the gravel bars of the Fraser River canyon, coastal service was expanded to include Puget Sound and Victoria. Two side-wheel steamers, the *Pacific* and *Brother Jonathan*, soon to be followed by the *Oregon*, had been reassigned from their regular routes to provide passenger and freight transportation up and down the lucrative Pacific Northwest coastal run.

The voyage to Victoria would take over two weeks, with stops to take on yet more passengers and freight in Astoria and Portland. As good fortune would have it, the Pattersons' journey was an uneventful one with fair wind and calm seas under a pleasantly warm mid-summer sun. Emily would spend long hours on deck with the children, watching in fascination as the *Pacific* slipped past the Cape Flattery headland before making a marked turn eastward into the Strait of Juan de Fuca. Gentle whitecaps played upon a sparkling sea and bevies of seagulls soared overhead, their shrill cries reverberating amidst the chatter of passengers. At one point a pod of orcas was spotted off the portside bow, their curved fins arcing and descending amidst the waves, fine mist spraying forth intermittently from their blowholes.

"What amazing creatures," Emily said to herself, watching them intently.

Near the end of the *Pacific*'s voyage, one of the ship's crewmen pointed out two tall poles, set apart on a shoreline hilltop.

"Beacon Hill," he announced. "Marks the location of Brotchie Ledge. That old ledge claimed many a ship before they installed the beacons."

The *Pacific* nosed its way up a narrow channel, which gradually opened into the sheltered inner harbour of Victoria. Numerous ships lay at anchor and buildings constructed of wood and stone lined the harbourfront. Founded as Fort Victoria on March 14, 1843, Victoria had been a Hudson's Bay Company trading post under the jurisdiction of Company Chief Factor James Douglas. By 1849, the trading post was officially designated the seat of government for the British Crown Colony of Vancouver Island. Like that of San Francisco, Victoria's population had grown rapidly, stimulated by the profits of gold, and was now a bustling population centre of five thousand-plus inhabitants. The network of streets hummed with industry, and plans were well underway for Victoria's official incorporation as a city.

But Victoria, place of vigour and optimism, was presently under a shadow. On March 19, 1862, the *British Colonist* newspaper reported that a miner from San Francisco had been discovered to have smallpox en route to Victoria and local residents were urged to take heed:

As our city is now in almost weekly communication with the Bay City, the danger of contagion from that quarter is necessarily very great, and we therefore hope that we shall not be regarded as alarmist when we advise our citizens—and more especially those who design proceeding to the mines, where proper medical treatment and good nursing are not to be obtained at any price—to proceed at once to a physician and undergo vaccination. The cost is but a trifle when compared with the perfect immunity from the loathsome disease, which those who may take this precaution will enjoy.

Two new cases were reported on March 26—passengers who had arrived from San Francisco aboard the *Brother Jonathan* and *Oregon*, respectively. After the vessels reached their destination, inadequate quarantine measures had allowed the disease to infiltrate the general city populace. The *British Colonist* echoed public sentiments in Victoria:

> Imagine for a moment what a fearful calamity it would be, were the horde of Indians on the outskirts of town to take the disease. Their filthy habits would only perpetuate the evil; keep it alive in the community, sacrificing the lives of all classes.

Smallpox—once the terrible scourge that had decimated entire civilizations over the course of centuries—was now entirely preventable, thanks to the groundbreaking discoveries of English physician Edward Jenner and other early pioneers of medical science. But lacking the natural antibodies that individuals of European descent had built up over centuries of exposure, Indigenous civilizations throughout North America were particularly vulnerable to infection. A smallpox outbreak in the 1780s had all but wiped out entire villages across the continent, claiming thousands of lives.

Camosack (rush of water), as the Victoria region was known by the people of the Songhees Nation, had long been a traditional gathering place for hunting and fishing. Despite the influx of white settlers, several native communities continued to live in close proximity to Victoria. The Songhees Reserve, which had been set aside by treaty in 1850–51, was situated due west across the city's inner harbour. Other Indigenous groups had travelled a great distance for the economic benefit of conducting trade at the fort. Members of the Tsimshian were encamped near the beach of James Bay. Haida camps were located at Ogden Point and Cadboro Bay. A Stikine camp was established at Laurel Point. All told, there were approximately 2,500 Indigenous people living on the outskirts of Victoria in 1862.

As Emily and her family watched from aboard the *Pacific*, several men gathered at dockside with buckets and mops, preparing to embark and scrub the vessel from stem to stern with disinfectant. As passengers descended the gangway, they were immediately herded into a closely guarded reception centre.

"This way for smallpox quarantine debriefing, ma'am," a man said briskly, ushering Emily towards a building which appeared to be a converted warehouse. Signs emblazoned "SMALLPOX QUARANTINE" were posted everywhere.

"Thank heaven we've all been vaccinated," Emily said quietly to John. "I have the papers to prove it if they need them."

Emily had long ago recognized the importance of smallpox vaccination. While mandatory inoculation programs were still few and far between, vaccine production was on the rise, and public acceptance of the simple solution to contracting smallpox was slowly gaining ground. Still, there were those who were skeptical of allowing themselves to be vaccinated.

"What does quarantine mean?" Edward asked.

"It's a place where people must go if they have a contagious disease, to prevent the disease from spreading," Emily explained.

"Why do we have to go to quarantine? We don't have smallpox."

"It's because they're worried we *might* have smallpox . . . and I suppose there are people in Victoria who have not been vaccinated to protect themselves."

Edward frowned, impatient. Emily sat down beside him on a trunk, bidding Abbie to do the same while she held a sleeping Beckie.

"I'll tell you a story," she began. "A long time ago in England there lived a man named Edward Jenner. He was a doctor who tended to patients in a small country village called Berkeley. One year, there was a smallpox epidemic in Berkeley, but Dr. Jenner noticed that many of his patients came down only with a very mild form of the disease and fully recovered. The one thing these patients had in common was that they were all farmhands who worked with cattle.

Dr. Jenner was puzzled. How were farmhands avoiding the dreaded smallpox? He knew that cows occasionally came down with a virus called cowpox, which could be transmitted to humans. One day, when a young milkmaid named Sarah Nelmes came to Dr. Jenner with the blister-like sores on her hands indicative of cowpox, he decided that he would try a bold experiment. He syringed up some liquid from Sarah's sores and then some liquid from the sores of a patient with a mild case of smallpox. Next, he found a very brave farmer with an even braver little eight-year-old boy named James Phipps. Dr. Jenner explained that he wanted to try deliberately infecting young James with the cowpox virus taken from milkmaid Sarah, followed a few weeks later by the smallpox virus.

Dr. Jenner believed that if his plan worked, James Phipps would forever be protected against smallpox. It was a very dangerous experiment, but amazingly, both the farmer and James consented. Dr. Jenner made two small cuts on James's left arm, inserted the cowpox liquid, and carefully bandaged the wounds. As expected, James came down with cowpox but was not very sick. Six weeks later, Dr. Jenner vaccinated James with the smallpox virus."

"And did he get smallpox?" Edward asked.

"No, he did not." Emily smiled. "He was perfectly healthy, grew up, married, had children, and lived to old age. Dr. Jenner was given a very large cash prize by the British government and was able to reward James Phipps for his bravery by giving him a house to live in. How is that for a happy ending?"

Edward peered around the busy quarantine centre, as one at a time individuals and families were being interviewed and various official-looking papers exchanged hands.

"But if Dr. Jenner's experiment worked, why are people still getting smallpox?" he asked simply.

"Well," Emily replied, "I guess there are still people that fear the idea of having a vaccination, especially one that contains a virus."

When the Pattersons were finally given clearance to depart the dockside quarantine area, Emily made inquiries about local treatment facilities. Public vaccination, while strongly being encouraged, was not mandatory in Victoria. Some victims were being quarantined and cared for at locations a good distance away from healthy populations. Others were forcibly expelled to endure their illness in solitude. It deeply saddened Emily to realize that certain smallpox victims would be condemned to a lonely and painful death, far from any semblance of comfort and care. But there was little she could do. She had her own family to think of, and John Patterson desired to get to Alberni as quickly as possible. The *Meg Merrilies* lay at anchor in the harbour, taking on passengers and freight for the journey northward.

CHAPTER 5

Alberni

It was not difficult for Emily to understand why the west coast of Vancouver Island was often being referred to as the "graveyard of the Pacific"—part of a notoriously dangerous region extending all the way from the northernmost tip of Vancouver Island at Cape Scott down to Cape Flattery and beyond to the treacherous bar at the mouth of the Columbia River. From the earliest days of the Russian fur trade, numerous vessels had met their end amidst wild winter storms, fog-shrouded headlands and hidden shoals. Cape Beale, a hulking mass of barnacle-encrusted rocks and sheer cliffs at the southern entrance to Barkley Sound, met the full force of Pacific breakers. Here the *Meg Merrilies* bore eastward to enter the Alberni Inlet. It would be a lengthy but steady sail to the milltown, with the prevailing wind filling *Meg Merrilies'* canvas and propelling her forward on a true course—a godsend wind in Emily's mind, as she noticed that there were few places to make landfall. Steep cliffs flanked the inlet on both sides for miles upon end, with nary a trace of beach in sight. The occasional dugout canoe travelled past, its paddlers barely acknowledging the presence of the *Meg Merrilies*, although Emily noticed that a crewman standing watch kept an eye steadily trained upon each craft as it came and went.

"Tseshaht, ma'am," he commented, noticing her inquiring look. "They'll leave us alone."

"Who is this inlet named after?" Emily asked him.

"Pedro de Alberni, a Spanish officer who had commanded the West Coast fort at Nootka Sound," he replied. "It's been a pretty well-travelled waterway over the years, this inlet, by both Europeans and the Nootka."

"Who are the Nootka?"

"The natives. There are many bands that make up the Nootka here on the West Coast, Tseshaht being one of them."

John Patterson was standing beside Emily, gazing at the surrounding thickly forested mountainsides with a look of fascination.

"You see that!" he exclaimed. "That's what we're here for! Nothing in the entire state of Maine ever compared!"

At the end of the afternoon, a familiar smell of woodsmoke crept into the air. The inlet terminated at a broad estuary, with a cluster of wood-frame structures clearly visible on the eastern side. Beyond the structures there appeared to be a virtual sea of stumps. A great hulking mountain with multiple peaks, some still bearing patches of snow, dominated the eastern horizon.

"Hello there, Stamp!"

John Patterson waved down to a stout gentleman who had come to the edge of the dock as *Meg Merrilies* nosed its way wharfside with the assistance of a steam-driven pilot tug. This time around there were no delays or questions as the Pattersons disembarked and John introduced everyone to Captain Edward Stamp, owner and manager of the saw-mill operation.

"Good afternoon, ma'am," Stamp said to Emily, doffing his hat. "I trust you've had a pleasant voyage to Alberni?"

"Yes indeed, very pleasant," Emily replied.

Captain Stamp seemed genuinely pleased to welcome each and every passenger off the *Meg Merrilies*, urging everyone to visit the cookhouse for coffee and "a delicious salmon dinner."

It was plain for Emily and John to see that Stamp had planned his venture carefully at Alberni. Backed by a consortium of London financiers and £400 of capital, he had received approval for a Crown grant of

fifteen thousand acres of timberland and two thousand acres of agricultural land in the region. After some deliberation, agreement was reached that the ideal location for construction of the mill was on a beach where the Somass River met the Alberni Inlet. Fresh water from local streams was diverted by flume to generate steam power for the machinery. Having run a general store in Victoria years previously, Stamp had a good working knowledge of what was needed to adequately provide for his employees. Steam engines, ploughs,

Captain Edward Stamp

oxen, horses, sheep and pigs were shipped from Victoria, along with tools, dry goods and seed for planting.

Emily had long resigned herself to the fact that life in a remote logging camp on the Pacific Northwest Coast would be entirely different from anything that she had ever experienced before. Long gone were the days of strolling the conveniently situated shopping precincts of Bath, New York and San Francisco, calling in upon local merchants for all of her day-to-day needs. A solitary wood-frame building served as Alberni's supply depot for groceries, hardware, medicines, bedding and crockery. Alberni's streets—if she could call them streets—were mud-laden wagon trails cut through a stark wasteland of stumps, which led straight to the skid roads. Here, amidst the rank smell of dogfish oil used to grease the skids, teams of oxen would haul logs of enormous girth down to the sawmill for processing. The mill itself was by far the largest structure in the settlement, built atop pilings that had been driven into stone-filled wooden cribs near the mouth of the Somass Estuary.

Home for the Pattersons, like other Alberni families, was a rustic company cabin of cedar planking, with a split-cedar shake roof. Captain Stamp had demanded quality workmanship, for every cabin was of sound construction, each complete with a cast iron wood stove, rope beds, cupboards and wash basins. Across the estuary, a group of men had been hired to cultivate a two-hundred-and-fifty-acre company farm on the fertile flatlands. Emily learned that plummeting temperatures in January of 1861 had caused the inland reaches of Alberni Inlet to freeze solid beneath a four-foot layer of snow. Mill workers and their families were forced to walk for ten miles in bitter cold before they could reach supply vessels anchored in open water. Locally sourced food had been given high priority ever since. Each day throughout the height of the growing season, an abundance of freshly harvested potatoes, beans, peas, lettuce and carrots were rowed across to the cookhouse. The well-being of the all-crucial livestock was not to be forgotten, and fields of hay, oats and barley grew tall and robust under the warm summer sun.

However idyllic life appeared to be in Alberni, there was one problem that Captain Stamp had evidently not foreseen. The Tseshaht had a seasonal encampment at the site of the mill and had not been pleased when told that they would have to move elsewhere. Gilbert Malcolm Sproat, a native of Scotland and Stamp's right-hand man, came to meet with John and Emily in their home late one evening to explain the situation. Emily poured him a cup of tea while they spoke in low tones around the dining table.

"When we dropped anchor off Alberni with our first load of supplies, I sent a boat for the Tseshaht chief and explained that the tribe must move their encampment, as we'd bought all the surrounding land from the Queen of England, and wished to occupy the site of the village for a particular purpose," Sproat told them.

"I suppose they know who the Queen of England is," Emily said flatly.

Stamp's Mill, Alberni, 1861.

John shot her a warning glance. Sproat momentarily raised his eyebrows and continued.

"On the following day the encampment was in commotion. Speeches were made, faces blackened, guns and pikes got out, barricades formed. . . . Outnumbered as we were, ten to one by Tseshaht men armed with muskets, and our communications with the sea cut off by the impossibility of sailing steadily down the Alberni Inlet against the prevailing wind, there was some cause for alarm. But both of our vessels were provided with cannon—of which the natives were very much afraid. After a little show of force on our side, they saw that resistance would be useless and began to move from the spot."

"Do you continue to have trouble with the Tseshaht?" John Patterson asked.

"Yes, and that is why I meet with all families as they arrive here in Alberni. I do not want to alarm you, but it is best that you are made aware of the situation we are dealing with."

"Can anything be done to win their trust?" Emily wondered. "Show them that we mean no harm?"

Sproat shook his head, appearing somewhat resigned.

"We're making progress with some, but for others, I'm afraid too much harm has already happened," he said grimly. "Captain Stamp has written a letter to the colonial secretary requesting that a vessel of war be sent to Barkley Sound. He has been appointed Justice of the Peace at the townsite and recently took it upon himself to sentence members of the Tseshaht to four months of hard labour in Victoria for committing sundry thefts."

Emily decided that she should best say no more.

CHAPTER 6

"Not King George"

As Emily had suspected, no facilities existed for schooling in Alberni, and once again she would need to draw upon her own resources to ensure the continuation of Edward's education. The farm was at peak production and one summer afternoon she arranged for herself and the children to be rowed across the Somass Estuary to view harvest operations. Potatoes were a favourite crop, both among the mill residents and the Tseshaht. Stepping off on the opposite shore, Emily noticed Gilbert Sproat and a pair of Tseshaht men conversing nearby. The Tseshaht had relocated their seasonal encampment upstream on the Somass after Stamp's arrival, and some had taken on employment with the company. Emily routinely smiled at any member of the Tseshaht that she encountered but found that her social overtures were most often greeted with indifference or outright resentment. Such was the case once again this particular afternoon, as the two men stalked away to work in a different area of the field after Sproat introduced them to her.

"I'd like to get to know the Tseshaht," Emily commented to Sproat, "but they seem to dislike me intently. Have I personally done something wrong in their eyes?"

Sproat merely chuckled. "It's probably because you're not 'King George'!"

"Not who?" Emily asked.

"King George," Sproat replied with his distinctive Scottish burr. "From the fine old isles of Great Britain that so many of us here in Alberni call home. Not to offend, but you Pattersons are 'Boston' . . . Americans that is, in the Chinook Jargon. The Tseshaht don't take kindly to Americans."

"But that's ridiculous," Emily protested. "We've done nothing to harm them."

"Well, it seems that long ago, possibly right back to Captain Barkley's time, native tribes up and down the coast were coaxed into believing that Americans were bad, not to be trusted, while the British were the good guys. It was all about colonialism and loyalty to King George the Third in the late 1700s."

Emily sighed. She could see that it would take more than the occasional friendly greeting to win the trust and respect of the Tseshaht.

"You mentioned Chinook Jargon . . . what is that?" she queried.

"It's a trade language," Sproat explained. "A little English, a little French, a lot of native dialect. Used up and down the coast by just about anybody who wants to make themselves understood. Better start practising Chinook, Mrs. Patterson, because you'll be hearing a lot of it around here!"

Indeed Emily could see that learning Chinook would do much to improve her chances for social exchange in the community. It rattled off the tongue of virtually every individual she came in contact with, young or old, "King George," "Boston," Tseshaht or otherwise. With no such thing as a Chinook dictionary, the best that she could do was muddle through, for word was beginning to circulate about her nursing skills.

Gilbert Malcolm Sproat

One evening, she was surprised to see a young Tseshaht man abruptly enter her house without knocking while she and the rest of the family ate dinner.

"Nika sick!" he announced.

Emily, despite being somewhat taken aback, heard the word "sick" and presumed that someone named Nika was ill.

"Where is Nika?" she asked, reaching for her medical bag, which she routinely kept by the door. "*Kah Nika?*"

The Tseshaht man looked confused. John Patterson merely laughed.

"You just asked 'where am I?' Nika means 'I' or 'me' in Chinook. Sick is the same word in Chinook as it is in English. He's telling you that he is sick."

"Thank you for that explanation, John," Emily said testily, as she bid the Tseshaht man to sit down. She quickly determined that there was no fever present and her patient appeared to be suffering from a mild inflammation of the tonsils. Boiling up a solution of milk and water, she demonstrated that he was to gargle with it while she prepared a linseed poultice to place around his throat. A half hour later, the man left, as indifferently as he had arrived, with nary a word of gratitude.

Interactions with the Tseshaht did not always transpire as cooperatively, or be resolved as peaceably, as Emily was soon to learn. On occasion, and as it seemed, most frequently right when she was in the midst of an important task, word spread that the women and children were to head immediately for safety to the cookhouse. There had been another Tseshaht uprising and, "for the sake of caution," Captain Stamp would order the cannons to be made ready and request that any man owning a firearm "ensure that it was loaded and on his person."

Whenever such alarms were raised, Emily would quickly douse the wood stove fire if it was lit, shoulder a few blankets, grab up Beckie, her medical bag, and while directing Edward to assist Abbie, hurry to the cookhouse as instructed. Seated at rough-hewn tables with cups of hot coffee, some of the young wives and mothers were clearly agitated and a few of the children were crying. Emily moved from group to group with Beckie in her arms, quietly seeking to calm fears. A few men, including Captain Stamp and John Patterson, came into the cookhouse a few hours later to bring everyone up to date.

"I believe we have the situation in hand," Captain Stamp announced, "but I suggest that you all remain in the cookhouse until further notice."

Emily gave her husband a meaningful look, indicating that she wanted more detailed information.

"I don't think there will be any more trouble," he told her quietly as Stamp's audience dispersed. "The mere sight of the cannons is a very effective deterrent."

"There must not be any bloodshed!" Emily replied, her voice equally low but firm. "From what I have learned, the Tseshaht have every right to be angry. They've been moved off land that they have lived upon for thousands of years, their fishing weirs on the Somass have been all but destroyed, our interactions with them have brought disease and loss of culture. . . . Is it any wonder they're rebelling?"

"Well then, what do you suggest we do?"

John was tired and irritable. Emily could see that her words had touched a nerve, but at the same time she was grateful for the men's protection and had no desire to see any of the frightened individuals in her midst suffer a worse fate.

"I'll look after things here," she said softly. "Please thank Mr. Stamp and the others for their efforts on our behalf."

Life returned to normal relatively quickly in Alberni after each uprising. It seemed that if everyone was given the opportunity to posture on occasion, the threat of an outright attack lessened. But as time wore on, Emily found that a new enemy was emerging in the milltown—that of economic downturn. Alberni's readily accessible stands of timber— those flanking the townsite and in the vicinity of a nearby lake recently named after Gilbert Sproat—had been completely logged off. The steep, rocky terrain remaining posed major challenges for access, not to mention getting the raw logs to port in a timely and convenient fashion. Captain Stamp did not have any machinery in place to harvest trees that were not within easy reach of his oxen and skid roads. Thus far, the entire operation had been profitable, but barely so. To compound matters, there was the issue of Alberni's isolation. Several mill workers and their families decided that they had seen enough of living in a town where most amenities were far beyond reach. Arguments ensued between Stamp and his employees and financial backers. Under the looming shadow of bankruptcy, a thoroughly frustrated and disillusioned Stamp resigned in January of 1863, selling his business to the Anderson family, who had been among his chief financiers. Gilbert Sproat, delegated to manage the mill after Stamp's departure, carried on as best he could, but the mill was struggling and employees were resigning at a rapid rate.

Emily had come to feel a special regard for Alberni and its surroundings. From her cabin door, she could enjoy the spectacular vista of Mount Arrowsmith, or Kulth-ka-choolth (jagged face) as it was known by the Tseshaht, towering over the Alberni Valley landscape—its snow-capped peaks reflecting hues of violet and gold at sundown. Alberni Inlet sparkled on summer afternoons and the entire valley basked in warm inland temperatures. If low tide occurred in early evening, there was a good chance of seeing black bears on the shoreline of the Somass Estuary feasting upon the plentiful salmon that darted through the shallows. Food sources were boundless for every living occupant of the land. To cap it all off in the summer of 1863, Emily learned that she was pregnant once again.

Christmas that same year in Alberni was a festive time, though tinged with sadness. A total of ninety-seven mill hands and their families would be departing for Victoria aboard the steamer *Thames*, under command of Captain John Henderson, immediately following the holiday. The Pattersons would not be among them.

"I will not travel that wicked coast in the depths of winter!" Emily's resolve had been as firm as her rounded belly. She would not be leaving Alberni while heavily expectant with her next child. John Patterson, for all his discouragement over the failure of the Alberni mill, had to agree. The family remained behind in a virtually empty settlement. Snow swirled about the doorsteps of abandoned cabins, still festooned with garlands of Christmas greenery. Edward and Abbie felt the loneliness most, seated on the cabin floor with their books and toys as opposed to searching outdoors for long-departed playmates.

Through much perseverance, Emily had managed to win the friendship of some local Tseshaht women. When her third daughter, Alice Frances, was born on February 26, 1864—reputedly the first white baby to be born on the west coast of Vancouver Island—Emily was delighted when several of them came to visit bearing gifts of dried salmon and soft deer-hide moccasins. Much to the women's surprise and admiration, newborn Alice already had the Patterson trademark of her mother and sisters—a head of thick black hair.

"*Klale yak'so!*" they exclaimed, as Emily allowed Alice to be passed from one onlooker to the next. "Black hair! Beautiful baby! Hee!"

"*Mahsie!* Thank you!" Emily smiled.

※

The Anderson Company attempted new ventures to save their Alberni investment, including the establishment of copper mines on the Tzartus and Santa Maria Islands in Barkley Sound. A fishing station was established on Effingham Island. It was clear, however, that the sawmill was not to reopen in the short term. In due course, the entire facility would close permanently at a loss of £50,000. With no future options to his liking in sight, John Patterson soon stated the inevitable to Emily.

"It's time for us to leave Alberni. We'll head back down to Victoria and weigh up our options. Perhaps I'll look into Oregon—good timber down there, so they say."

"I will always remember our time here," Emily said sadly a few weeks later, while she and John watched the mill and empty cottages of Alberni disappear from view as the *Meg Merrilies* rounded a gentle turn in the inlet. "I wonder if Alberni will ever come back to life?"

"No one can say that for sure, but I certainly hope so!" John replied.

CHAPTER 7

Champoeg

Emily gaped in wonder at the astonishing volume of water pouring over the forty-foot Willamette Falls, as she and her family rode past aboard the newly opened portage railway. It was early in the spring of 1867 and the Pattersons were making their way from Victoria to a new home and new life in Oregon's fertile Willamette Valley. By the mid-1860s, steamer service up and down the Pacific Northwest Coast had become well-established and frequent, with regular calls between Victoria and the sawmilling community of Portland, Oregon. While Emily and the children had resided in Victoria for the past two years, John had been absent for lengthy periods, seeking employment in places near and not-so-near. After such a lengthy period of waiting, Emily was grateful when he announced that he had purchased a small sawmill and that the family was finally going to be whole again. One more member had been added to the Patterson fold since their departure from Alberni—baby Frank, born in Victoria on May 12, 1866.

The portage railway transported passengers comfortably and safely past the falls to Oregon City, terminus of the Oregon Trail. "They must have been a disheartening sight in bygone years!" Emily remarked, well imagining how the frothing cascades must have confounded many a trail pioneer within striking distance of their goal.

"Oregon City has been quieter since the Panama Railway was completed," John told her, "but steam power generated by the falls is giving the community new life."

He pointed out several structures, identifying them as lumber, flour and woollen mills. Beyond Oregon City, the Willamette River meandered its way through timbered forest and open rangeland, every so often punctuated with houses, barns and small settlements. With the exception of a few distant rolling hills and buttes, the landscape was virtually unchanging. Grasses grew tall and lush on either riverbank and the occasional bluebird flitted past. It was an entirely peaceful and captivating scene. Emily found herself thinking back upon the newspaper reports that she had read in Victoria, and hoping that other regions of the United States were reverting to similar settings. The Civil War bloodbath was over but peace had come at a terrible price, with the assassination of President Abraham Lincoln on April 14, 1865.

"How much further?" Abbie asked, as the small steamer chugged its way along the seemingly endless miles.

"Not far!" her father replied cheerfully. "We'll land at Butteville shortly and then travel by wagon to Champoeg Creek."

"Cham-poh-egg . . ." Emily repeated. "Strange sounding name . . ."

"Nobody seems to know for sure what it means," John explained. "It may have stemmed from the language of the Kalapuya Indians, who were the original occupants of this land, or the French-Canadian fur trappers who arrived about sixty years ago and set up a Hudson's Bay Company trading post."

The Kalapuya, as John described, along with the Chinook and Clackamus people had lived off the bounty of the Willamette region for thousands of years. They had fished the river and its numerous tributaries for salmon, steelhead and sturgeon. By setting fire to the lush prairie grasslands, they created vast, open sightlines for hunting deer and elk. They had a sophisticated knowledge of plant life, harvesting the plentiful acorns, hazelnuts and berries in season for year-round sustenance.

"A resourceful society," Emily commented admiringly, "just like the Tseshaht."

"Sadly, it seems that most of the Kalapuya are long gone," John told her. "Between 1830 and 1833, a fever epidemic struck them hard throughout the Lower Columbia and Willamette valleys. There were once over thirteen thousand Kalapuya . . . now there are only about three hundred left."

Gazing over the pastoral setting before her, Emily found it hard to imagine that such tragedy had ever occurred.

After their steamboat pulled up at the Butteville landing, the Pattersons disembarked. John Patterson went off to collect his dray wagon while Emily, after putting Abbie in charge of Beckie, Alice and Frank, proceeded to unload trunks with the help of Edward. She quietly considered it a miracle that the steamboat had managed to stay afloat with all of her family's worldly possessions aboard. Several residents of Butteville had come down to the landing and before long, many helping hands materialized to lift the heaviest loads. Exceedingly grateful, Emily noted that Butteville appeared a tidy, close-knit community, with whitewashed buildings, several supply depots, at least one church, a school and a network of wooden sidewalks to keep pedestrians high and dry out of the muddy roads.

The most welcome act of all came when a local man offered to drive the family aboard his express wagon to the Pattersons' new home. The sawmill operation that John Patterson had purchased was located approximately three miles from Butteville, high up on the river benchlands near a smaller watercourse called Champoeg Creek.

"Too far for the little ones to walk," the man muttered, hoisting Alice aboard his wagon as if she were less than the weight of a piece of kindling. He introduced himself as Albion Chenery, but beyond that had very little to say. Through a few painstaking attempts at conversation, Emily was surprised and pleased to learn that he had been born in the village of Livermore Falls, Maine, not that far from Bath. She would have longed to hear more, but Albion Chenery was clearly something of a mystery man. Owing more to his strength and agility than appearance, she judged him to be approximately fifty years of age. His eyes bore an unmistakable sadness and he stared straight ahead as he guided his team of horses up the road. Lurching from side to side aboard the express wagon, the Pattersons passed the occasional farmhouse and expansive fields of wheat and hay in early spring production. Emily was grateful that she would have plenty of weeks ahead to begin planning and sowing her kitchen garden.

John Patterson's sawmill was a small operation—one of several log and grist mills that had sprung up along the banks of Champoeg and Case creeks. Emily was pleased to learn that the sawmill purchase had come part and parcel with a log cabin—still rather small, but larger than the one that the family had resided in at Alberni. Closer inspection revealed that it had a sizeable loft accessed via a sturdy ladder, a small wood stove, a cupboard still containing a few pieces of crockery and a couple of rope beds with feather-tick mattresses. The rope would need to be restrung and the mattresses washed and restuffed, but everything appeared to be in good order—clean, tidy and very much in a state of abandonment.

"I wonder who lived here before us?" Emily asked John, as they carried a trunk between them.

"It was a couple, I believe," John replied. "Don't know very much about them at all, though. My guess is that they moved on and decided that they had more than they could carry."

Neighbours of the Pattersons were scattered over a wide area up and down the Willamette benchlands. Emily resolved to introduce herself to as many as she could. Leaving the older children to their school books, she regularly set off with Alice and Frank aboard the dray wagon if John wasn't in need of it. In the days and weeks ahead, she learned much about the Champoeg area including how a remarkable happening on a spring day in 1843 had laid the groundwork for Oregon's journey to official statehood. Through the early years of the 1800s, a steady influx of Americans arrived to establish farms and communities in the resource-rich Willamette region. Following its merger with the British-owned North West Company in 1821, the Hudson's Bay Company (also British-owned) gained prominence with a wide network of trading posts. Tensions began to mount among large numbers of new American settlers over the influence of the HBC.

On May 2, 1843, a crowd of approximately one hundred white men, both American and British-allied French Canadians, gathered at the Hudson's Bay Company granary and trade store in the riverside community of Champoeg. Officially, the meeting had been called to discuss the best options for dealing with local predators. Wolves, grizzly bears and cougars continued to inhabit the region and were killing livestock. Unbeknownst to the French Canadians, word had quietly circulated on the meeting's real purpose—a vote to determine whether or not Oregon Territory should be strictly under American governance. In a close (52–50) decision, the Americans won. To everyone's relief, the results of the vote were accepted peacefully, without the violence and bloodshed that had so often marred similar proceedings in other parts of the country. Thus the backwoods Willamette community of Champoeg, with its total population of approximately two hundred, became the unlikely setting for Oregon Territory's first provisional government. Salem, Oregon, would be approved by Congress as the official capital in 1852.

During her outings, Emily noticed that few structures occupied the Willamette River shorelines, and with good reason. Back in 1861, the month of November had been exceptionally cold and wet in northwestern Oregon. A heavy snowpack had already accumulated upon Mount Hood and higher elevations of the Columbia and Willamette valleys. Temperatures warmed towards the end of the month but were accompanied by eighteen days of steady rain. On the afternoon of December 6, residents of Champoeg had noticed that unusually large pools of water were forming on the town streets. At the schoolhouse, the local teacher Mr. King told the children to get their wraps and go right home.

"Don't loiter on the way!" he said firmly.

By nightfall, the Willamette River had overflowed its banks and torrents of water descended upon the township of Champoeg. Those who had not heeded previous warnings to get to higher ground now scrambled to escape. Rowboats and canoes were quickly deployed to rescue terrified families clustered upon rooftops. Horses were coaxed through swirling eddies. The town baker and his assistant clung to their establishment as it slowly drifted downstream. The church bell gonged intermittently as it crashed into the muddy waters. At the foot of Napoleon Street, the steamboat landing—wharf, pilings, boathouse and gangways—were swept away with nary a trace remaining.

Miraculously, no lives were lost, although nearly every structure in the town of Champoeg—stores, blacksmiths, liveries, saloons, the church, hotel, and schoolhouse—had been wiped from the face of the earth that December night. At their peak, the raging floodwaters had reached a depth of twenty feet above river level. The once-thriving economy of the entire Willamette region took a severe blow. Lots that had previously cost $500 plummeted in value and an entire acre could now be purchased for less than $50. In the six years since the flood, Champoeg townsite—the seat of so much history in its brief existence —had largely returned to its natural state, a lonely stretch of prairie alongside a gentle bend in the Willamette River.

It was difficult for Emily to imagine the destruction as she gazed over the idyllic grasslands which had once been home to a bustling settlement. Of those individuals and families who had been fortunate enough to reside on higher ground before the days of the flood, only a handful now remained. One April afternoon, Emily came upon a large house situated well up on the Willamette benchland. She knocked at the door but no one came to answer and the place seemed deserted. Peering through the filmy lace curtains of a front window pane, she could make out a few pieces of furniture draped in bedsheets.

"Where is everybody, Mama?" Alice asked.

"I don't know," Emily replied, trying to hang on to a wriggling Frank, who was desperately wanting to explore of his own accord.

They walked around to the back where they found a middle-aged woman tending to a small garden plot.

"Hello," Emily said politely. "Do you live here?"

"Over there," the woman replied briefly, pointing in the direction of a smaller farmhouse and barn not too far distant.

"We're the Pattersons. I'm Emily, and these are my children, Alice and Frank. We live over by Champoeg Creek. My husband just bought one of the sawmills."

If the woman heard, she gave little indication. Emily noticed that she breathed heavily as she worked. It was an abnormally warm day for April and time was ripe for planting season.

"Would you care for a piece of johnnycake?" Emily asked, taking a sealed tin out of her saddle bag.

At that, the woman promptly dropped her hoe and eagerly accepted the offer. Emily bid her to sit down on the porch stairs, handing pieces of johnnycake to Alice and Frank as well.

"This is such a beautiful place," Emily commented, as they sat together munching.

The woman made no reply. Emily decided that the only way she would have a chance to strike up a two-way conversation would be to ask questions.

"What is your name?"

"Felicité Manson," the woman replied, licking crumbs off her fingers.

"Felicité ..." Emily repeated. "What a pretty name ... it sounds French. Are you of French background?"

"Métis," Felicité replied.

"Métis ... that would be part French Canadian, part Indian, would it not?"

"Father was from Quebec, mother Indian."

Emily wanted to ask Felicité if her mother was Kalapuya, but decided not to appear too inquisitive. Through much gentle coaxing, she managed to learn that Felicité was born in Champoeg back in 1814 and had married a Scottish Hudson's Bay Company trader by the name of Donald Manson in or around 1828. The couple had eight children and everyone had managed to escape with their lives but little else during the great flood. They had rebuilt their house on higher ground and, with what Emily imagined to have been a monumental effort, had salvaged sections of their flood-damaged barn. The rebuilt Manson barn was said to be the only surviving structure from the town of Champoeg.

Felicité had brightened somewhat while talking about the barn, but quickly returned to her dour side once the johnnycake was finished, grabbing her hoe and proceeding to scratch at the earth, pausing now and again to cough and wheeze.

"Have you had that cough long?" Emily asked.

Felicité merely waved her hand dismissively in reply, muttering something unintelligible.

"Well," Emily said boldly, "if it continues, you might well consider seeing a doctor."

Robert Newell

"Doc Newell's gone," Felicité replied. "Newells took in just about the entire town of Champoeg the night of the flood . . . two hundred or more. Some of them stayed and stayed. Doc Newell pauperized himself, looking after everyone else. Moved on just a few months ago, to live with his wife's people in Idaho. I come over here now and then to look after the place."

Emily put two and two together.

"Was this Doc Newell's house?"

"It was. He was a good man, Doc Newell."

Emily could see that Alice was getting restless and Frank tired, so she stood up, carefully sweeping the remains of johnnycake off the porch steps back into her tin. The Newell house did not need a mouse infestation. She longed to hear more about the Newells and the flood and everything else about the people of Champoeg, for Felicité clearly had a wealth of fascinating recollections that occasionally bubbled their way to the surface—only to simmer into submission according to her mood of the moment. But there would be limited afternoon daylight for returning home and John would be wanting a hot meal after his day at the sawmill.

"Well goodbye, Felicité," she said. "It was lovely to meet you, and please let me know if there is anything I can do for you."

Felicité nodded, but before returning to her hoeing, she surprised Emily by asking her a question.

"You say you live up by the creek?"

"Yes," Emily replied. "About midway between Champoeg and Case creeks, well up on the benchland."

Felicité frowned. "Lots of stagnant water up there in the summer."

Frank was squirming and fussing, and Emily had not quite heard Felicité's exact words. She waved goodbye and they parted ways.

Emily was saddened in the months to come, learning that Felicité Manson had died on June 10 and was buried two days later in the St. Paul Catholic Church Cemetery. For whatever reason, she had chosen to bear her unknown illness alone, despite Emily's best efforts to inquire with various locals after her whereabouts and well-being. Few people seemed to know much about Felicité, but one thing had become abundantly clear: Doctor Robert Newell had been one of the most likeable and well-respected gentlemen ever to walk the streets of Champoeg. Emily grew to admire him without ever having known him. Born in Ohio, Newell was a true mountain man who had made his way to the Rockies at the age of twenty-two, working traplines and blazing trails ever westward through the harshest of environments. He married "Kitty," the daughter of a Nez Perce sub-chief, and together the couple and their four sons were among the very first families to travel the Oregon Trail to the Willamette River Valley. Although never formally trained in medicine, Newell had taught himself how to treat various illnesses and perform rudimentary surgery. It was said that on occasion, he would be seen holding a scalpel in one hand, while consulting a book of medical instruction in the other. Quite literally every displaced citizen of Champoeg had been given food and shelter at the Newell residence in the days and weeks following the 1861 flood. Having lost his grocery store and keelboat business to the floodwaters, Newell himself eventually faced bankruptcy and was forced to move on with his family.

"He had no training," Emily remarked to John, as they sat together at the dinner table. "And yet they actually called him a doctor. How I wish that I could have met him."

"I would like to have known how he managed to perform surgery without proper training," John replied somewhat dubiously. "I suppose people will go to any lengths when they are desperate."

"He saved a lot of lives and many people were grateful for it," Emily said wistfully. "I hope that someday I can be of half as much service."

During the late days of spring, much of the Willamette Valley was studded with wildflowers, including vast expanses of camas lilies. Following the advice of locals, Emily would hunt and dig up the plentiful camas lily bulbs. Only those lilies with a blue flower were to be harvested. The white "death camas" lilies were highly toxic and as deadly as they were beautiful. Encased for two and a half days within an earthen firepit, the edible camas bulbs baked to a golden brown. Served whole, they provided a delicious side dish reminiscent of sweet potatoes, or they could be ground down into a coarse meal for use as a thickener.

Summertime in the valley could be festering hot beneath a relentless sun, or soaked with rain, as nature dictated. The summer of 1867 proved to be ideal, with just the right combination of heat and moisture to enable Emily to cultivate a lush kitchen garden. The region had a much longer growing season than that of Maine or Alberni, and several varieties of lettuce, onions, carrots, and potatoes soon began to emerge from the soil. As the months progressed, the more well-established farms in the area yielded wheat, oats and hay, while orchard trees bore cascades of fruit in a riot of colours—cherry, peach, pear and plum, all to be enjoyed fresh off the tree or bottled for the root cellar.

By the end of their first year in the Willamette region, Emily had decided that she and her family were living in a veritable land of plenty —the kind of place where she could happily settle down for the remainder of her days. John Patterson's sawmill was fully refurbished and humming with production. Edward, Abbie and Beckie attended school in Butteville. Alice gallivanted about the house and garden with the ever-adventurous Frank toddling behind. Friendly neighbours came calling to chat over tea. Emily had been able to provide her nursing and midwifery skills on many an occasion as word spread through the community of her expertise. Life was good by the shores of Champoeg Creek.

CHAPTER 8

Journey of Sorrow

"Mama, I don't feel so well."

Nine-year-old Abbie had been listless for a day or two, unwilling to help with the garden plot. The summer of 1868, unlike that of the previous year, was excessively hot and dry in the Willamette region. Emily and the children had spent long hours in the out-of-doors, working hard to keep this season's kitchen garden well established and thriving. Lack of rainfall had necessitated frequent trips to the creek to obtain water for irrigating the crops. Good, clean well water was reserved for drinking and washing. To cool off under the glare of the sun, Emily had allowed the children to wade in the creek shallows—an activity particularly enjoyed by Frank, who at the age of two was well into the pleasures of discovering the world around him. Champoeg and Case creeks had numerous quiet bends and shaded eddies, somewhat stagnant and mosquito-infested by late summer, but still delightful for exploring. Emily tried to ensure that everyone wore sun hats and slathered on plenty of citronella oil or rubbed their bare arms with lemon grass to avoid mosquito bites. By early evening, the irksome beasts were out in full force.

Emily packed Abbie off to bed with a cup of water and a warm blanket, but her daughter failed to show improvement in the hours and days ahead. Alarmingly, John and the rest of the children soon began coming down with the same symptoms in varying degrees of severity—dry cough, aching muscles, and nausea all soon made worse by fever and chills. Emily herself soon began to feel lethargic. At this time of the year, she knew that her mind should have been set upon harvesting the second planting of late-summer vegetables and beginning the annual home preserving regimen—yet her energies did not seem to be up to the most mundane of household tasks.

Convinced that her family was under attack with a severe strain of influenza, Emily summoned every ounce of her limited energies to lift the lid of the heavy medicine chest and rummage amongst its contents. Castor oil was her most trusted remedy—gagging to the taste but well proven in treating a wide variety of ills. She insisted upon each of the children slurping down a dose from their own individual spoons. Beckie retched hers back up almost immediately. Alice was crying softly, curled up in a miserable ball upon her feather mattress. Frank, his breathing laboured and shallow, whimpered in a disturbed sleep, his skin hot to the touch. Emily struggled to stay on her feet as she moved from child to child, dabbing sweaty foreheads with pieces of damp flannel and speaking gentle words of reassurance.

"John, what is this!" she cried in exhaustion and frustration, after a week had passed with no improvement. Her husband merely shook his head in reply, his expression vacant. He had given up on working at the sawmill after three days of valiant perseverance and had thrown himself into bed, flecks of sawdust clinging to his sweat-soaked body from head to toe. Emily slumped into a kitchen chair and pored over her medical books, pausing every so often to lay her head down upon the open volume before her and close her eyes. Fever was the family's main complaint—a burning, sweat-inducing fever that seemed to subside after a day or two only to reoccur hours later. No amount of traditional remedies seemed to be having any desired effect. Flipping through pages, Emily considered the various possibilities. There was no discoloration or rash, so measles, chickenpox and scarlet fever were ruled out. Bronchial infection and pneumonia produced a wracking, phlegmy cough that clogged the airways but no one seemed to have reached this stage. There was no presence of a thick grey membrane coating the throat and tonsils, ruling out diphtheria. Emily bathed her face with water and resumed her search, turning pages half-heartedly. Her eyes met the heading of a chapter entitled "Diseases of the Tropics." She paused to reread the heading. *Tropical disease*. She had read through this chapter before as the Pattersons had steamed southward for the Panama isthmus. She had never for a moment considered the state of Oregon as "tropical," although this particular summer locals had told her that the weather was much warmer than usual. Rising painfully, she made her way over to the medicine chest and once again dug through its contents, closely examining each and every bottle that she had carefully nested amidst straw inside. Larger bottles affixed with paper labels and clear sealing wax had been wrapped in layers of muslin cloth to protect their contents within. The black ink had run on some of the labels, but it did not take Emily long to find what she had been looking for: a brown glass bottle labelled Warburg's Tincture.

Before travelling to China, Emily had researched every source of information she could find on treating malaria—scourge of tropical regions throughout the world. The name for the disease had originated from the Medieval Italian *mala aria* or "bad air" and malaria had long been associated with swamps and marshland. Emily learned that centuries ago, legend told of a feverish Indian who came across a pool of stagnant water somewhere on the eastern slopes of the Andes mountain range in South America. Delirious with thirst, he drank quantities of the water despite its bitter taste. Much to the man's amazement his fever quickly abated. The pool happened to be surrounded by a grove of evergreens, later to become known as *chinchona* or *quina-quina* trees. Word quickly spread of the Indian's seemingly miraculous recovery, and the bark of these trees would later become renowned among Indigenous communities ranging from Venezuela to Bolivia as cure for fever. Jesuit missionaries introduced the bark to European medical circles around 1640 and in ensuing years it became widely accepted that quinine, the chemical compound derived from the bark, contained active anti-malarial properties. The full formula for Warburg's Tincture, invented by Dr. Carl Warburg of Germany in 1834, had yet to be published, but as it contained disulphate of quinine, it had become recognized as an effective treatment.

Emily had always been cautious in her selection of medicines. For every legitimate treatment that had come on the market over the years, there seemed to be an equal number of quack "miracle cures"—products which promised much but delivered little in the way of relief. Now she held an almost-full bottle of Warburg's Tincture in her hands, purchased eight long years ago in New York. There was no information as to shelf life. She knew that alcohol was a preservative, which could effectively sustain active ingredients in a variety of products for an indefinite time period. Could the cure for her family's illness have begun days ago, simply by taking a spoonful of medicine from a long-forgotten bottle buried deep within her own medicine chest? Emily decided to take the first dose herself and find out. She poured a small amount in a glass, quaffed it down with a liberal amount of water and collapsed into a chair, surrendering herself to sleep.

"Edward! Wake up!"

Edward, at fifteen, was difficult to waken at the best of times. He had built himself his own small shack in a clearing off to the side of the Patterson house, well removed for privacy but within close enough reach to the outhouse.

"Go away!" he muttered, burying his face in his pillow.

"Edward Patterson!" Emily repeated in a loud firm voice. "You must drink this. It's medicine that will make you feel better. Come on! Sit up now and drink it."

She brought her arm behind him and forced him up, carefully keeping the rim of the cup in her opposite hand covered to prevent spillage while he thrashed in protest.

"Leave me alone, Mum!"

Edward was still burning with fever, and to Emily's mind, hallucinating. He had never acknowledged her as his mother and it seemed that in recent years, no matter how much she tried to be a friend and engage in conversation, his attitude had become sullen and distant. John had assured her that the behaviour was normal for a young adolescent man and she was not to take it to heart.

"Edward Patterson, you are going to drink down this medicine!"

In days ahead, Emily would emphatically state "it was purely by the grace of God" that she had managed to get every last member of her family to swallow a dose of the bitter-tasting Warburg's Tincture, leading to their gradual but steady recovery. No one knew exactly what had caused the dreadful malady, although down through the centuries, there had been sporadic outbreaks of fever in the Columbia/Willamette region. Little did anyone realize that if a solitary traveller unwittingly infected with malaria ventured upriver in the heat of summer's day and chanced to be bitten by a mosquito, an epidemic was in the making.

As the cooler days of fall descended, Emily returned to her chores of preparing the family's winter food supply. There were tomatoes and cucumbers to be pickled, apples purchased from neighbouring farms to be cooked into sauce and bottled, not to mention a couple of turkeys to fatten. She sent Edward to the store in Butteville time and again for quantities of salt, sugar and cider vinegar, along with orders for fall rye and additional sacks of flour for Thanksgiving and Christmas baking. All the while she kept a worried eye upon Frank, who had not recovered in the same satisfactory manner as the rest of the Pattersons. Her normally bright and extrovert little boy continued to appear wan and listless, reluctant to eat or drink and explore the world as a curious toddler should. Young as he was, Frank had not yet developed the natural resilience and antibodies to fend off disease. The family could only watch helplessly as Frank's condition further deteriorated. Emily set up a bed near the wood stove and lay with him day and night. He lapsed in and out of consciousness while she gently massaged his swollen feet and legs, murmuring words of love and encouragement. Thanksgiving celebrations were all but cast aside. Surrounded by his family, Frank Patterson died on December 12, 1868.

It was a lonely and dreary journey to Butteville cemetery no matter the season but especially so in the depths of winter. Gnarled branches of oak and cottonwood trees hung like black talons over the wagon road and a coating of frost lay thick upon the bent-over prairie grasses. Emily was in readiness for the inevitable day, having arranged for the delivery of new black dresses for her daughters and making repairs on funeral attire that she had carefully set aside for herself, John and Edward. One never knew when there was going to be a funeral. John had taken her up to the sawmill shortly after Frank's death to show her the little coffin that he had built days previously. He had kept it a secret from her and it was the only time that she had submitted herself to wracking tears of sorrow.

"I'm supposed to make people better!" she sobbed, falling into her husband's arms. "Isn't that what a nurse is supposed to do? But I couldn't make my own son better!"

Shortly into the New Year, the Pattersons relocated to Butteville, abandoning their Champoeg Creek home. Emily had decided that she simply could not bear constant reminders of Frank. A new start in new surroundings would surely help to ease the pain of loss. Albion Chenery, the mystery man who had originally driven the Pattersons to Champoeg Creek the year previously, had kindly offered to share his home with them, while in his words, they "reorganized their lives." Mr. Chenery had learned of Frank's death just after Christmas and had dropped by to pay his respects. Not ordinarily prone to sharing her troubles, Emily had surprised herself by speaking openly of her grief and desire to leave.

"I've got a small place just south of Butteville . . . subdivision of the Case property," Mr. Chenery remarked casually, as if he were offering a cup of tea. "Nothing fancy, but there's room for yourself and your husband, along with the kids. Near enough that the sawmill would still be in reach. Could use some of the wood myself for my carpentry business."

"We wouldn't want to impose," Emily protested. "What of your own people . . . your wife and children?"

"All dead," Mr. Chenery said simply, barely raising an eyebrow.

Emily was horrified at her faux pas and inwardly vowed to make amends as her husband graciously accepted Mr. Chenery's offer of a roof over their heads and a working partnership.

In the months ahead, Emily would come to realize what a fortuitous blessing it was that the lonely gentleman had come into their lives. Albion Chenery was a skilled carpenter and provided much backup support for John Patterson at the sawmill. The Chenery home was of sound construction and spotlessly clean throughout with a nearby enclosure for livestock and a well-tended orchard. There were the sad indicators that the home had once been a lively one. Toys and books were packed neatly into boxes, a wooden rocking horse stood idle, and an exquisite china tea service was elegantly displayed in a glass-framed cabinet. Emily often wondered about the Chenery family and how they met their sad end, but she knew well enough not to ask further questions. Mr. Chenery never broached the subject. But one day, while visiting Butteville Cemetery to lay fresh flowers upon Frank's grave and pull some weeds, she happened upon the Chenery family graves. Once again, her eyes filled with tears as she read the dates and names chiselled on the weathered gravestones. Albion and Harriet Chenery's son, Clark A. Chenery, died the same day he was born, on January 20, 1856. Two daughters, Leonori A. Chenery, age three and a half, and Loren M. Chenery, age one and a half, had died four days apart in January of 1861. Albion's wife, Harriet Ann Clark Chenery, had died on September 10, 1861, at the age of twenty-two.

Never had Emily felt as much empathy for an individual as she did for Albion Chenery. Somehow this poor brave soul had managed to carry on, all the while bearing the grievous weight of so much loss upon his shoulders. She wondered at times how he managed to cope. To be sure, there were days when she found him seated alone in the barn, head in his hands, looking the picture of abject misery. She would bring him a cup of tea and offer to pray with him. He did not seem to be a devoutly religious man, although he did attend the little Butteville

The Champoeg church bell on permanent display.

Church on occasion, sitting quietly at the back and not joining in with the hymns. He did seem to take particular fascination in the church bell, which he pointed out one day to Emily and the children as they left the service.

"An old survivor, that bell," he said with a smile. "You know that bell used to belong to the church in Champoeg town? They dug it out of the mud a few days after the flood of 1861, cleaned it up and it was as good as new—ringing just as well as it ever did."

"How amazing!" Emily exclaimed. "A very lucky find . . . it could have lain buried forever."

It was not long before Emily realized the true significance for Albion Chenery of the bell's resurrection. The year of 1861 had been a terrible one for him. To see the Champoeg bell rescued from the mud and destruction at the end of that very same year had undoubtedly given him some small semblance of hope and renewal. Gazing at the beautiful bell—its metallic sheen glimmering brightly in the morning sun— Emily had a profound sense that she too could recover, after her journey of sorrow.

CHAPTER 9

Family Reunions

On May 16, 1869, John and Emily welcomed their fourth baby daughter, Adelaide (Addie) Agnes. They continued to reside on the outskirts of Butteville with Albion Chenery, who seemed perfectly at ease with sharing his home indefinitely. But John Patterson's sawmilling business was failing. When it was clear that the Northern Pacific Railway connections would bypass Butteville for the neighbouring community of Aurora, industrial growth stagnated and Butteville fell into a slow but steady decline. Emily could see that her husband was restless, and she was not the least bit surprised when he came to her one day and announced that he was selling out.

"Can't afford to keep losing money," he said simply. "I'll go back to my steamboating for a while and see where it leads us."

Albion Chenery was visibly sad when he heard of the family's plans to up stakes, but acknowledged that times were proving difficult in Butteville.

"We will be forever grateful to you for taking us in, Mr. Chenery," Emily told him.

She inwardly worried about their dear friend's well-being. He told them that he was formulating plans of his own . . . perhaps a move to Portland, or "wherever the compass points."

The Pattersons moved to Rainier, Oregon, a lumber and grist milling community at the confluence of the Columbia and Cowlitz rivers. Steamboat service was fast and frequent, with the industrial hubs of Portland, Astoria and Oregon City in relatively close proximity. John Patterson went back to his former work of delivering mail via steamboat up and downriver. In the early days of 1872, the family received the surprise and welcome word that John's younger brother, Calvin Patterson, was headed for Oregon in command of the sailing vessel *Edward James*. As contact with their families on the East Coast had been sporadic over the years during the Civil War, Emily and John eagerly anticipated his arrival. Calvin Patterson, still youthful at the age of forty, showed up at the door of the Pattersons' Rainier home late one spring evening and ushered himself inside to a round of hugs and handshakes.

"Well, who do we have here?" he asked, giving a laughing two-year-old Addie a joyous toss in the air. "You've been busy, haven't you, John! What a splendid family!"

Emily blushed demurely at the "you've been busy" comment and decided she would not reveal that she was pregnant again—just yet. She could see that her husband and Calvin enjoyed a deep brotherly comradery. They talked together by the hour, immersed in reminiscence of their seagoing journeys and the general economic state of the West Coast. Before long, John took up a position as first mate aboard the *Edward James* and seemed to bear no disgruntlement to working under the command of his younger sibling.

Neighbours of the Pattersons were scattered over a broad area in Rainier. With John away from home for days at a time, Emily often ventured out on lengthy walks with Addie in her arms for afternoon visitations. She was delighted to find that one nearby couple, Abington and Harriet Ridley, had also made their way out west from Maine. Harriet was also alone more often than not, explaining that her husband had found work at a sawmill "up in Canada," and came home only on rare occasions. Abington Ridley was away when his first-born son Gideon died, and Harriet had born her grief in solitude. The Ridleys' second son, Leon, was still a babe in arms, but he was a sickly child, often prone to infections of the upper respiratory tract. By the fall of 1872, it was clear that he was fighting the same malady that had claimed his older brother. Emily could see that Harriet had become severely rundown with worry and sleepless nights.

"Where exactly is your husband?" Emily asked one morning, as she prepared a soothing mustard plaster to place upon Leon's congested chest. The mustard seed would dilate capillaries in the lungs, allowing Leon to cough more productively. She had left Addie in the care of her elder sisters, not wishing to expose her to anything potentially contagious.

"A small sawmill up the coast," Harriet replied. "Hastings Mill, it's called."

"Is it very far from here?"

"I believe about two or three days' journey by sail with favourable winds. . . . Can you help my Leon?"

"I'll do my very best," Emily said, "but I do feel that your husband should be sent for as quickly as possible."

Harriet promptly burst into tears, wringing her hands. Emily gave her a gentle hug.

"I'll write a note," she told the distraught mother. "My husband and his brother are due back tomorrow from Astoria aboard the *Edward James*. We'll insist that they sail for Hastings Mill straight away."

Calvin Patterson needed no persuading when Emily confronted him the next day to ask if he could delay whatever responsibilities were pending to deliver an important message up the coast.

"But I cannot promise a two-day journey," he told her truthfully. "If conditions are rough around Cape Flattery, or if we get hit with an easterly wind, we won't be entering Canadian waters any time soon, let alone making Stamp's Mill."

"It's called Hastings Mill," Emily said patiently.

Calvin Patterson chuckled. "It used to be called Stamp's Mill when it

Harriet Ridley and her first child, c. 1870s.

opened for business back in '67, very first sawmill operation on the south shore of the Burrard Inlet, but of course Captain Stamp did what he was best at and got himself ousted a few years back. There's still a few folks around that call it by the old name."

"Was that Captain Edward Stamp? The one who owned the mill at Alberni on Vancouver Island?"

"The very one." Calvin nodded. "The place seems to be running well under the new management. I can't say I blame Ridley for taking on employment up there."

"Well he's needed here!" Emily said firmly. "Can you please find him and tell him that."

In less than a week's time, Abington Ridley arrived in Rainier by horseback. He galloped right up to the very door of the Ridley cottage late one evening and barged inside to find Emily tending to a much improved Leon. Harriet was sleeping soundly in the loft upstairs. Emily sternly put a finger to her lips.

"Thank you for coming, Mr. Ridley," she said quietly. "Your family is fine."

The exhausted man slumped into a chair. He was soaking wet and caked with mud—in no way appearing like someone who had just embarked from a sailing vessel. After a few minutes rest and a hot cup of coffee, he told her how he had received the message from Calvin Patterson, directly off the *Edward James*. Calvin had warned him

Abington Herbert Ridley

that stormy weather brewing off Cape Flattery had delayed their arrival and, with the barometer dropping, there was no sign of any immediate improvement. Not to be deterred, Abington Ridley had quickly gone off and recruited four native men to help him paddle south through the inland waters of Puget Sound to the sawmilling community of Steilacoom. From there he had travelled the rest of the way via horseback—a distance of over one hundred miles factoring in river crossings and various detours. It was remarkable that he had made the journey in such a short span of time, and Emily was favourably impressed despite her dislike for chronically absent husbands.

"I suppose my husband and his brother will be making their way back shortly aboard the *Edward James*," she remarked.

"I suppose," Abington replied. "Last time I saw them they were touring the sawmill."

>‹

It would be yet another week before Captain Calvin Patterson and John Patterson returned to Rainier. John spoke in glowing terms about what he had seen north of the Canadian border at Hastings Sawmill.

"Marvellous operation. Canadian chap from Halifax by the name of Raymur has the place running like clockwork. All the latest equipment, trees by the score, plenty of good moorage. . . . I've never seen anything quite like it."

"I hear that Captain Edward Stamp was involved," Emily said with just a hint of suspicion as she carefully eased herself into a rocking chair.

"Yes, that he was." John nodded understandingly. "And yes, I recall full well how things went wrong in Alberni. But now he's long gone and there is new investment flowing at Hastings Mill from good reliable sources. They've offered me a very good position and, damn it, Emily, I am inclined to accept. Yes, I know, bad language, but imagine! You and the children will have a proper home . . . there's a store, a school, a few hotels are starting to spring up . . . there's even the promise of a national railway line. You know British Columbia is a Canadian province now . . . the railway sealed the deal."

Emily sighed, instantly recognizing that her long unspoken dream of a stable, permanent home was about to be quashed yet again.

"And what of your brother? Aren't you supposed to be his first mate?"

"Little brother Calvin will do just fine!" came a voice from the door.

Calvin Patterson ushered himself inside, having caught the tail end of their conversation.

"I'll be happy to see the last of him!" he bellowed. "Big know-it-all brother, every minute of the day, telling me what to do and how to do it . . . a bona fide Captain Bligh if there ever was one! Even had to fish him out of the drink one day when he decided to go for a swim with his clothes on."

In the next instant, John and Calvin Patterson were on the floor, tussling and cuffing each other amidst hearty gales of laughter. They paid no heed to Emily's frantic calls for minding the dining table with its neatly arranged cups and saucers—the first china ones that she had dared purchase since leaving San Francisco. There would be weeks of packing once again, endless decisions over what to take and what to leave behind, weighing up the options for modes of transportation . . . it was exhausting to think about. Emily felt a sharp kick in her belly, as if the little developing Patterson within shared her thoughts of annoyance. On November 29, 1872, Calvin Oric Patterson, named in honour of his uncle, was born in Rainier.

John Patterson returned to Hastings Sawmill early in 1873 to begin his new position and make arrangements for some sort of living quarters for his family. The prospect of relocating to yet another remote inlet in wilderness surroundings carried its share of worries, but one consoling factor for Emily was that a move back north also meant a return to the birth land of Alice and dear departed Frank. Emily had listened with interest to Abington Ridley's description of travelling the sheltered inland waters of Puget Sound via canoe. The sound could be prone to rough seas like anywhere else but was definitely preferable to rounding Cape Flattery in an overcrowded, overloaded steamer.

Once again, Emily began the familiar task of hauling out the family trunks and sorting essentials from expendables. She was delighted to learn that Harriet Ridley and fully recovered Leon would be joining them in the move. It was evident that Abington Ridley had firmly established himself at Hastings Mill and had no intention of searching for work closer to Rainier. Despite the trepidation of leaving her much beloved homeland, Harriet had come to trust Emily, stoically declaring that she would follow her "to the ends of the earth."

One individual, however, would not be joining them. Edward

Patterson, at nearly twenty years of age, had decided that the time had come to strike out on his own. He had greatly matured over the past couple of years and was clearly eager to chart his own course.

"But where will you go?" Emily asked, watching him pack up what appeared to be a rather inadequate quantity of supplies into a canvas rucksack.

"Oh, I don't know," he mused nonchalantly. "Maybe back east . . . New York, Boston perhaps."

"I wish you the very best of success!" Emily said firmly. "It is only natural that you should want to venture out into the world and forge your own path."

Edward seemed surprised at Emily's open declaration of understanding and spontaneously planted a gentle kiss upon her cheek. Emily knew that she would deeply miss her husband's first-born son, having relied upon him so many times over the years to watch over his half-siblings— while no doubt eager to carry on with activities more akin to his own interests.

"Take care, son!" she added.

The Pattersons and Ridleys initially had to travel in the wrong direction before they could turn to the north. In early April, they took a short steamboat journey southward on the Columbia to the townsite of Kalama in Washington Territory, terminus of a four-horse stagecoach service to Olympia over the Cowlitz Trail. The Cowlitz, infamous for its mudholes, treacherous creek crossings and surrounding forest canopy so thick that sunlight could barely penetrate, was gradually being widened and improved—but still harrowing enough to persuade motion sickness-prone coach passengers to disembark and walk their way north.

Olympia, at the southernmost end of Puget Sound, was the official seat of government for Washington Territory and a thriving centre of maritime commerce. From Olympia, merchant and passenger vessels of all kinds navigated through Puget Sound's vast maze of channels and islands, calling in at the seaport communities of Tacoma, Seattle, Port Townsend among others. As always, Emily marvelled at the beauty of the region she was passing through. To the east, the snow-covered mass of 14,000-foot Mount Rainier was truly the highest mountain that she had ever seen—its solitary, majestic form in stark contrast to the craggy landscape of the Olympic Peninsula to the west. Before long, Puget Sound spilled open into the wide expanse of the Strait of Juan de Fuca, invisibly bisected by the U.S.–Canada border.

There was no direct passenger service from Olympia to Hastings Sawmill, necessitating a stopover in Victoria. Emily wondered if being back in the place where Frank was born would trigger a certain degree of melancholy, but Victoria of 1873 had grown substantially from the town that she had known some seven years previously. Now officially the capital of the province of British Columbia, Victoria was a lively and prospering centre of commerce with a population in excess of five thousand, its busy streets lined with all manner of shops, lodgings, restaurants and saloons. The crowded inner harbour, along with neighbouring Esquimalt, had evolved into major ports of call, providing moorage facilities for vessels from the farthest reaches of the Pacific and beyond.

"Where is our ship, Mama?" Alice asked, peering quizzically over the forest of masts in the harbour flanking Wharf Street.

"Papa told us to look for the steamer *Maude*," Emily replied. Her husband had sent funds for travel and specific instructions by mail, but had been unable to take time off work to accompany them. At present, the side-wheel steamer SS *Maude* was the only vessel providing passenger service between Victoria and Hastings Mill. Sailings were sparse —only once a week or even less frequent—causing Emily to ask herself another question as she set about searching for a rooming house with vacancy for a three-night stay: *Just where on earth is Hastings Mill?*

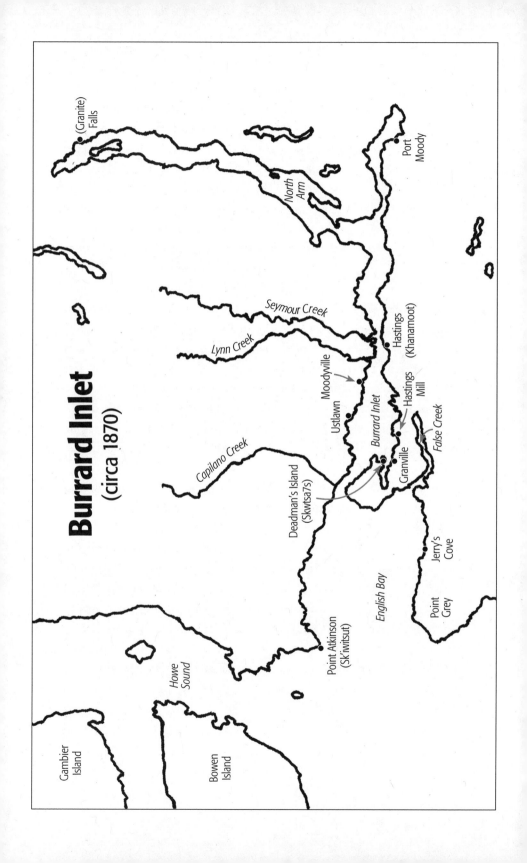

Burrard Inlet
(circa 1870)

(Granite)
Falls

Port
Moody

North
Arm

Seymour Creek

Hastings
(Khanamoot)

Lynn Creek

Moodyville

Ustlawn

Hastings
Mill

Burrard Inlet

False Creek

Capilano Creek

Granville

Deadman's Island
(Skwtsa7s)

Jerry's
Cove

English Bay

Point
Grey

Point Atkinson
(Sk'iwitsut)

Howe
Sound

Gambier
Island

Bowen
Island

CHAPTER 10

Hastings Mill

Georgia Strait could be notoriously fickle at any time of the year and April of 1873 was no exception. Emily tried to soothe a seasick Alice, miserably curled up on a passenger bench aboard the SS *Maude*. The vessel had departed Victoria just after daybreak and ten hours later was still grinding its way through a gentle swell—insignificant enough for large, ocean-going vessels, but resulting in a bumpy ride for craft of smaller dimensions.

"Not far to go!" the captain called out cheerfully from the pilothouse. "Narrows dead ahead!"

"I think we may all be dead before we reach those narrows," Harriet Ridley murmured to Emily.

It was nearly dusk by the time the *Maude* drew past the Prospect Point signalling station and entered the sheltered waters of Burrard Inlet. To the north, an expanse of thickly forested mountains, still snow-laden at their highest peaks, spread as far as the eye could see.

Along the flatter south shore, there appeared to be clusters of small communities, flanked by more thick stands of ancient forest.

At long last, as the *Maude* was powered down in preparation for docking at the south shore, Emily and her fellow passengers had their first up-close and unobstructed view of Hastings Mill. The sawmill itself was by far the largest of the small collection of structures clustered on the waterfront—its refuse burner belching smoke, which drifted lazily down-inlet. As they drew closer, Emily noted a wooden building perched upon a wharf, which appeared to be a store, with plenty of adjacent moorage space. Directly in front of the building a large damaged sailing vessel lay moored, listing precariously to one side—something of a blight upon an otherwise well-ordered scene.

"The *Cornelius*," *Maude*'s captain retorted dryly in response to Emily's query about the vessel. "Got blown into Howe Sound after the captain tried to pilot her out of Burrard Inlet under full sail . . . foolish idiot! Wish they'd hurry up and scrap the damn thing . . . takes up valuable moorage!"

"I can see Papa!" Addie called out excitedly.

John Patterson and Abington Ridley waved their arms and called

SS Maude *at Nanaimo, c. 1872.*

out greetings as the *Maude* drew up dockside. In the next instant the men were being swarmed by children, while Emily and Harriet descended the gangway as gingerly as they could with their full skirts, baby Calvin and numerous pieces of hand luggage.

"Hello, my darling!" John Patterson greeted Emily with a hug and a kiss. "How was your journey from Rainier?"

"Queasy," Emily replied truthfully.

"I've got a dray ordered for the luggage. Come on up and see your new home! It's not a far walk."

"Did you build us a house, Papa?" Abbie asked.

"Well, I'm working on it," he replied, as they trudged up a sawdust-laden street from the wharf.

The mill grounds seemed relatively quiet at day's end and Emily inquired as to where everyone was.

"The early shift workers are probably asleep," her husband told her. "Or drinking away their earnings over at Gassy's."

"Gassy's?"

"Gassy Jack Deighton. Local character . . . quite the talker, that's why they call him Gassy. I'm sure you'll meet him before long."

John Patterson led his family up a gentle slope, pointing out various amenities as they went. The sawmill itself was a long, narrow building, clearly designed to facilitate processing logs of massive dimensions. Equipment had been shut down as evening darkness descended, although the orange glow from the giant refuse burner indicated that plenty of mill waste was still being disposed of. A flume carried fresh water to generate steam for the mill machinery and service the nearby cookhouse. The building that Emily had noticed from the *Maude* was indeed a general store—a large, wooden structure built atop pylons, adjacent to the cookhouse. A large building opposite served as a storage warehouse, library and community hall. Bleachers had been built alongside its north-facing wall facing an expansive sawdust field.

"For sporting events on holidays," John explained. "Lots of fun, I'm told."

Emily was curious to know what had happened to Captain Edward Stamp, and her husband related everything that he knew. Apparently

Hastings Sawmill and townsite, 1872.

undaunted by the failed Alberni venture, Stamp had continued in his quest to build a new mill, searching for trees of exceptional quality and easy access. In 1864, that search led him to Burrard's Inlet—so named by Captain George Vancouver, who had explored the region some seventy-two years earlier. After some deliberation, Stamp settled upon a location about halfway along the inlet's south shore just west of the seasonal Squamish community of Kumkumlye (big leaf maple trees). The surroundings met his criteria perfectly. There were vast stands of ancient-growth cedar and Douglas fir spread across miles of gently undulating flatlands. Experimental soundings revealed water levels easily deep enough to establish port facilities for the largest of sea-going vessels. Access to fresh water for powering the steam engines would be achieved by constructing a flume to a nearby lake.

As per custom, Stamp returned to England to secure financial backers. By April of 1865, he had organized and incorporated the B.C. and Vancouver Island Spar, Lumber and Sawmill Company with £100,000 of British capital. Determined not to see a repeat of the mistakes made in Alberni, Stamp presented a lengthy document of strict pre-sale conditions to British Columbia's Colonial Secretary Frederick Seymour. Anxious to encourage industrial development on the British Columbia mainland, Seymour approved all of Stamp's demands and the mill was fully operational by June of 1867.

"But John, I recall you mentioning that Stamp is no longer here?" Emily asked.

Her husband nodded.

"For a time, everything seemed rosy for Stamp at Hastings Mill. Orders were filled for port cities of Australia, China, Hawaii, South America. . . . Douglas fir spars from Burrard Inlet were said to be the best ever shipped from any part of the world. But just as it was in Alberni, Stamp fell into disagreement with his financial backers and wound up resigning early in 1869. The mill has been sold a couple of times since but lately it has been doing very well under the management of Captain Raymur."

Walking a little farther the family passed several cottages, some of substantial size, others little more than rudimentary shacks. John stopped alongside one of the shacks, which appeared to be of recent construction.

Captain James Raymur

"Here we are," he said cheerfully. "I know it's going to be rather tight for space, but I can assure you it will only be temporary. There's your real new home, just over there."

He pointed to the nearby wooden foundation of what was clearly to become a much larger dwelling.

Emily could almost feel Abbie and Beckie's dismay, although she recognized that her husband must have worked long and hard in his off-duty hours to prepare some sort of interim shelter for his family. Closer inspection revealed that the two-room shack did have its advantages. Everything was of solid construction, with a clean, level floor, walls built high enough that there was no need to stoop, and a corrugated metal roof to keep out the rain. John had constructed new rope beds, and had even prepared feather-tick mattresses—a task that normally would have been taken on by Emily and her daughters. There was no room for a stove or kitchen of any kind, but in John's words, "everyone would be welcome to eat at the cookhouse."

"I guess it's all not quite what you were expecting," he said apologetically.

. "It's perfectly fine," Emily responded, with a reproachful look at her elder daughters. "We'll make do just fine."

><

Some Hastings Mill townsite amenities had been constructed very recently, including—much to Emily's pleasure—the first schoolhouse, an eighteen-by-forty-foot wood-frame building virtually across the street from their shack. Despite it being late in the 1873 school year, Emily insisted that her children be enrolled. The Public Schools Act had recently stipulated that any school in British Columbia required a minimum of ten students in attendance to be eligible for government funding. Owing to the townsite's transient population, Hastings Mill School had sporadically been operating well short of the legal quota. At present, Ada, Carrie and Fred Miller attended the school, along with Dick Alexander and one or two mixed-race children. The addition of Abbie, Beckie and Alice would bring attendance figures up to nine, but the school was still one student short of meeting the government standard. Emily decided that she would try to resolve the situation by approaching little Addie, not quite four years old.

"Addie, how would you like to go to school with your sisters?" she asked.

Addie appeared somewhat undecided. Alice, keen to attend classes, put forward a simple suggestion.

"Why don't you bring along your doll and a book? That would make you feel better, wouldn't it, Addie?"

Much to Emily's relief, Addie took an immediate liking to school, more due to the fact that she and her sisters made up nearly half of the classroom population than any personal comforts. The schoolroom was still something of a bare-bones affair, with one long table and benches as opposed to desks, but each child had a slate for writing, and a small cordwood stove had been installed for winter heating.

Delighted with the way things were falling into place, Emily decided to organize a birthday party for Addie, who would be turning four on May 10th. Realizing that the Pattersons' temporary lodging would be impossibly small and not wishing to chance the frequently wet weather for an outdoor picnic, she boldly arranged for the party to be held in the next most logical location—Hastings Mill School. After school dismissal at three on Addie's birthday, she enlisted the help of some native women to sweep out the room and carry over tin plates and cups from the Patterson shack. The weather cooperated so races and games were held outside on the mill grounds.

Much to everyone's pleasure, Captain Fry of the *Niagara*, in port to take on lumber, contributed a surprise treat of freshly baked currant buns. Everyone agreed that this was a special offering and well deserving of some added fun—a contest to see who could eat their currant bun the fastest. The prize was claimed by Leon Nahu, a Hawaiian boy who lived in the nearby Coal Harbour community of Kanaka Ranch. Emily did not discriminate on who attended Addie's party—a fact not unnoticed by Emma Alexander, wife of Hastings Mill Store manager Richard Alexander, who had helped with the festivities.

"I think it's wonderful that you've invited all the children," she remarked. "They play together so well."

"I'm happy that they're having fun," Emily replied. "My daughters have endured a lot of upheaval over the years."

"I can certainly appreciate that!"

Emily was to make several friends at Hastings Mill, but she found an especially kindred spirit in Emma Alexander. Like Emily, Emma had faced her own series of epic adventures. Years earlier, she had departed from her native London, England, aboard the SS *Tynemouth*—one of the infamous Bride Ships which had been commissioned to transport willing, eligible young women to Victoria. The bride ship saga was a social experiment, specifically intended to provide a stabilizing, Christian environment for single young men in the Crown Colony of British Columbia. Emma, one of sixty prospective brides aboard the cramped living quarters of the *Tynemouth*, had endured a hellish voyage beset

Emma Helen Alexander, one of Emily's closest friends.

with gales and two violent crew uprisings. Many of the women would later claim it was "truly miraculous" that the *Tynemouth* reached its final destination. Unlike some of her shipboard colleagues, Emma deliberately took her time to get established in her new setting. She worked as a nanny in Victoria, where she eventually met and married Scotsman Richard Alexander in 1867. After Richard took up employment at Hastings Mill, Emma followed in December of 1870, journeying to Burrard Inlet with two baby boys and all the fixings for a Christmas dinner aboard the steamer *Grappler*. Now at twenty-nine years of age, Emma Alexander had accumulated a lifetime's worth of character-building experiences.

"Eliza Scott Alexander, what a mess you are!"

Emma brought out a handkerchief and dabbed at the cheeks of a little girl who had been toddling about the racecourse with the remnants of a sawdust-coated currant bun in her hand.

"My daughter," Emma sighed. "Into everything, as usual!"

"How old is she?" Emily asked.

"She'll be two in September."

Emily noticed that Emma seemed concerned as she spoke about Eliza and wondered if anything was wrong.

"I'm expecting again," Emma confided. "The baby is due around Christmas and I'll have to travel to Victoria for my confinement. I don't know how I'll ever manage with the children."

"Why do you have to travel to Victoria?" Emily asked.

Emma explained that the nearest doctor to Hastings Mill resided in New Westminster. Obtaining his services often meant sending a native messenger on a three-mile paddle up Burrard Inlet to the "End of the Road" at Hastings, then on an arduous, ten-mile journey via horseback along the rough Douglas Road, which had been hacked through the wilderness in 1865 by the Royal Engineers. Of course the return journey would then have to be made by the doctor—if one happened to be available at all. The attending doctor would then charge fifteen dollars for his services. With professional medical help at least one full day away, white women had always opted to travel to Victoria or New Westminster well in advance of their anticipated delivery.

"There was a terrible accident a couple of years ago," Emma went on. "Dr. Black of New Westminster received word late in the night that a man here by the name of Brooks had attempted suicide. Brooks was alive but very much in need of medical attention. Dr. Black had travelled the road between New Westminster and Burrard Inlet so many times the journey was more or less routine for him, but that night his horse evidently slipped in a stream bed and crushed him to death."

"How dreadful!" Emily gasped.

"I don't know anyone in New Westminster," Emma said, "but I have friends in Victoria that I can stay with. It's just a question of what to do with Eliza and the boys."

"Well, this time, why don't you have your baby here at Hastings Mill?" Emily suggested. "I'm a nurse. I can help you."

Emma appeared startled and uncertain at the suggestion.

"You're a nurse?"

"Not officially," Emily admitted, "but I've delivered many babies in my time and I can assure you that I am very competent at what I do. Please give it some thought."

Emma promised that she would.

As evening descended, more adults arrived to join in the festivities for music and card games. Much to Emily's satisfaction, Addie's birthday party was pronounced a resounding success.

CHAPTER 11

Crossroads of Cultures

It did not take Emily long to learn that there were clearly defined social boundaries at Hastings Mill. Mill employees were an eclectic assortment of multi-nationals—Canadians, Americans, British, Europeans, Chinese and Hawaiians among others, as well as members of the Indigenous Squamish, Musqueam and Tsleil-Waututh communities. Employees of mixed race, Chinese and other nationalities lived in small shacks at the eastern perimeter of the property. Chinese employees were singularly forbidden to reside any closer to the sawmill precincts. Middle-class family cottages and services were clustered upon the land due south of the sawmill. Hastings Mill's "blueblood residents"—those of higher social status such as Captain Raymur—occupied the more spacious properties up on the hillside to the west. The Patterson house, when complete, would occupy a lot midway between the blueblood quarter and the family cottages.

The consumption of alcohol was strictly forbidden at Hastings

Mill—a policy decreed years ago by Captain Stamp. On September 30, 1867, an English sea captain by the name of John Deighton paddled his canoe into a cove known to the Squamish as Lucklucky (beautiful grove of maple trees) to the west of the mill boundary. Deighton had fallen on hard times while working as a riverboat pilot on the Fraser River and was hoping to begin a new venture. He had no shortage of eager volunteers when he produced a keg of whiskey and loudly requested help in building a drinking establishment at the western edge of the mill boundary, beyond the area of prohibition. Within twenty-four hours, John Deighton's Globe Saloon was open for business and lively with customers. It was not long before additional saloons were constructed, their proprietors eager to cash in on the zero-tolerance policy at the sawmill. Businesses offering everything from groceries to dry goods to laundry services were established along a waterfront wagon road. On March 1, 1870, the emerging townsite was officially named Granville. For the sake of convenience, Granville's post office operated out of the entry vestibule to Hastings Mill Store, which had long been used as the traditional drop-off point for mail. Official as it now was, Granville continued to be called "Gastown," in tribute to its colourful and ever-talkative founder, John "Gassy Jack" Deighton.

The more Emily came to know Hastings Mill and Granville, the more she realized that she was living at a cultural crossroads, populated by a diverse assortment of colourful characters. The non-Indigenous residents were predominantly male, from a host of ethnic backgrounds. Mill manager Captain James Raymur was a Nova Scotia-born, no-nonsense individual, who (much to Emily's liking) insisted upon cleanliness throughout the mill grounds. Mill accountant and store manager Richard Alexander, husband of Emma, was a handsome and energetic Scotsman who had travelled overland from Minneapolis to the Fraser River goldfields. Ontario-born Jonathan Miller was the region's first and only police officer, appointed in 1871 by a New Westminster magistrate. To Emily's knowledge, his wife Margaret was the only white woman in the community aside from herself, Harriet Ridley and Emma Alexander.

A large contingent of Kanakas—Hawaiian-born mill workers and their families—lived at Kanaka Ranch, a community on the shore of

Coal Harbour, down-inlet from the mill property. Across the harbour, communities of native residents inhabited the large peninsula which had been set aside as a military reserve. There were many mixed-race couples living in the region such as Joseph Silvey of the Azores and his native wife Kwahama Kwatleematt, Englishman Thomas Fisher and his fourteen-year-old child bride, Chilean-born Lavinia, and Irishman Joe Mannion, who had married a young Squamish woman by the name of Takood. In Emily's mind, the inhabitants of Burrard Inlet's south shore were as unique and diverse a population as she had ever come across.

Emily was more than relieved when her husband announced that the new Patterson home was finally ready for occupation. The weeks of living in a cramped and crowded shack had been starting to take their toll on everyone, and a two-storey house would seem like a palace by comparison. Windows were yet to be installed and there was a considerable amount of construction material still lying about, but temperatures were warming rapidly and the children had grown accustomed to spending more time outdoors than in. John had also been putting together their basic furniture needs—chairs, cabinets, and lantern stands —from the abundance of scrap lumber on hand at the mill. The Patterson dining table, however, took extra consideration. Dining tables were routinely built to accommodate large families at mealtimes but as Emily had observed over the years, they were also a convenient place to lay out a patient in need of medical care. Protected with a covering of oil-treated canvas, the family dining table could serve as a steady base upon which to splint a broken limb, stitch a laceration or perform emergency surgery. Emily decided that if she was to serve as both doctor and nurse in a community devoid of either, she would require a sizeable dining table. John complied by building her a sturdy extension table that could be lengthened or shortened as necessary.

Over ensuing weeks, word quickly circulated that a new arrival by the name of Emily Patterson was skilled in medical care. Hastings Mill

Hastings Mill, c. 1890s. The Pattersons' house is centre-left in foreground.

residents came or were brought to her door at all hours of the day or night with all manner of complaints—everything from splinters in fingers to more serious injuries like lacerations from mill saws or broken bones from logs sliding errantly on the skid roads. Shifts at the mill were long and employees would regularly be performing precision tasks with few hours of sleep in between. As Captain Raymur strictly upheld Captain Stamp's zero-tolerance policy on alcohol, many of the crewmen chose to head straight for the Granville saloons at day's end. Emily's conversations with patients took on a typical pattern while she staunched the flow of blood from an injury:

"How did this happen?" she would ask.

"Missed my mark with the planing saw."

"Hmm . . . and how much sleep did you get last night?"

"'Bout two or three hours . . . maybe more. Can't recall."

The odour of whiskey would be unmistakable in the air and often there was marked evidence of a fist fight or two. Emily would carefully wash any open wounds and douse them liberally with iodine, ignoring yelps of protest. She would finish off by applying bandage material purchased from the mill store or torn from her own bedsheets as the case warranted.

"There—now at the end of your next shift, you're to go straight home and get a proper amount of sleep!" she said firmly, knowing full well that her good advice would not be followed.

"Yes, much obliged, Missus Patterson," the patient would mutter, before slinking away.

Much as she enjoyed meeting and socializing with the various inhabitants of her community, Emily found herself most drawn to the Squamish, Musqueam and Tsleil-Waututh peoples who had populated Burrard Inlet and its surrounding regions from ancient times. Not so many years ago they had lived a well-ordered life, carving fish hooks of bone and antler, stripping select pieces of bark from the cedar tree to fashion baskets and clothing, harvesting the bounty of land and sea without any outside interference. Now, as had happened in Alberni, local native families were being rapidly assimilated under a tidal wave of foreign influence. They used metal coins to pay for tools and clothing, crockery and glassware. They were more likely to be seen wearing coveralls or long dresses of cotton print than apparel of deerskin and mountain goat hair. They sat dutifully in the newly built Methodist church at the western edge of Granville, listening to sermons and singing songs in a new and unfamiliar language.

Among the many native residents Emily came to know, Qua-hail-ya, wife of Gassy Jack Deighton, tended to be on her mind most frequently. Also known by her English name of Madeline, Qua-hail-ya was the niece of Deighton's first wife, who had died some years previously. At the age of twelve, young Qua-hail-ya had been told by her seriously ill aunt that she would be married off to Deighton. A year later in 1871, she had given birth to a son, Richard Mason Deighton. By the spring of 1873, Gassy Jack had expanded his business fortunes with the opening of Deighton House, a prestigious new hotel in the heart of Granville. He built and furnished a small cottage for himself and his family to reside in, well back in the forest behind the hotel. Gassy, a stout Englishman with a short beard and ruddy complexion, was a regular passerby on the boardwalk between Granville and Hastings Mill, occasionally accompanied by his wife and son.

At Gassy's bidding, his brother Thomas and sister-in-law Emma had recently arrived from England to take over day-to-day operations at the hotel. Upon their first meeting, Emma Deighton had seemed pleased to make Emily's acquaintance—overjoyed, in fact—and had almost immediately asked if Emily could assist her with some sewing for the hotel. Despite her already busy schedule, Emily had inadvertently found herself agreeing to the proposal. One late-summer morning, Emily and Alice strolled together down the boardwalk. Emily carried a full basket of slipcovers to deliver to Deighton House and Alice had made arrangements to spend the day with her friend Carrie Miller, who lived nearby. On route, they encountered Gassy Jack.

"Good morning, Mr. Deighton, how are you?" Emily greeted him.

"Ah, not so well," he chuffed in his loud, characteristic drawl. "Thinkin' about heading over to New Westminster for a spell. My brother's wife doesn't care much for Madeline and Richard. Madeline's not happy. Keeps disappearin' off to the north shore. I have to keep goin' over there to fetch her back."

"Qua-hail-ya has family over on the north shore, does she not?" Emily asked evenly.

Gassy did not reply, distracted by Alice, who had suddenly taken refuge behind her mother's skirts. A couple of Squamish men were sauntering up the boardwalk with fur pelts draped over their shoulders.

"What's the matter, young lady? You afraid of Indians?" Gassy asked.

"Her half-brother filled her with some stories years ago from our Alberni days," Emily sighed. "I'm afraid she hasn't forgotten."

"Well, they wouldn't dare lay a hand on you!" Gassy said flatly, before continuing on his way with a tip of the hat.

"Alice, you really should try to get over this irrational fear of Indians," Emily said annoyedly, as they carried on past the two men. "They're human like the rest of us."

"But they're so different from us," Alice meekly protested.

"Nonsense!"

John "Gassy Jack" Deighton, c. 1870s.

Emily and Alice parted ways after arriving at Deighton House, Alice having spotted Carrie Miller waiting for her outside her house further down the street. Emily climbed the low staircase to enter Gassy Jack's new establishment. With its carpeted floors, brocade chaise longues, varnished reading tables and ornate gas lamps protruding from floral print-papered walls, the Deighton House lobby was truly a small oasis of European ambiance in rough-and-ready Granville.

"Good morning, Mrs. Patterson," a woman greeted her, emerging from the back kitchen.

"Good morning, Mrs. Deighton," Emily replied. "Here are the slip-covers you ordered."

"Thank you very much," Emma Deighton said, accepting the basket. "It's so difficult to find a good seamstress here. But I'm afraid I'll have to delay your payment until Thomas writes up this month's accounts."

Emily decided that she would ignore the issue of payment, which seemed to be a recurrent problem.

"How are you enjoying Granville?" she asked pleasantly.

"I detest it!" Emma uttered. "Mud-laden streets, men coming into our premises smelling to high heaven of manure and dropping sawdust everywhere, drinking and carousing going on all night—truthfully, I can't imagine a sorrier excuse for a town on God's earth!"

"Well, I'm sure your husband's brother must appreciate the fine job you have done. Deighton House looks lovely!"

Emma bristled yet again. "My husband's brother is a boorish lout who has married a child and sired a half-breed little ruffian. He asked Thomas and me to come all the way out here to run this place and we agreed in good faith, but I can only say that we have been outright deceived!"

Suggesting a cup of tea, Emma Deighton sounded as if she would enjoy continuing with her rant for hours. Emily made a vague excuse about work needing to be done at home and quickly made her escape, inwardly deciding that she would prefer to avoid any visits to Deighton House in the foreseeable future. But in the same token, she could not help but worry over Qua-hail-ya and her little son and vowed to keep their well-being in her sights.

→←

Hastings Sawmill School's new teacher, a widow by the name of Mrs. Frances "Fanny" Richards, proved to be quite popular with the schoolchildren as fall classes recommenced. Emily was also full of admiration for Fanny. Born in Bath, Somerset, England, in 1854, Frances Nias had immigrated with her parents and siblings to San Francisco while still an infant. The Nias family travelled up the coast after losing everything in a San Francisco fire, eventually settling in Victoria. But more tragedy was soon to follow, when in the fall of 1860 nine of the thirteen Nias children succumbed to diphtheria. As one of the four surviving siblings, Fanny attended Victoria's St. Ann's Academy. When the Nias

Frances "Fanny" Richards

family immigrated to Australia a few years later, Fanny chose to remain behind, having met and fallen in love with a gentleman by the name of Louis Richards. Fanny and Louis were married on December 6, 1870 in Victoria. Tragedy struck yet again when Louis died of consumption two years later, while Fanny was pregnant with their first child. Louis Richards Junior was born in Victoria on October 7, 1872. With her parents far away in Australia and an infant son to support, Fanny took it upon herself to complete her studies to obtain her teaching certificate and successfully apply for the vacant teaching position at Hastings Mill.

Emily was deeply saddened upon learning of Fanny's difficult background from Emma Alexander. Although not prone to being a gossip monger, Emma took the lead in any situation at the mill that involved child welfare.

"She doesn't know how she will be able to manage with young Louis while she is teaching, poor little mite. I want to help as much as I can, but I'm afraid that soon I may not be able to move very quickly if he gets into mischief."

Emma was nearing the third term of pregnancy and her belly had ballooned over the past few months.

"Well then, we'll call on everyone to help," Emily said firmly. "That young lad will have every bit of care and attention he deserves with an entire community to look after him."

True to her word, Emily had soon arranged for a full schedule of child minders to attend to Louis while his mother taught classes. As Emma Alexander's due date approached, her times with Louis were greatly reduced and eventually eliminated. Numerous well-meaning individuals had suggested that "she would surely be leaving soon for Victoria?"

"Wait and see," Emma simply replied.

On December 13, 1873, Emma gave birth to a baby boy at her Hastings Mill home with Emily in attendance as midwife.

"The delivery of your son went very well," Emily reported minutes later to an exceedingly nervous Richard Alexander, who had been pacing the yard outside the Alexander residence with a small gaggle of mill colleagues.

"It's a boy!" Richard exulted.

A round of cheers arose for Henry Osborne Alexander—the first white baby to be born at Hastings Mill. In addition to prompting congratulatory handshakes, thumps on the back and the lighting of cigars, the milestone event firmly established Emily's reputation as a skilled and knowledgeable midwife. Emma spoke of her expertise in glowing terms. Harriet Ridley confidently declared that her next baby would be born at Hastings Mill.

Christmas was a time for festive celebration at Hastings Mill and Granville, and local residents had decided that the Christmas of 1873 would be no exception, despite the fact that a global depression had recently cast its economic shadow over the lumber industry. Mill production continued and there was a general sense of optimism that recovery "was just around the corner." Rollicking dances and parties were held in the upper floor Reading Room of the Hastings Literary Institute, a building which had originally served as Hastings Mill's first warehouse and company store. The spacious Reading Room, though still somewhat devoid of books, was ideal for neighbourhood gatherings. There was no shortage of greenery for decorating, and buildings all over town were gaily festooned. Emily purchased extra quantities of flour, sugar and spices from Hastings Mill Store to bake up a vast assortment of decadent treats for family and friends. It was a time of bustle and last-minute preparations, marked with giggles and secrets and the hurried hiding of mysterious packages. The Pattersons, like other residents of Hastings Mill and Granville, were sound asleep in their homes during the early morning hours of December 22, 1873, as flames erupted on the north shore of Burrard Inlet.

CHAPTER 12

"A Funny Little Place"

The geography on the north side of Burrard Inlet contrasts starkly with that of the south. Mountains carved and shaped over thousands of years by glacial ice rise to lofty heights from the forested ridges, punctuated with deep river valleys that gush with water from melting alpine snows and rainfall. In 1862, business partners Thomas Wilson Graham, George Scrimgeour and Phillip Hick pre-empted 480 acres of heavily timbered land on Burrard Inlet's north shore to construct a water-powered sawmill. The venture was short-lived. Transportation costs and stiff competition from established sawmills on Vancouver Island and in New Westminster forced the owners of Pioneer Mills into bankruptcy.

On January 29, 1865, a gentleman from Hartland, Maine, by the name of Sewell Moody, in partnership with James van Bramer, James Howe, John Polmere and Moses Ireland, purchased the mill and surrounding property for $6,900. Sewell Moody, an innovative and energetic young man in his late twenties, proved to have the winning formula when it came to turning the company, now known as Burrard Inlet Lumber Mills, into a profitable enterprise. Leases were obtained to gain access to thousands of additional acres of harvestable timber on the north shore ridges. As the fine quality of Burrard Inlet timber gained international recognition, fully loaded ships were soon departing for Mexico, China, Peru, Hawaii and other destinations.

A small community grew around the mill site as business increased. In June of 1866, the *British Columbian* described the scene:

> The beautiful sunny side of the slope is now dotted with the neat cabins of hardy workmen . . . wharf accommodations and a dozen ships . . . a large store built on the wharf is well stocked with general merchandise for employees and visitors. A new building is being constructed as a lecture and reading room for employees of the mill.

As yet, the community had no official name but was locally referred to as "Moody's Mill." As more and more families took up residence, additional buildings materialized, including a two-storey structure which served multiple purposes as a Masonic Lodge, library and community centre. Mrs. Margaret Thain, born in New Brunswick and trained in England, took up her duties as schoolteacher in 1871. She soon decided that Moody's Mill should have a more befitting name—one that reflected the presence of a town with amenities like a store, school and library. In years henceforth, she would recollect:

Mrs. Margaret Thain

"It was a funny little place named after Mr. Moody and called Moody's Mill when we went there. But I had the honour of naming it properly, for I was not going to live in a place without a name, so I suggested 'Moodyville' and that has been its name ever since."

⇥⇤

"Fire! Fire in Moodyville!"

Shouts rang across Hastings Mill townsite, and residents, bleary-eyed from their winter solstice slumber, emerged from darkened cottages in the pre-dawn chill. Shrill blasts from the Hastings Sawmill steam whistle pierced the air, while dozens of hastily lit lanterns carried by men on the run bobbled their way to the wharf.

"What's happening, John?" Emily asked. Her husband, having made a quick assessment down at the waterfront, had hurried back home to grab up buckets and blankets.

"Fire across the inlet!" he told her. "Looks like Moody's entire business is going up!"

The door banged shut as John departed. The children had awoken with the commotion and Addie started to cry.

"It's all right, Addie," Abbie said comfortingly. "The fire is on the other side of the inlet . . . we're perfectly safe here."

"But others may not be!" Emily said. She quickly began assembling a voluminous kit of bandaging and burn remedies in preparation for casualties. Directing Abbie to look after the younger children, she ran down to the sawmill wharf with a bulging satchel. Across the water she could see the bright flames virtually turning night into day on Burrard Inlet as they voraciously devoured Sewell Moody's sawmill. Boats were pulling away steadily from the Hastings Mill wharf and her husband was nowhere in sight.

"I want to get over there!" she called. "Would someone take me, please?"

Most of the men ignored her or seemingly pretended that they didn't hear.

"Looks dangerous, Mrs. Patterson," a nearby mill worker told her finally. "Best stay on this side. If there are any casualties, we'll bring them over."

Emily decided to take matters into her own hands and muscled her way onto one of the steamers hastily being made ready for departure.

"Please don't waste any valuable time!" she brusquely informed anyone who tried to dissuade her.

As luck would have it, a steady rain was falling, preventing the fire from making much headway beyond the mill itself. The entire population of Moodyville townsite had come down to the shoreline to watch as the blaze burned itself out. Emily quickly disembarked after her steamer pulled up at one of the many landings on the Moodyville waterfront. She circulated amongst the crowd, inquiring if there were any burn victims. Much to her relief it appeared that everyone was safe and unharmed. Moodyville townsite had been spared, but Sewell Moody's magnificent steam-powered mill, along with much valuable equipment —saws, belting, conveyors and other machinery—had been completely gutted.

In the days following Christmas—this year celebrated with less fanfare on both sides of Burrard Inlet—there was much debate as to the cause of the fire. Sewell Moody managed to determine that the only persons in attendance when the blaze broke out in the sawmill lamp room were a watchman and fireman, who had quickly given the alarm. But with little in the way of firefighting equipment, responders could only stand and watch as most of the mill facilities were quickly consumed. Suspicion circulated over a disgruntled employee but nothing could be proven and no charges would be laid. Moody and his business partners had no insurance and would have to begin the arduous process of rebuilding the steam-powered mill facilities using materials from the old water-powered mill, which had been spared the inferno.

"That Moody's an amazing chap!" John Patterson told Emily one evening not long after the fire as she served up a piping-hot venison stew with freshly baked biscuits. "He's off the ground and running, lining up new financiers, ordering new materials. . . . I believe Raymur's given him a good deal on fresh lumber. Did you know he's from Maine?"

"Yes, I believe I knew," Emily sighed, inwardly bracing herself for what she knew would be coming next. Her husband, with his knowledge and skills as a master mechanic, had been spending lengthy hours across the inlet to assist with reconstruction.

"I've been offered a full-time position at the Moodyville sawmill when it's up and running again."

"That's wonderful, John!"

Emily was not exactly overjoyed at the thought of a move across the inlet so soon after the family had settled into their Hastings Mill home, but in the days ahead, the plan would provide some welcome distraction. Tragically, John Patterson's brother Calvin died on January 25, 1874, of complications from injuries sustained aboard his steamer, the *Edward James*. Emily had been sent for immediately but there was little that she could do other than administer liberal doses of morphine to ease Calvin's final hours. Calvin had a young wife, Theresa, who had immigrated to the West Coast from her native Ireland two years previously. John was heartbroken over the loss of his brother and threw himself into the task of reconstruction at Moodyville.

The Pattersons' move took place gradually over the spring of 1874, to a house which had recently been vacated by a family by the name of DeBeck, on a massive slab and sawdust pile known locally as "the Spit." Great was Emily's surprise and delight when she learned that she would soon have familiar faces nearby. On April 14, 1874, schoolteacher Fanny Richards married Benjamin Springer, son of an upper-class, United Empire Loyalist family from Delaware, Middlesex, Ontario. Springer was a member of the local school board that had hired Fanny, and also served as tallyman and bookkeeper for the Moodyville sawmill. Fanny and Benjamin's marriage ceremony, the first recorded European-style wedding at Granville, was held in the Methodist Church. Fanny would finish her year of teaching at Hastings Mill, whereupon the couple and young Louis would move into a house not far from the Pattersons on the Spit.

CHAPTER 13

The Custom of the Country

Emily soon discovered that Moodyville, like Hastings Mill, had well-established social enclaves. The Rookeries—a Chinese laundry district —sprawled along the shoreline west of the mill. To the east stood Kanaka Row, comprising homes built on pilings for the Hawaiian employees. Midway up the hillside behind the mill, a perpetually muddy lane occupied by a number of shacks and cottages had been dubbed "Brigham Terrace." Emily was curious as to who "Brigham" was, and asked the question of schoolteacher Margaret Thain, not long after the two ladies met.

"That," Margaret said dryly, "is in tribute to Mr. Brigham Young."

"Brigham Young . . ." Emily repeated, searching her memory. "He is the leader of the Mormon Church in Utah Territory, is he not?"

"Yes, and as you may well be aware, the Mormons practise polygamy, the custom of having more than one wife at the same time. I've heard some say that Mr. Brigham Young has over fifty wives, and has fathered dozens of children!"

"I understand. . . ." Emily nodded with a disapproving tone.

Brigham Terrace was Moodyville's polygamist district. In the very early days of Canadian settlement, relationships between Hudson's Bay Company fur traders and Aboriginal women were strictly discouraged. Acknowledging the general scarcity of European women, the HBC's London Committee eventually bowed to pressure and accepted inter-racial marriage. Marriages "according to the custom of the country" were not officially sanctioned by church or state, but with so few mar-riageable women of white ancestry, many men struck up relationships with native women. As greater numbers of European women began to arrive on Canadian shores, a man would often take two wives—his life partner of native origin, strong in her knowledge of the land—and his "proper" Christian-bred wife of white heritage. By the early 1870s it had become common knowledge in Moodyville that some men practised polygamy and fathered multiple children with more than one wife.

Margaret Thain was a cheerful and industrious woman, well settled into her teaching position at the Moodyville schoolhouse. But she cast her eyes furtively from side to side as she strolled along with Emily on the Spit.

"I'm afraid our Mr. Moody himself is a polygamist," she reported in a low voice.

Emily had noticed that a number of mixed-race children played in the yards outside of Moodyville residences, among them George and Anita Moody, son and daughter of Sewell Moody and a native woman. But Sewell Moody, according to Margaret Thain, had also married a Scottish woman, Janet Watson, in a July 1869 Anglican ceremony in Victoria.

"He has a little daughter named Florence and a newborn son living with their mother in Victoria," Margaret Thain went on. "He desper-ately wants Janet and the children to join him in Moodyville, even built them a lovely new house, but of course when she came over and met the little half-breed children who called themselves Moody, she put two and two together and went straight back to Victoria, angry as sin!"

Emily disliked gossip and decided that she preferred not to hear more of Sewell Moody's unfaithful ways. It was becoming abundantly clear to her however that country marriages were occurring with increasing frequency in the communities of Burrard Inlet. There was a conspicuous shortage of white women in the region and lovelorn mill workers would gravitate towards any eligible young lady who happened to catch their eye, regardless of racial background. Of course following, or often not following marriage, there would be babies, and they were arriving by the score. Emily's midwifery skills were much in demand, and her conversations with new young fathers took on a familiar refrain:

"You have a healthy little daughter, Mr. Jackson."

"A girl? Well . . . that's real nice. Thank you, Mrs. Patterson."

"Now your wife is going to need plenty of rest and you are going to have to look after her needs. Is the woodbox full and do you have plenty of soap on hand for washing diapers?"

"Uh . . . well, I'm not rightly sure about the soap, but I'll get right to filling that woodbox."

In addition to demanding cleanliness and warmth for her tiny newborn charges, Emily would staunchly advocate for proper nutrition and the prevention of spoilage. On April 2, 1869, an elderly English sailor by the name of William Bridge had jumped ship and pre-empted 160 acres of land on the north shore, approximately one mile to the west of Moody's Mill. With the help of his native wife and others, he planted an orchard and cleared a cow pasture, gradually developing a productive local farm. Residents from both sides of Burrard Inlet would arrive by boat or on horseback to purchase fresh milk and produce at Bridge's farm. Well aware that food-borne illnesses had claimed thousands of lives over the centuries, Emily would make inquiries into William Bridge's preservation techniques. Milk that had not been properly boiled and treated with boracic acid would not be fit for consumption. A French scientist by the name of Louis Pasteur had made public his recent studies on eliminating harmful bacteria from raw milk and other food products, arousing much interest worldwide, but mandatory pasteurization was still years away.

➤‹

Throughout the summer months of 1874, Emily had not seen Gassy Jack and his family. She learned from Emma Alexander that they had relocated to New Westminster, where Gassy had taken full charge of the steamboat *Onward*, ferrying passengers and freight up and down the navigable lengths of the Fraser River. Gassy had been a steamboat pilot in the years leading up to his Gastown venture, but this time, the move would be short-lived. Once again experiencing the chronic pains in his legs and feet that had been repeatedly troubling him for a number of years, Gassy had soon found the steamboating workload intolerable. He returned to Granville with Qua-hail-ya and Richard, much to the outright annoyance of Thomas and Emma Deighton, who moved to Victoria almost immediately, their distaste most evident.

On a chill December 2 evening in 1874, a bevy of guests from both the north and south side of Burrard Inlet were welcomed to the first-ever marriage ceremony conducted at Hastings Mill townsite, between Abbie Patterson and Frederick William Jordan, captain of the barque *Marmion*. In port to take on a load of lumber for China, the *Marmion* had been docked at Hastings Mill for several weeks, and pretty Abbie was quickly swept off her feet by the dashing Captain Jordan. The Ridley family had moved into the vacated Patterson house at Hastings Mill and graciously offered the use of their sitting room for the wedding ceremony.

The Reverend James Turner, first resident minister on Burrard Inlet, presided over the service, after which guests were invited into the kitchen for refreshments. Emily had spared no expense in baking a vast array of desserts for her eldest daughter's special day. After dinner, everyone walked across the road to the mill warehouse, where the party would continue upstairs in the Reading Room. Abbie, flushed with excitement, was presented with a treasure trove of gifts—exquisite pieces of jewellery, china, silver and "just about every other wonderful thing imaginable," as she would later declare. A local man, George Bone, struck up his concertina and with violin accompaniment, dancing went on well into the night.

At one point during the festivities, two burly mill men waded into the crowd lugging a large wooden case between them.

Abbie Lowell (Patterson) Jordan, c. 1880s.

"For the newlyweds!" one of them announced triumphantly, placing the case on the wedding table before a seated Abbie and Captain Jordan.

A small label was fastened to the twine binding the case, which read, "To Mr. and Mrs. Jordan, with compliments, Mr. and Mrs. John Deighton."

"My word!" Abbie exclaimed. "What could this be?"

"Open it!" Beckie urged.

Captain Jordan attacked the twine with a knife and carefully pried up the wooden lid to find the case filled with bottles of wine and spirits nested in straw.

The room fell silent as everyone realized the impropriety of Gassy Jack's gift. Alcohol at Hastings Mill continued to be strictly forbidden. Dumbfounded, Abbie looked from her parents to her new husband, quite uncertain of what to do next. One of the delivery men grinned sheepishly.

"Well, ma'am, it's kinda Mr. Deighton's custom to give away liquor when there's a special occasion."

"How very thoughtful!" Emily spoke up. "Perhaps the newlyweds might consider sharing these bottles with their generous guests . . . to perhaps take on a picnic sometime?"

Emily had carefully chosen the word "picnic" to subtly emphasize that rules were rules and Mr. Deighton's alcohol was not to be consumed anywhere on Hastings Mill property. Everyone readily agreed that this would be the perfect solution and Mr. and Mrs. Jordan happily began distributing bottles. The case was quickly emptied and Emily could not help noticing that some of the wedding guests made a rather hasty departure following. She decided that it would be better to remain ignorant of the reason why.

A few days after the wedding, Abbie and her husband made final preparations to sail away from Burrard Inlet aboard the *Marmion*. The ship was bound for China, and Abbie, like her mother before her, would soon be leading the typical existence of a seafaring wife.

"I can't wait to see China, Mama," Abbie said resolutely, clearly trying to disguise the doubt in her voice.

There was no deceiving Emily. She took her daughter's hands in her own and squeezed them tight.

"You will be just fine!" she said firmly. "I can see that Mr. Jordan is a fine gentleman and he will take good care of you. There will be only one ocean between us and we will see each other again. I shall look forward to that day very much!"

CHAPTER 14

The Passing of the Founders

Early into the new year of 1875, Emily paid a brief visit to Gassy Jack at Deighton House, with the intention of thanking him for his kind wedding gift. She was surprised and concerned to see how much he had deteriorated in health since they had last crossed paths. He struggled with ongoing pain and swelling in his feet and legs, and his breath came in short, laboured wheezes.

"Did you see a doctor in New Westminster?" Emily asked.

"Waste of time," he muttered, waving his hand dismissively. "Good shot of whiskey will do the job as well as any dose of medicine they keep wantin' me to take!"

"Well," Emily said sternly, "I do recommend that you take it easy and rest those legs from time to time. That should help with the inflammation."

But it was abundantly clear that there would be no restraining Granville's colourful founder. Gassy Jack Deighton soldiered on, beginning an ambitious renovation and enlargement of Deighton House that same January. Proposals were being drawn up for a new carriage road to connect Granville with the up-inlet community of Hastings (not to be confused with Hastings Mill), otherwise known as the "end of the road" from New Westminster, and Gassy was more than eager for it to become a reality. Known as Khanamoot to the local Musqueam and Tsleil-Waututh natives who came ashore to dig for clams and pick berries, Hastings (formerly called New Brighton), had been established around 1865 as a resort community where mosquito and woodsmoke-weary New Westminster residents could come to enjoy Burrard Inlet's fresh ocean breezes. Hastings had grown to include a wharf, post office and the Hastings Hotel, run by Maximilien Michaud. "Maxie's" was one of the more popular locales for social gatherings on Burrard Inlet —largely due to the unhindered and prolific sale of alcohol. Emily deliberately avoided Maxie's and insisted that her daughters do likewise.

On April 29, Emily assisted in the delivery of Benjamin and Fanny Springer's daughter, Mabel Ellen Springer, the first white girl baby to be born at Moodyville.

"How my life has turned around!" Fanny said with a smile. She was tired but radiant as she held tiny Mabel in her arms and marvelled over her good fate while Emily prepared her a cup of tea. "A little over a year ago I was in despair, with the death of my first husband and a fatherless son to care for. Now I couldn't be happier!"

"I'm very happy to hear it!" Emily replied.

Unbeknownst to Emily, fate was simultaneously being less than kind to Gassy Jack. Ongoing pain forced him to take to his bed in early May. Not wishing to involve Qua-hail-ya, he hired a friend by the name of Arthur Mackreth to be his full-time caregiver. Dr. Charles Trew of New Westminster was called out several times but could not prescribe a cure. Impatient for results, Gassy demanded another doctor. On May 20 and 22, he was treated by Dr. McInnes, but again without success. Gassy was not the most cooperative of patients and it was clear that nothing could be done to halt the progression of his descent. Certain Granville residents would recall that on the night of May 29, 1875, Gassy's pet dog, a bull mastiff, began to howl somewhere off in the dark. Lying on his bed,

Gassy was said to have muttered his final prophetic words: "You son of a bitch! There's something going to happen!" Moments later, John "Gassy Jack" Deighton—unofficial founder of Granville townsite—passed away at the age of forty-four.

Emily was saddened and outraged upon learning that Gassy Jack's body had lain in bed for six days before any plans for internment were arranged. She chided herself for not calling in on him more regularly, but he had been stubborn to the last and flatly rejected most offers of help. Qua-hail-ya was not to be blamed, for she was little more than a frightened child whose one ongoing desire had been to return to her own people. Constable Jonathan Miller arranged for the purchase of grave clothes—long underwear, a white shirt and necktie. Dressed in these, along with one of his best suits, Gassy Jack was gently placed in a coffin. After a funeral service conducted by the Reverend J. Turner at Deighton House, his remains were transported to New Westminster for burial.

>‹

While John "Gassy Jack" Deighton had been British to the core, Maine-born Sewell Moody was decidedly American, through and through. Just as communities on the south shore of Burrard Inlet celebrated Dominion Day every July 1, Moody pointedly arranged for Independence Day to be celebrated at Moodyville in fine patriotic style every July 4. There would be boat races on the inlet, decorations of red, white and blue festooning mill structures and family picnics on the Seymour flats pastureland. During the summer of 1875, ships of all sizes and descriptions were arriving and departing from Burrard Inlet. This year, the 4th of July fell upon a Sunday, and Emily, along with Alice, was offered a special way to celebrate. The twelve-gun man-of-war HMS *Repulse* was anchored in the harbour and selected residents from both sides of the inlet had been invited by the ship's paymaster and chaplain to come aboard the vessel for an on-deck church service and luncheon. Launched in 1868, the *Repulse* was a leviathan—at 3,749 tons, one of the largest vessels ever to call into port. Emily and Alice, together with

Sewell Moody, Richard and Emma Alexander, and Moodyville store-keeper David Milligan, were piloted out to the vessel aboard a steam pinnace—the *Repulse* being far too large for docking facilities at Hastings Mill or Moodyville. Following the service, the group was served up

a meal of cold steak and kidney pie, buttered bread and ale. Emily politely tucked in to her serving, while frequently casting stern glances at Alice, who had clearly hoped for something more elegant to be offered aboard such an impressive ship.

"I thought they would give us something grand," eleven-year-old Alice admitted to her mother later that afternoon as they walked home. "Something sweet and pink in colour!"

"I somehow doubt that the men aboard the *Repulse* would be concerned

Sewell Prescott Moody

as to whether or not their food was pink," Emily said with a smile. "If you are at sea for months on end, all you really desire is something that is filling and nourishing."

Emily understood Alice's disappointment, however, and had arranged for the paymaster and chaplain of the *Repulse* to visit the Patterson home for afternoon tea. She would not have the time or ingredients to bake up "something pink," but made sure that the dining table was gaily decorated with a centrepiece of pink silk flowers.

"That looks so pretty, Mama." Alice smiled appreciatively.

"We must also remember to send a note of thanks to Mr. Moody," Emily said. "I suspect that he played a part in arranging our visit to the *Repulse*."

Sewell Moody, despite his hard-nosed managerial style, was well liked among the residents of Moodyville. In early fall, upon learning that Emily and John were expecting another child, he congratulated them heartily. Moody had made a point of getting to know each and every one of his employees and their families. Tall and stately, he was popularly known as Tyee or "chief" in Chinook.

One November morning in 1875, Emily was surprised when her husband returned from work early, an expression of shock and sorrow plain to see upon his face.

"What's wrong, John?" she asked.

"Mr. Moody has died," John told her solemnly. "Drowned off Cape Flattery, aboard the *Pacific*. We just received word via telegram."

Emily stared in outright dismay. "I can't believe it!" she exclaimed.

Shock waves reverberated through the entire Moodyville community with word that Sewell Moody, en route to do business in San Francisco, had drowned when the side-wheel steamer *Pacific* collided with the SS *Orpheus* in heavy seas off Cape Flattery. The *Pacific* had left Victoria on the morning of November 4 with a full complement of 275 passengers and crew aboard. By nightfall, all had perished aside from two men who had managed to cling to pieces of wreckage for many hours before being rescued. There were no local newspapers in the Burrard Inlet communities and full details were slow to arrive from Victoria and New Westminster. The November 9 issue of the *Daily British Colonist* reported a graphic account of the wreck:

> American ship *Messenger*, Captain J.F. Gilkey arrived nine days from San Francisco and reports picking up part of the pilot house twenty miles south of Cape Flattery and Henry L. Jelley, the only survivor of the steamship *Pacific*, which sailed from Victoria at 9 Thursday morning and foundered 40 miles south of Cape Flattery at 8 Thursday evening. Jelley lashed himself to the pilot house.

Later reports confirmed that a second man, quartermaster Neil Henley had also survived, having been rescued by a passing vessel after enduring seventy-eight hours adrift on a piece of wreckage.

Days of searching ensued, but Sewell Moody's body was never recovered. Emily was deeply saddened, realizing that two families would be affected by the loss. Janet Moody, upon hearing the news in Victoria, had allegedly collapsed in a faint. There was no mention of Moody's native wife, who had returned to live at the Mission Reserve with her children. Two weeks after the tragedy, a small piece of white-painted wood floated to shore beneath Victoria's Beacon Hill, not far from Moody's Victoria home. Closer examination revealed that a message had been hastily scrawled upon it in pencil—"S.P. Moody all lost." Initial thoughts were that someone had played a cruel hoax, until several individuals confirmed that the writing style indeed matched Moody's. On December 18, Moodyville residents gathered at the Mechanic's Institute for a memorial service officiated by the Reverend Mr. Derrick of the Wesleyan Mission. During his lengthy sermon, Derrick spoke thoughtfully about the piece of wood. "It was a letter to us," he said, "a last letter and written—not only for his, but for the three hundred dying ones—and what a picture does that engraving on wood point to our hearts today."

With Sewell Moody's death, his business partner, an Irishman by the name of Hugh Nelson, took over management of the sawmill. The Springer family moved into the vacant Moody house on the Spit. The Spit was a lively place by day, where mill workers strode to and fro, while children played upon the expansive sawdust field. Early on Sunday mornings, the Reverend Edwards, who conducted Anglican church services in the Masonic Hall, joined the loggers in rousing matches of football. Emily and her family would laugh at the antics of their minister charging about the sawdust, his clergy robes tied up high around his waist. When the church bell rang at 10:30 a.m., he would cheerfully announce to the loggers, "Now I've played your game, you come play mine." But after dark the Spit took on a more sombre air. Lantern light emitted a soft glow from the cottage windows—small islands of illumination in a shadowy, brooding landscape. Rumours had lately begun to circulate among Moodyville residents that something out of the ordinary was occurring in the house formerly occupied by Sewell Moody.

"Some say Moody's house is haunted, Mama!" Beckie told her mother, as she set out plates for dinner one evening.

"That's utter nonsense!" Emily retorted.

As a Christian woman, Emily did not believe in ghosts or paranormal spectra of any kind, but nevertheless, she was hard-pressed to later explain an event which took place one night. Benjamin Springer was ill, and Emily had been staying over late to tend to him while the rest of the family slept. As she was getting ready to return to her home for bed, she heard a loud "bang" in another room, which sounded like the sash of a window being violently closed. A moment later she heard it go up again. Emily immediately hurried over to the window where the noise had occurred and peered outside.

"Who's there!" she called out into the night.

There was no telltale laughter or sight of any mischief-maker running away and ultimately no clear explanation for why the window had apparently closed and reopened itself.

John Patterson could not resist a chuckle when Emily told him of the occurrence the next morning.

"I should imagine that was Mr. Moody. He wants us to know he's still in charge."

"Nonsense, John!" Emily scolded.

CHAPTER 15

Prestigious Company

Moodyville continued to flourish under Hugh Nelson's direction. The firm was reorganized under the name Moodyville Sawmill Company, and Nelson recruited an elite circle of professional business partners: bank manager James Burns, barrister Montague William Tyrwhitt Drake, ship's chandler Peter McQuade and riverboat captain John Irving. Construction of the Canadian Pacific Railway, Canada's first transcontinental railway line, was well underway and Nelson lobbied hard for Moodyville to be made the western terminus. Emily closely followed reports of the railway's progress, knowing full well from the family's experience in Butteville that rail service—or lack thereof—could have dramatic implications.

"Come what may," she reasoned, "British Columbia became a Canadian province on the condition of a coast-to-coast railway. At some point in time, the railway must surely reach Burrard Inlet."

"We will all be grey-haired before it does," John Patterson commented dryly.

Nonetheless, when Hugh Nelson began talking of plans to build a grandiose mansion on the hillside above the mill, John Patterson liked the idea and began exploring the possibilities of building a larger home himself. Life on the Spit was noisy, sooty and crowded, whereas some two hundred or more feet up the hill the air was fresher, and on a clear day, the view up- and down-inlet was spectacular. Emily, much to her own surprise, completely agreed that another move would make good sense. The children would still be able to attend the same school and she would have a quick downhill run whenever a medical situation below demanded her immediate attention.

The Pattersons' new house would occupy the highest point of a developing neighbourhood whimsically dubbed "Nob Hill" after its San Francisco counterpart. Emily had her own set of specifications as to how the house should be constructed.

"I would like it to be two storeys in height with plenty of bedrooms, a full-width veranda for entertaining on sunny days and a fenced front yard to keep out the deer," she enthused. "Perhaps in time we could have an addition to use as a patient consulting room."

"Hmm," was her husband's only response.

Over time, most of the managerial staff and highest skilled tradesmen of the Moodyville community—chief engineer, foreman, paymaster, accountants and their families—would gravitate to Nob Hill, creating an elite social enclave, well removed from the dust and clamour down on the Spit. Conscious of the fact that a stark division was beginning to form between Moodyville's privileged few and the poorer, working-class households, Emily encouraged her husband to become actively involved with the Moodyville School. School attendance had grown steadily under the tutorage of Margaret Thain, and at a public meeting held on January 30, 1876, John Patterson was unanimously elected as Moodyville's first school trustee. Thirteen-year-old Beckie, eleven-year-old Alice, and five-year-old Addie all attended the school, while three-year-old Calvin eagerly awaited his turn. On March 12, Emily, John and the rest of the Patterson family celebrated the birth of baby Frederick, who would affectionately become known as Freddie.

Victoria and New Westminster still had the highest concentration of European settlers in British Columbia during the mid-1870s, but as

Moodyville, 1898. The Pattersons' house on Nob Hill is highest on left.

The Pattersons' house on Nob Hill, c. 1890.

new settlers continued to arrive in the Burrard Inlet milltowns, word spread both locally and internationally of the region's steady emergence on the lumbering scene. There was a local twitter of excitement when word was received that Lord Dufferin—Governor General of Canada

—and his wife, Lady Dufferin, were calling into Burrard Inlet during their West Coast tour. On the morning of September 4, 1876, the HMS *Amethyst*, alongside the escort vessel *Rocket*, entered the harbour. Emily, preoccupied with baby Freddie and household chores, decided that she would be unable to join the festivities on the south shore. She would later enjoy a vivid description of the day's events, provided by Alice.

Brimming with excitement at the prospect of a royal encounter, Alice had made advance arrangements to be on the south shore in time for the *Amethyst*'s arrival. She joined up with her friend Carrie Miller and other children, all hoping for a good vantage point—a plan quickly stymied by Mrs. Miller, who firmly insisted that the group remain behind the garden fence of the Raymur property and not get underfoot. Crestfallen, Alice could only watch from a distance as the *Amethyst* glided into the harbour before a waiting group of VIPs.

A small shuttle boat would be dispatched to transport Lord and Lady Dufferin from the *Amethyst* to the dockside adjacent to the mill store, where straw matting had been laid down to disguise the weather-beaten floorboards. The small organ which normally occupied the mill schoolhouse had been carried over to the welcoming platform, the plan being for it to accompany a rousing chorus of "God Save the Queen," led by Mr. Clarkson, the customs officer. As Alice and her friends looked on, the mayor and council of New Westminster trotted past on horseback—the horses having acquired a good deal of mud on the journey. Soon afterwards, a red-faced Mr. Clarkson came running up to the children.

"Quickly!" he urged. "Remind me of the words to 'God Save the Queen'!"

Emily laughed heartily when Alice described the day's events upon returning home. She was also pleased to learn that there had been an unexpected change of plan in the official itinerary. Lady Dufferin, expressly fond of Aboriginal culture, had asked if she could visit the native community of Kumkumlye, to the east of Hastings Mill townsite. Caught off guard but duty-bound, a small group of escorts willingly guided her down the narrow, meandering trail to the cluster of board-and-batten shacks at Kumkumlye. Lady Dufferin nodded her head in

greeting to many a curious onlooker and then stopped when she noticed a very old and frail woman known locally as the Virgin Mary. The
woman was little more than skin and bones—in no way pleasant to
look upon—but much to the amazement of the entourage, Lady Dufferin shook her hand.

"It's the talk of all Granville!" Alice reported. "Imagine, Queen Victoria's representative, shaking hands with an Indian!"

"Well, I'm certain that it didn't do her ladyship any harm!" Emily
retorted.

><

Despite the occasional flirtations with high society, the milltown populations of Burrard Inlet were still largely made up of loggers and aimless
drifters—wayfaring young men with a thirst for liquor and gambling
pursuits, long on swagger and short on maturity. Although Moodyville
was officially an alcohol-free zone, Harry Hogan had openly defied the
ban by opening the Terminus Hotel and saloon in 1874. There was also
an active smuggling trade across the inlet and liquor-fuelled brawls
were an all-too-regular occurrence. Emily's knack for diffusing tensions as she tended to various cuts and bruises in the aftermath of a fray
won her much respect among the guilty parties. But however tolerant
she appeared, she was also of a firm disposition not to be trifled with.
One day she received word that a fist fight was happening in Maiden's
Lane, the pathway which led up the hill above the sawmill. A man had
fallen and badly split his lip. Hurrying to the scene with her medical
bag, Emily quietly bade the victim to be seated so that she could dab
and sew up the profusely bleeding wound. The man was raving angrily,
and nearby, his terrified wife was crying.

"Be careful, Mrs. Patterson!" she warned. "He will strike you!"

"No, he won't," Emily said simply. With that, she glared at her
patient. "You dare move and I'll hit you over the head with a club!"
Instantly, he fell silent.

Often on the run to the scene of an injury, Emily kept her medical
bag within easy reach and topped up with a wide selection of first-aid

Lady Dufferin, c. 1876.

supplies. John Patterson made a good living at his profession and gave her free rein to purchase any items she deemed necessary. What she could not obtain from the mill store, she would mail order from New Westminster or Victoria, trying to keep abreast of the latest tried-and-true remedies. In conversation with members of the Squamish, Musqueam and Tsleil-Waututh communities, she also came to know and appreciate the abundance of natural remedies available virtually within her own back yard. She would learn that boiling the tips of western red cedar produced a wonderfully fragrant steam that helped to clear upper respiratory tract infections. Salal leaves, plentiful throughout the year, could be made into an effective poultice for insect bites and stings. When the root of devil's club was burned to white ash, it could be applied to open sores to prevent infection and reduce inflammation.

Emily would also put simple ingredients from her own kitchen to use medicinally. One day a native woman known locally as "Little Tommy" brought her baby to Emily. The baby's eyes were practically sealed shut with yellowish mucus.

"*Okoke tenas seahost sick*!" Little Tommy said.

"Ah yes, you are right. This child's eye is sick indeed," Emily replied knowingly. "Okoke conjunctivitis. Let's see what we can do."

Emily gently washed the baby's eyes with a little milk and diluted boracic acid, and then directed the woman to go to the mill store "to ask for some Steadman's Teething Powder." The woman returned some time later with baking soda.

"*Halo*! No!" Emily said firmly. "This is baking soda. It is *cultus* . . . worthless for helping the child."

Emily proceeded to write a note for the woman, requesting Steadman's Teething Powder.

"Now you must remember to wash your hands!" she added. "Wash *le mah*! Otherwise the entire town will be coming down with conjunctivitis."

One spring morning in 1877, Emily came over to Hastings Mill to check up on one of the Miller daughters who had been down with a cold. Before returning to Moodyville, she decided to call in at the Hastings Mill Store in hopes of finding some much-coveted Spanish lace for Alice. Strolling up the boardwalk, she was surprised to come across a newly built structure near the townsite entrance, with a sign prominently displayed in the window, "Dr. W.W. Walkem, Physician and Surgeon." As she approached, a man appearing to be in his mid-twenties stepped outside, with a mop and pail of water in hand.

"Morning, ma'am," he called out, noticing her.

"Good morning." Emily smiled. "Are you the new doctor?"

"Dr. William Wymond Walkem," he replied. "Just getting ready to open the practice tomorrow, all being well. Know of anyone who requires a doctor in this town?"

"Oh, I'm sure there will be more than a few patients coming your way."

"Very good! Don't want all that hard study at McGill to go to waste!"

Emily decided that she would not appear foolish by asking where McGill was. Despite her relief in knowing that a qualified physician would now be on hand to ease her workload, she felt an odd prickle of annoyance. She had resided in the Burrard Inlet region for five years now, had forged friendships and trust among residents from all walks of life, delivered babies, bandaged cuts, soothed feverish brows, had in the words of many, gone above and beyond the call of duty when it came to medical matters. Now all of a sudden this young upstart by the name of Dr. Walkem had emerged in her community like an energetic young horse, chomping at the bit to lead off at the races.

"From what I understand, he's to receive payment of one dollar per month from every mill employee on the inlet," John Patterson told Emily later that evening. "He's also being given a one hundred dollar per month honorarium from the B.C. government—but I strongly doubt that he let many people know about it."

"I told him that I was a nurse and could offer my assistance, but when he found out that I was untrained, he simply said 'Well, we'll see what we can come up with.' How patronizing was that!"

John laughed and gave her an affectionate hug.

"Perhaps he'll change his mind when he sees how wonderfully efficient you are!"

Despite her misgivings, Emily realized that she would have to be mindful of not encroaching upon Dr. Walkem's business. One afternoon, while she was seated on her veranda entertaining a number of captain's wives, a native woman came along in tears, calling out "Jinnie Douglas bit my lip!" Despite the fact that she easily could have treated the injury herself with a short length of suture, Emily gave the woman a cotton compress to staunch the blood flow and encouraged her to "go right over and see the doctor."

But on the afternoon of August 20, 1878, medical urgency struck closer to home.

"Mrs. Patterson! Mrs. Patterson! Come quickly!"

Emily answered her door to find a young mill worker puffing in agitation.

"It's your husband, Mrs. Patterson! He's hurt bad!"

Not waiting to hear another word, Emily grabbed up her medical bag. Bidding a frightened Beckie to mind her younger brothers and sisters, she tore off for the mill as fast as she could manage in her house slippers. The mill saws had been silenced and a cluster of men stood on the dock gathered about a stretcher, upon which lay a distraught John Patterson.

"John!" Emily cried, reaching his side. "What has happened?"

"Caught his arm in a piece of machinery, ma'am," one of the men spoke up. "Looks like it's broken."

Emily was anxious to hear from John himself to try and determine if there was any head injury as well.

"Can you move your fingers, John, and tell me what day it is?" she asked.

"Tuesday," John answered through gritted teeth. "Now stop asking damn fool questions and somebody get me some painkiller!"

"A bottle of ether, please," Emily directed over her shoulder, "and two strips of wood, thick enough to make a splint but not too heavy."

Within short order, Emily had her husband sedated with his arm immobilized, and he was carefully stretchered up to the Patterson home. Dr. Walkem arrived in the late afternoon, having been summoned from Hastings Mill. Emily stood silently by while he made a full assessment of the splinted arm.

"The fracture is not to be of a serious character," he reported. "It appears that you've dealt with the situation very well, Mrs. Patterson."

"Thank you, Dr. Walkem."

Dr. Walkem made a few gentle adjustments to the splint and retied the bindings, all the while chatting animatedly about the attractiveness of the north shore mountains and excellent fishing prospects in the local streams. At length he doffed his hat and departed, mentioning that he would like to get back across the inlet before darkness set in.

"He certainly likes to talk," Beckie remarked disapprovingly.

"Everyone calls him Windy Wymond," Alice said with a giggle.

"Well, that will be enough of that!" Emily said sternly.

CHAPTER 16

Days of Pain
and Solace

For all their expertise, neither Emily nor Dr. Walkem was able to avert tragedy. That same summer of 1878, the first wedding at Moodyville took place between Mr. Palmer and Harriet Mitchell. Harriet had been feeling unwell of late with a cold, but had resolutely managed to summon enough strength to attend her own wedding. The couple was to begin their married life in a three-room house down the hill from the Pattersons. Emily had noted Harriet's ashen face as the young bride wavered unsteadily on her betrothed's arm throughout the service.

"I'm rather worried about Harriet," she remarked to Alice not long after the Pattersons returned home. "I'd like you to take her this package of sweets and let me know how she is doing."

Within brief minutes, Alice was back.

"She's not well at all, Mama. She's lying in bed, all moaning and delirious and Mr. Palmer would like you to come."

Emily rushed down the hill, only to find that the new bride had lapsed into unconsciousness. Dr. Walkem was sent for but there was nothing he could do. Within a week of her wedding, Harriet Palmer was dead. The devastated bridegroom told Emily to "spare no expense for anything that was needed." Accustomed to her occasional role as mortician, Emily arranged for a coffin and prepared Harriet's body, clad in her wedding dress, for burial.

Moodyville did not have an official cemetery at this time, nor did Granville. The eastern side of Brockton Point had been officially designated as a burial plot, as well as Deadman's Island. The latter, a bleak place known as Skwtsa7s or simply "island" to the local Squamish, had long ago been the scene of a bloody battle and was now used as a cemetery for both natives and non-natives. Those seeking burial for their loved ones in accordance with Christian tradition had to travel by boat or make the long journey along Douglas Road to reach the officially designated Fraser Cemetery in New Westminster. The entire community of Moodyville came down to the dock to watch in sorrow as Harriet Palmer's casket was loaded aboard a small steamer. There was not a dry eye in the crowd.

While life often had its low points for residents on both sides of Burrard Inlet, there were also memorable days of solace amidst the breathtaking scenery of the surrounding region. One pastime which gave Emily particular enjoyment was a day excursion via steamer up the North Arm, a sheltered fjord which adjoined Burrard Inlet near its easternmost point and meandered far into the pristine wilderness of the Coast Range. After a twenty-mile journey past lofty, forested peaks and isolated pockets of boulder-strewn beach, the steamer pilot would drop anchor alongside a rushing waterfall which bubbled over granite cliffs in a series of cascades.

The yet-to-be-named Granite Falls became a regular summer getaway for Burrard Inlet residents and visitors from foreign ports. Emily and other wives would pack massive picnic baskets full of treats— cucumber sandwiches, dried fruit, cakes fresh from ovens and all the

The yet-to-be-named Granite Falls, on the north arm of the Burrard Inlet, 1887.

fixings for tea brewed upon the campfire. Ladies would sit upon logs or cut rounds of wood, chatting and employing busy fingers hour by hour on their various fancywork projects, while their children took delight in the many outflow streams which coursed their way from the base of the falls to the shoreline. The volume of water would range from torrential in the spring runoff, when one had to shout above the roar, to meagre rivulets by the end of a long dry summer.

When the weather turned foul, as it could invariably do at any time of the year, Emily and her friends would host "at homes," singing songs around the piano or absorbing themselves in card games or cribbage. High society gained considerable momentum at Moodyville in 1879, with the construction of Invermere—a British colonial mansion—the likes of which had never been seen before among Burrard Inlet communities. Invermere, otherwise popularly known as "the Big House," was built under the direction of Moodyville mill manager Hugh Nelson. Formerly a member of the colonial Legislative Assembly of British Columbia and representative for New Westminster District in the federal House of Commons, Nelson had recently been appointed to the Senate of Canada. His appointment thereby called for a home that reflected power and prestige. The pounding of hammers and drawing of saws resounded daily over Moodyville as Invermere grew. With its wide, shady verandas and rooftop "widow's walk," Invermere would become the social magnet for the elite residents of Burrard Inlet, Emily and her family among them.

Emily always looked forward to letters from Abbie, as well as the occasional visit. Captain Frederick Jordan was now assigned to regular coal runs between San Francisco and Nanaimo on Vancouver Island. During the early fall of 1879, while the barque *Marmion* was docked in Nanaimo to take on a load of coal, Abbie and her family travelled across the Georgia Strait via steamer for what should have been another joyful family reunion with her parents and siblings. Typically when the Jordans arrived, there was much news to share and lively conversations would take place at the Patterson dining table amidst a gaggle of children. Emily took great delight in getting to know her first grandchildren—William, born at sea, and baby Edward Burrard, born December 22, 1878.

Invermere, or "the Big House," in Moodyville, c. 1887.

"This is your uncle!" she would say with a smile, introducing William and Edward to three-year-old Freddie.

But this visit was much different, for Emily and John's youngest daughter Addie became ill. After a brief time, she lost the power of speech, would not respond to any sound and lapsed into complete unconsciousness. On October 20, 1879, Adelaide Agnes Patterson died at the age of ten. A service was conducted at the Mechanics Institute by the Reverend Bryant, after which Addie was to be interred in the Church of England section of Fraser Cemetery. The *Daily British Colonist* published a death notice on October 26, referring to Addie Patterson as "a bright and interesting daughter of Mr. J.P. Patterson of Burrard Inlet. . . ."

Emily had attended at many a child's deathbed over the course of years, gently reading the words of the 23rd Psalm and encouraging family members to talk to their departing loved ones. When child mortality statistics began to emerge in certain countries during the seventeenth century, it was estimated that a third of children died before the age of nine. In some societies, midwives were permitted to give emergency baptisms to little souls that were not destined to survive their first few hours of life. It was commonplace for parents to experience the death of at least one child—a grim reality that was only starting to improve in the latter half of the nineteenth century. Emily had inwardly reminded herself many times that parents who never lost at least one child were rare in the extreme.

"Are you all right, my dear?" Emma Alexander asked softly, supporting Emily's arm as the women made their way along the rough trail from New Westminster's Columbia Street to the burial ground. John Patterson and a group of other men led the procession, bearing Addie's little casket between them. Abbie, Beckie, Calvin and Freddie followed behind, as the bell tolled steadily from nearby St. Mary the Virgin Anglican Church.

"Not quite yet," Emily replied stoically, "but I will be."

><

On the morning of November 7, the Jordans reboarded the *Marmion*—fully loaded with coal at its Nanaimo berth—for the southward journey back to San Francisco. Abbie, dressed in black, had been disheartened to leave Moodyville.

"You must take care of that arm, Papa," she said firmly.

John Patterson's injury had healed well, although he still complained of the occasional soreness. Abbie turned to her mother.

"I'll write lots of letters," she promised tearfully. "I hate to be so far away at a time like this!"

"Take care of yourself," Emily told her simply, "and the boys. Do not worry about us. We will continue as we always have."

By mid-November, residents up and down Burrard Inlet were preparing to settle in for the long winter. The logging operations continued full force as a thin layer of white hoarfrost appeared with increasing frequency each morning on the skid roads, creating the ideal slippery slide for transporting cut logs to the mills. Emily took advantage of any brief hours of sunlight to hang out laundry or beat the Moodyville dust from her growing collection of rag rugs. She was hard at work rug beating one morning when she noticed John climbing up the hill, having what appeared to be a sheet of paper clutched in his hand. As he drew nearer, she perceived that his face wore a markedly sombre expression.

"We have a telegram from Abbie," John said.

Emily stopped her beating and waited expectantly. John unfolded the sheet and read aloud, "MARMION FOUNDERED CAPE FLATTERY. ALL SAFE. ABBIE."

"All safe," Emily repeated.

Over the years, Emily had become very proficient at hiding her true emotions. More or less mechanically she returned to her beating with renewed vigour. "Well John, thank heaven it's a dry day."

Despite carefully scouring newspapers from Victoria and New Westminster in the days ahead, neither Emily nor John could find any mention of the *Marmion*'s loss. It seemed that the notorious water off Cape Flattery had claimed so many vessels over the years that unless there was significant loss of life, little or no press coverage was merited.

It would be another month before the Pattersons would learn more details of the shipwreck in a lengthy letter from Abbie. The *Marmion*, heavily laden with thirteen hundred tons of coal, had sailed out of Departure Bay as scheduled on November 7. By late evening, a strong southeaster with a heavy cross sea was battering the ship as it plied the Juan de Fuca Strait towards Cape Flattery. Daybreak brought no relief and the ship's barometer had plunged. Abbie described how she had prayed throughout the night, hanging on to William and Edward:

> I lost my grip on Edward during one of the swells and he was thrown against some trunks, breaking his leg below the knee, although I did not have knowledge of it at the time. His cries were heartrending. The crewmen were working constantly at the pumps, but *Marmion*'s hull was leaking badly and no amount of effort could slow the steady accumulation of seawater. We all came up on deck and the blessed crew of the vessel *Tam O'Shanter*, which had providentially been in the same area, dropped anchor off our port bow and prepared to take us aboard. The seas continued to be rough but had calmed sufficiently enough for an orderly transfer of passengers and crew. You will be pleased to hear that I saved my sewing machine. . . .

"Gracious!" Emily exclaimed, stopping mid-sentence. "I hope she didn't risk anyone's life to save the wretched sewing machine!"

"Keep reading, Mama," Beckie urged. She, Alice and Calvin had gathered at the dining table to hear Abbie's account of the disaster. Emily continued:

> From the deck of the *Tam O'Shanter*, we watched and saw the *Marmion* sink to its watery grave. My husband recorded its final position, 48 degrees 6 north and 125 degrees 40 west. Perhaps he has designs on attempting to salvage the lost coal but I think that would be foolhardy in the extreme. Please rest safe in the knowledge that we arrived in San Francisco without further incident and Edward's leg is on the mend. Insurance will help with our financial losses, so all is well. Your affectionate daughter, Abbie.

The silence that prevailed around the dining table was finally broken by John.

"It seems that all is well then . . . sad about the *Marmion*. She was a grand old workhorse!"

Emily folded Abbie's letter and carefully tucked it within the pages of the family Bible.

"Yes," she said simply. "It's good that all is well."

><

Emily was outwardly delighted yet quietly dismayed that her eligible daughters continued to attract the attention of visiting sea captains. On September 18, 1880, eighteen-year-old Beckie married Captain George

Beckie Park Patterson

Henry Pierce of the ship *El Dorado* in New Westminster. After the morning ceremony, the wedding party sailed back down the Fraser River and up Burrard Inlet to Moodyville, where a sit-down supper for fifty was held aboard the *El Dorado*. Two days later, the ship was towed out of Burrard Inlet for departure. Beckie would settle with her husband in Alameda, California, across the bay from San Francisco.

Finding all the trips back and forth to New Westminster for various religious observances lengthy and exhaustive, many Burrard Inlet residents agreed that the time was long overdue for another local house of worship to be built. The Methodist Church in Granville was largely attended by the native population. Emily had great admiration for the Methodists, staunchly declaring them "the real pioneers on Burrard Inlet," but recognized fully well that additional worship space was in dire need. Meetings were held and word soon spread that an Anglican church "in the finest tradition" would be constructed on Burrard Inlet's south shore. Heatley, Campbell and Company, owners of Hastings Sawmill, had generously offered a plot of land at the western edge of the mill property, on the condition that no formal land title would be given to church trustees.

Church committee members could not agree upon a name for the new church as it was being constructed and decided to put the question to Captain Raymur. He consulted his wife, who suggested, "Why not call it after you, James?" St. James Anglican, a church that Emily would be heavily involved with for the rest of her life, was a small and comparatively rustic structure when completed, holding little more than sixty people at capacity, but it attracted a full congregation of parishioners each Sunday from both sides of Burrard Inlet. Leon Ridley, now a strapping young lad of nine, was the first to toll the bell. The church was dedicated by Bishop Sillitoe of New Westminster on May 15, 1881. Thanks to her name beginning with the letter "A," Alice Patterson was the first inductee of the first confirmation class. She looked beautiful and serene as she walked down the aisle in her white confirmation dress and Emily could not have been prouder.

Emily, along with other ladies of Moodyville and Hastings Mill, continued to raise funds to fully pay off the church's construction costs.

"We'll hold a charity bazaar!" Emma Alexander declared. "We'll spread the word as far and wide as we can . . . Port Moody, New Westminster . . . perhaps even Nanaimo and Victoria, if we can manage it."

Regular meetings were held at the Raymur home to sew clothing and create beautiful fancywork projects. The ladies debated over which date

The first St. James Anglican Church, 1884.

to hold the bazaar, originally proposing Dominion Day, but there were races and games on the mill sawdust field which no one wanted to miss, so eventually the 4th of July was settled upon. Held in the schoolhouse, the bazaar lasted for two days and two evenings, attracting visitors from as far away as Victoria. The church's future minister, Reverend George Ditcham, stopped by the lunch sale table to thank the ladies for all their hard work while he ordered a sandwich and a piece of cake.

"Everything has gone splendidly!" he beamed. "You are all to be congratulated on such fine efforts."

"Thank you, Reverend," Emma replied, at the same time cutting him an extra substantial piece of lemon cake and attempting to balance it upon her carving knife while transferring it to a china plate. Her fingers had become somewhat greasy over the past few hours with handling all of the various sweets, and in the next instant, much to Emma's horror, the knife slipped from her fingers and landed solidly upon Reverend Ditcham's foot.

"Oh my heavens!" she shrieked. "What have I done!"

If the reverend's shoes had been made entirely of leather, it is likely that the mishap would not have caused much damage, but Reverend Ditcham was wearing a pair fashioned of leather soles with thin woven serge on top. The knife neatly penetrated the serge and a small amount of blood began to ooze through.

"Well . . . it seems we have a problem!" the reverend said, trying to sound lighthearted but clearly somewhat concerned.

Emily, who had been pouring tea at an adjacent table, quickly ushered Reverend Ditcham out the door and seated him on the schoolhouse steps. While Emma Alexander apologized profusely, she brushed away crumbs of lemon cake and gently drew off the damaged shoe and sock, revealing a not-too-severe cut beneath.

"Not a problem, Reverend Ditcham," she said with a smile. "A little bandaging and you'll heal just fine. I'm a little concerned about your shoe though."

"We'll find him another pair," Emma said determinedly.

"I can see that I'm going to feel very welcome in your new church," the reverend chuckled, clearly enjoying all the fuss being made of him.

CHAPTER 17

Modern Times

Communities along the Burrard Inlet shores continued to experience rapid growth through the early 1880s. Construction had been comparatively slow on the transcontinental Canadian Pacific Railway as one challenge after another presented itself in British Columbia's rugged mountainous terrain. Nevertheless, there was rampant speculation in development property in anticipation of the railway's impending arrival. Emily did not fail to notice the burgeoning value of lots in the region and, ever conscious of boosting family coffers, she shrewdly suggested to her husband that they consider purchasing real estate. John Patterson continued to be cynical. He did, however, consent to Emily's suggestion and the Patterson fortunes swelled with the buying and selling of lots.

On the evening of February 4, 1882, Emily heard a loud, insistent knocking at her door—not an unusual occurrence, given that her medical expertise would regularly be sought after at any time of day or night. She was surprised to be greeted by her next-door neighbour, Squire Jones Randall, in a state of great excitement. The Randalls had become acquainted with the Pattersons in Oregon and, inspired by Emily's favourable descriptions of life on Burrard Inlet, had also chosen to make their way north. Over the past few weeks, Randall had been hard at work on a "special project" down at the Moodyville Mill with equipment ordered up from the States. Like John Patterson, he was a master mechanic, whose passion was tinkering with any and all types of gadgetry. Young Freddie Patterson, not quite six years of age, was a fascinated onlooker and had been permitted to help with easier parts of the installation.

"I want you all to put on your best clothes and come on down tonight and see the electric lights turned on!" Randall announced proudly.

Moodyville—backwater milltown as it was on the shore of Burrard Inlet—would be the first location on the Pacific Coast north of San Francisco to be illuminated with electric lights. Emily and her family all trooped down to the shore to watch, along with virtually the entire population of the town.

"Are you ready?" Randall shouted.

The crowd answered with a resounding "ready!" In the next instant, it seemed that the entire mill complex was flooded with light. Gasps of amazement, cheers and applause rose in the air.

"They're beautiful!" Alice exclaimed. "What modern times we're living in."

There were ten electric lights in total, each composed of two carbon filaments surrounded by glass globes. They had been placed strategically about the mill complex, wherever light was needed most—above the saws, alongside the lumber chute and down by the loading dock.

"I should imagine we'll be able to cut and load twenty-four hours a day now," John remarked to Emily.

"I hope everyone will get adequate rest between their shifts," Emily replied, "but I do agree that they are quite amazing. I wonder how long before we can all enjoy them in our homes?"

If Emily and other Moodyville residents entertained any hopes that electric lights would soon replace the age-old coal oil lamps throughout

Squire Jones and Rebecca Edith Randall, c. 1875.

their community, they would soon be sorely disappointed. As John Patterson suspected, the lights were purely for the benefit of the mill workers, enabling raw logs to be processed and lumber to be loaded for shipment at any time of day or night. But another welcome improvement soon arrived that everyone could enjoy, with the inauguration of a new ferry, the SS *Senator*, built by Captain James van Bramer. The *Senator*, named in honour of Hugh Nelson, whose appointment to the Canadian Senate had established him as a local celebrity, was a full fifty-two feet in length, with enough cabin space to shelter up to twelve passengers.

For Emily, a trip across Burrard Inlet aboard the *Senator* was sheer luxury by comparison with other local vessels she had experienced. Previously, travel between inlet communities had often come down to relying upon the aid of friends and neighbours. Captain van Bramer had offered service aboard the steamer *Sea Foam* since 1866. In 1873, he expanded his fleet with the steamer *Chinaman*, soon to be followed by the *Union* and *Lily*. The *Union*, more often scoffingly referred to as the "Sudden Jerk," was a small scow that had been outfitted with side-wheels, powered by a threshing machine. With no reverse gear, the

SS Senator, *c. 1889.*

Union could travel only straight ahead. Captain George Odin, owner/ skipper of the vessel, employed a number of creative means to alleviate this deficiency. By sounding the whistle, enough steam pressure was diverted that the *Union*'s engine would die. If this technique failed, an empty burlap sack was thrown into the gears. As a last resort, Captain Odin would casually advise his horrified passengers to brace themselves while he drove the *Union* head-on into the wharf pilings. Emily had often declared that she would personally row a patient across the inlet for a visit with the doctor rather than risk a journey on the *Union*.

✦

Abbie arrived in Moodyville once again during the summer of 1882, well on in pregnancy with her fourth child. Edward was now an inquisitive young lad of three, and one-year-old Lewis had arrived into the Jordan fold. Sadly, first-born William had died some years previously. Captain Frederick Jordan had quickly re-established himself after the wreck of the *Marmion*, commanding a succession of vessels on the coal run between Nanaimo and San Francisco. Currently, he had charge over the steamer *Belvedere*.

"I know of no better midwife than you, Mama," Abbie had said flatly.

Emily was thrilled to deliver her own baby granddaughter, Emily Belvedere Jordan, on August 15 at the Patterson home.

Much to her added pleasure, Emily acquired new but familiar neighbours. Hugh Nelson's obligations as senatorial representative for Barkerville, B.C., required him to spend lengthy periods of time away from Moodyville, and he ultimately decided to step down as mill manager. Benjamin Springer took over and the Springer family moved into "the Big House," Invermere. Emily was delighted, as she had remained close friends with Fanny Springer—former schoolteacher of the Patterson children during their early days at Hastings Mill. Emily had delivered four of Fanny and Benjamin's children at the Springer residence on the Spit. On September 24, 1882, she delivered Ruby Maude Springer within the luxurious ambiance of Invermere—a markedly different scene from the sparsely furnished shacks where she so often attended births.

The Springers transformed the once untamed landscape surrounding Invermere into a lush country garden, reminiscent of the grandest English manor houses. Acres of stumps, long-dead foliage and other debris left in the wake of the logging operations were replaced with flower beds, manicured lawns and a tennis court. Inasmuch as Richard and Emma Alexander ruled the elite social circles on the south shore of Burrard Inlet, Benjamin and Fanny Springer did likewise in Moodyville. The Pattersons would receive invitations to elegant social soirees that contrasted starkly with the rough realities of life in a gritty milltown.

Life would have been just about perfect for Emily, had it not been for the fact that eighteen-year-old Alice was clearly suffering from a severe case of boredom. With both of her older sisters gone and her years of study at the Moodyville schoolhouse complete, there was little for Alice to do other than help her mother with housework or babysit for neighbours. She greatly enjoyed the social times, especially if dancing was included, but unlike Abbie and Beckie who had been married by this age, Alice had not found her ideal male companion. In her opinion, many of the young potential suitors about town were ruffians and "quite unsuitable." Despite her growing maturity, Alice continued to harbour a deep-seated fear of Indians. She did feel some sympathy, however, when Calvin described how an unpopular teacher named Mr. McMillan at the school often whipped misbehaving native boys mercilessly with a switch.

"I believe he's singling them out, just because they're Indian, Mama!" she commented one evening. "It's cruel and unfair!"

"I should have Papa make some inquiries," Emily promised. "Indeed that's not right!"

The next morning, Emily, together with Alice, was strolling in the vicinity of Mr. McMillan's home when Alice clapped her hand over her mouth to stifle a loud, guttural scream. Virtually every branch of an apple tree on the McMillan property had been festooned with dead snakes. Two young boys from the Mission Reserve dashed from behind a nearby bush and gave the tree a violent shake upon seeing Alice, caus-

Alice Frances Patterson, c. 1890.

ing some of the snakes to wriggle and drop to the ground as if they were still alive. Alice turned on her heels and ran, screaming at the top of her lungs.

"Don't you gentlemen have anything better to do?" Emily asked reprovingly, glaring at the two mischief-makers as they promptly raced off in the opposite direction.

"It was horrible!" a still shuddering Alice described to Calvin and Freddie later that evening. "I never saw so many snakes!"

John Patterson, listening to their conversation, could do little else than attempt to stifle a round of laughter, while Calvin and Freddie outright guffawed. Alice marched to her bedroom in disgust.

"I should hope that Mr. McMillan saw them!" Emily muttered to John after the rest of the children departed. "I suspect he received his deserved comeuppance!"

➜←

In the fall of 1882, not long after the snake incident, Alice started to feel physically unwell. Her illness began unobtrusively enough, with a sore throat and fever, but soon an unmistakable rash made its appearance— small red spots spreading over her body from the neck and upper chest, gritty like sand to the touch.

"What's wrong with me, Mama?" she asked weakly from her bed, while Emily bustled about the room, gathering up all of Alice's clothing, spare pillows and blankets. Throw rugs were rolled up and the pretty lace curtains were taken down from the window.

"It appears that you have scarlet fever," Emily said. "We'll have to remove a few of your things for the time being."

"Why?"

"They could become germ traps, I'm sorry to say. I'll boil them up and put them in storage. You'll have them back when you're better."

"Will I get better, Mama?"

"Of course you will," Emily said firmly. "But you must rest and drink whatever I offer you."

It was heart-wrenching for Emily to banish her normally healthy and active Alice into the isolation of an empty, cheerless bedroom. She zealously whisked away any item that her daughter had been in contact with. Bedclothes and nightgowns would require regular soaking in a tub of disinfectant solution. Any household item that Alice laid a hand upon, including china, cutlery, hairbrush or comb, had to be soaked in disinfectant or boiled for twenty minutes. Her used handkerchiefs were burned. Alice would remain in her mandatory exile for up to one month, or until all traces of the fever rash peeled away. Over the course of centuries, scarlet fever had taken a dismal toll worldwide and was still much feared, despite recent declines in mortality rates. The age-old treatment of blood-letting—a deliberate and prolonged draining of the patient's blood to the point where fainting ensued—was no longer in wide practice, having largely been discredited as a way of eliminating the source of the infection. Strict isolation and sterilization measures were the only known medical recourses of the day.

Alice's complete recovery was painfully slow and Emily consulted with Dr. Masters, who had taken charge as Granville's resident doctor in November of 1881 after Dr. Walkem moved to Nanaimo. Dr. Masters was a tough, no-nonsense Englishman, who flatly insisted that Alice, no longer contagious, needed to winter in the warmer climes of California to fully regain her strength.

"That would be wonderful!" Alice exclaimed, upon hearing the verdict. "I could visit Abbie and Beckie!"

While recognizing the wisdom of Dr. Master's advice, Emily frowned over the logistics of making such a journey.

"You'd need a chaperone," she said firmly, "and I don't know how Calvin and Freddie would manage without me all winter—not to mention your father and all of those little babies in waiting."

"I don't need a chaperone!" Alice protested. "I'm eighteen and I'm perfectly capable of looking after myself. I could eat oranges and strawberries and go to the Palace Hotel . . . it's the largest hotel in the world, Mama! Seven storeys!"

"Strawberries will be out of season," Emily retorted.

Dr. Masters could only sit by and offer subtle apologetic looks to Emily, but Alice finally received her wish through much melodramatic pleading and was soon happily waving goodbye from the deck of a southbound steamer. It was arranged that she would divide her time between the Jordan and Pierce family residences, for Beckie would make a trip north for Emily Belvedere's baptismal ceremony, held in Nanaimo on January 21, 1883.

During Alice's absence, Emily would have a measure of distraction as construction steadily progressed on Moodyville's first hotel. She watched as the two-storey building took shape on the waterfront with a

Moodyville Hotel, 1886.

protracted mixture of interest and unease. Located adjacent to the mill atop pylons driven three feet deep into the sawdust, the Moodyville Hotel was a grand structure that would accommodate visiting sailors and new migrants. Like Harry Hogan of the Terminus Hotel, manager Captain William Power, a veteran of the gold rush, would see to it that his venture would be a profitable one with the inclusion of a saloon. Much to Emily's displeasure, the days of prohibition, which had been openly defied once before in Moodyville, were now officially over.

"I hope Captain Power realizes that axe blades, high-speed saws and hard liquor are a bad combination," she told John, while seated at her sewing machine working on a new pair of trousers for Freddie. No one could stop Harry Hogan, however, and there was a marked increase in the number of on-site job injuries after he opened his saloon. "It's a foolish prospect in every way," she added.

"Kind of like trying to hold back the tide, I'm afraid," her husband replied. "Times are changing and we might as well get used to the fact."

Emily sighed and pumped the sewing machine treadle harder.

CHAPTER 18

Point Atkinson

Year by year, shipping traffic on Burrard Inlet was steadily increasing. Back in 1872, the Marine Department of the federal government in Ottawa had ordered construction of a lighthouse to safeguard the treacherous headland at Point Atkinson—Sk'iwitsut or "turning point" to Indigenous peoples of the region—where Burrard Inlet and Howe Sound converged in a swirl of hazardous currents. By 1875, the light-house—a wood-and-brick structure built on a granite outcrop—was fully functional, the beam from its catoptric lens shining ninety-five feet above the sea and visible to ships up to fifteen miles distant. Despite the vast improvement in navigational safety, the Marine Department's main problem was finding a lighthouse keeper willing to endure the loneliness of the remote point. Edwin Woodward, his wife Ann and their two children took up residence on March 17, 1875, but left in 1879, finding the isolation unbearable. The Wellwood family moved in next, but stayed only one year. Finally, Ontario-born Walter Erwin arrived with his wife Jane in the fall of 1880 to take on the job of Point Atkinson lightkeeper.

However hospitable and pleasant the waters of Burrard Inlet on a typical summer's day, the storm season inevitably descended and November winds could whip up a frenzy of whitecaps over the harbour with little notice. Late in the afternoon on a wet and blustery fall day in 1883, Emily answered a knock at her door to find a drenched and tired-looking Squamish man.

"Letter for Mrs. Patterson from Mr. Erwin at Atkinson," he said, handing her a small oilskin pouch.

Emily urged the man to come inside and dry off but he declined, indicating that he wanted to return to his home as soon as possible.

"Erwins need help," he said, before departing. "Come quick."

Emily hurriedly unfastened the twine wrapped around the pouch to find a smaller inner pouch, also made of oilskin. Whatever message Mr. Erwin wanted to convey, he had taken great care to ensure that it remained dry. Emily drew out a folded note, which bore a hastily scrawled line.

Point Atkinson Lighthouse and lightkeeper's residence, c. 1900.

"Mrs. Patterson, my wife is very ill. Please come to Point Atkinson at once, Walter Erwin, Lightkeeper."

Having just placed a full kettle of water atop brightly burning flames in the wood-stove firebox, Emily hastily moved it to the back burner. Alice, fully restored to good health after her California sojourn, was out visiting a friend, and Calvin and Freddie were doing homework in their bedroom. Racing upstairs, she first went to her large medicine chest. Walter Erwin had not described the nature of his wife's malady, so she would have to speculate and pack an assortment of remedies in her medical bag—camphorated oil, ether, Paine's Celery Compound, mustard seed, a tin of Pennyroyal tea, as well as her stethoscope and small supply of basic surgical instruments. Yanking open her bureau drawer, she dug out extra layers of clothing—woollen pantaloons, a thick, woollen fisherman's sweater of John's, woollen socks and gloves. A few minutes later, John Patterson, having arrived home from work, came into the room to change out of soaking wet overalls.

"Duty calls?" he asked, as Emily hastily threw on her oilskin cloak. Her slim frame virtually doubled in size every time she had finished readying herself for the elements.

"Mrs. Erwin is very ill at Point Atkinson," Emily told him quickly. "I need to find a boat . . . is the *Leonora* in dock? Or the *Etta White*?"

John stared at her incredulously. "Emily, it's blowing a gale out there! You can't seriously be thinking of heading out to Atkinson in conditions like this!"

"I don't have time to argue, my dear," Emily said simply, brushing past him with her bulging satchel. John followed her back down the stairs into the kitchen.

"Emily, this is ridiculous! No one is going to go out in this storm. How do we know if this request of Erwin's is even legitimate? Perhaps he didn't write it at all."

"I've received a message for help and I am going to answer it."

Emily resolutely added a small jar of coffee to her satchel. "I'm sure Mrs. Ridley can offer you a hand if you need help with anything. I may be some time."

John noticed that the kettle had been moved away from the hottest part of the wood stove and deliberately made a point of replacing it.

"You won't find anyone willing to put out in this weather," he told her.

>‹

Rain was falling heavily as Emily descended a muddy Nob Hill. The mill docking area was relatively deserted, rain puddles glistening beneath the electric lights. The saws had quieted for the day, their clamour replaced by the steady tinkling of ship's bells, lapping waves and the groan of wooden hulls rubbing against creosoted pilings. A number of mill workers and sea captains had taken refuge from the storm at the Moodyville Hotel bar. As John had warned, no one was willing to abandon their drinks and venture outside the door, let alone attempt a journey to Point Atkinson.

"Foolhardy proposition, Mrs. Patterson!" more than one of them rebuked. "Could try for tomorrow, perhaps."

In frustration, Emily left the bar with the intention of searching among the boats to see if she could find a willing pilot. She found one hardy soul checking the ropes of his craft to make sure they were fast to the dock, but he shook his head grimly when she asked about transport.

"Pure insanity!" he told her in disgust. "They say it's raging over Jericho way!"

"Jericho . . ." Emily murmured, half to herself. "Chinalset . . . Jericho Charlie! That's who I need!"

Racing back into the bar, she asked if anyone knew the whereabouts of Jericho Charlie.

"Believe he's over at the Mission," one of the men replied. "Saw him heading over in his canoe earlier this afternoon."

Emily had come to know Chinalset, also popularly known as Jericho Charlie, during his many visits to the Moodyville general store. He was a Squamish man who could be seen at any given time of the year plying the waters between Hastings Mill, Moodyville and the logging operation across English Bay at Jerry's Cove, his massive freight canoe loaded high with bales of oats and barley. The strength of Chinalset was well

Chinalset (standing at left), 1891.

known, a strength that clearly ran in the family. The story often circulated of how his father had once killed a grizzly bear with a single shot from a bow and arrow.

It was late evening by the time Emily had reached the Mission Reserve and managed to track down Chinalset, who was visiting his aunt in her small cottage home. He shrugged indifferently when she asked if he would take her to Point Atkinson that same night.

"Need to wait for full tide," he informed her. "Couple of hours ... then we start."

"Chinalset, there's no time to wait," Emily said patiently. "Mrs. Erwin is very ill."

"Full tide," he said flatly. "No sooner. Too hard to pull against incoming tide. Be crazy!"

Anxious as she was, Emily had to acknowledge that this was the only opportunity she would have of reaching Point Atkinson. She ceased her arguments and took the time to carefully re-examine the contents of her medical bag. Chinalset went off to locate another paddler.

The trio prepared to set off from the Mission dock just after midnight, as the storm continued to rage. Emily took her place in the middle of the canoe with the medical bag securely lashed to the seat beneath her. Chinalset's recruit paddler was a muscular young native lad who took up the bow position, while Chinalset himself manned the stern. The glimmer of Moodyville's electric lights quickly faded as the canoe headed down-inlet through sheets of rain. Chinalset was familiar enough with Burrard Inlet to make steady progress, despite the lack of moonlight and star positions to aid in navigation.

He and the native lad dug their paddles deep and strove to keep the canoe's bow aimed squarely at each cresting wave. Still, the vessel tossed about like a cork, forcing Emily to clutch tightly both sides with her gloved hands. As the group approached the Narrows, the going became rougher still. Volumes of Burrard Inlet sea water boiled through a gap less than half a mile wide between the north shore and the steep cliffs of Prospect Point to the south. Just past the Narrows, the confluence of the Capilano Creek added its own challenges with gravel bars and swirling rapids.

Emily could plainly see the distant, pulsating light of Point Atkinson and knew that Walter Erwin had a strict responsibility to keep it burning, no matter the circumstances. Point Atkinson jutted prominently into the merge of Burrard Inlet and Howe Sound like a thick finger. The topography of the headland—a labyrinth of sheer granite cliff faces and submerged rock shoals—had presented a formidable hazard to mariners in the years prior to the construction of the lighthouse. Chinalset and his fellow paddler struggled to keep their vessel on course, bringing Emily ever nearer to her destination. The lighthouse and keeper's residence stood at the most southerly location on the point, where waves pummelled the shore full force. Each pulse of light from the beacon revealed translucent foaming breakers, crashing in amidst a tangle of seaweed and wildly bucking pieces of driftwood.

Just as the group was coming tantalizingly close, Chinalset made a sudden move, plunging his paddle deep on the right-hand side of the canoe and dragging it backwards, forcing the craft to veer well off their intended course. The bow paddler responded by lunging forward with his paddle on the left, digging it hard and deep beneath the waves.

"Where are we going?" Emily shouted above the din. She knew that the Point Atkinson landing—a small pocket of beach with a wooden gangway—lay right at the base of the headland within easy reach of the lighthouse.

"Too rough!" Chinalset yelled back. "Pull into Skunk Cove, walk from there!"

Emily instinctively wanted to ask if there was any possible chance that they could make it all the way by water, but she could see that any attempt would be sheer madness. It was all she could do to hang on tight enough to avoid being abruptly thrown into the waves.

Skunk Cove was a welcome relief—a sheltered bay due east of the Point Atkinson headland, with calmer waters and a pebble beach. For untold centuries, it had been used as a convenient moorage by native inhabitants. Sheer cliffs—faintly illuminated from the beam of the now-obscured lighthouse—dominated the west side of the cove, cutting off direct access to the point. After beaching the canoe and tying it securely to a tree, Chinalset and his companion led Emily through the darkness to a narrow game trail which led uphill through the thick growth of salal. Clutching her bag, Emily walked midway between the two men, slogging along a zigzag, ridgetop course through a rain-drenched wilderness. Massive outcroppings of granite randomly protruded among thick trunks of ancient-growth cedar and Douglas fir.

Years earlier, federal legislation had decreed that the Point Atkinson Lighthouse would be set against a dark background of undisturbed forest, so that its navigational beam would never be confused with any other light of industry. Cold, wet and tired as she was, Emily had the distinct impression that under bright sunshine on a warm summer's day, she would have found great beauty in her surroundings.

Just as dawn was beginning to break, the trail broke open into a small clearing with a paddock for livestock. Ahead stood a giant mound of granite, atop of which stood the lighthouse and an adjoining cottage. Both precariously perched structures were surrounded by a fortress-like wall of whitewashed brick. A wooden staircase and series of cat-walks had somehow been constructed to bypass the many vertical rock faces of the headland. With the wind causing her sodden dress to flap noisily against her legs, Emily clutched the handrail as she mounted each step.

"Erwin house," said Chinalset, as they reached the door of the residence. He spoke casually, as if he had just dropped off a passenger from a summer picnic excursion.

Emily decided that she would forego knocking and drew open the unlocked door of the residence. Walter Erwin was nowhere to be seen, but in the solitary bedroom adjoining the kitchen, she found Jane Erwin lying in bed, her head propped up against thick pillows. By the faint light of a kerosene lantern placed upon a nearby table, Emily could see that her face was deathly pale.

"Hello Mrs. Erwin, how are you feeling?" Emily asked softly, removing her rain-soaked oilskin and taking a seat beside her.

"Emily Patterson," Jane rasped, as an expression of unmistakable joy crept over her face. "I knew you'd come! I knew you'd come!"

Emily was surprised twofold at this outburst. She had half-expected the woman to be on her deathbed, but Jane Erwin was clearly fully aware and coherent. Emily had met the Erwins on only one prior occasion, yet her reputation as a nurse on call, no matter the circumstances, had somehow spread to Point Atkinson.

Feeling Mrs. Erwin's forehead, Emily noted that she had a fever—high to be sure, but not to the point where rapid cooling would be required. Encouraging the woman to breathe deeply, Emily made a careful assessment with her stethoscope.

"Your lungs are clear, Mrs. Erwin. It appears that you are likely suffering from an upper respiratory tract infection, but it is nothing serious for the moment."

"Are you certain?" Jane Erwin asked, before emitting a volley of coughs.

"Yes, I am certain, and the coughing is a good thing," Emily said reassuringly. "It will help to clear away the catarrh. You must drink plenty of fluids and try to get as much sleep as you can. You will be just fine."

With that, Emily left the room to meet an exhausted-looking Walter

Erwin, who had just come inside. Chinalset and his paddler were sitting before the kitchen wood stove drinking cups of hot coffee, and Erwin bid her to do the same. She needed no encouragement, her body aching with exhaustion.

"I'm so very grateful to you all!" Walter Erwin said, sounding somewhat sheepish after learning Emily's diagnosis. "I couldn't properly take care of her and attend to the light. Damn mechanics need cranking up, lamp room windows need wiping . . . got to get up there again shortly to clean the lens. . . ."

"Not to worry, Mr. Erwin," Emily replied. "But you and your wife must take care of yourselves out here in this remote place. You really should have someone to relieve you of your duties, if not regularly, at least occasionally."

The storm abated by mid-morning and Emily was greatly relieved when the steamer *Leonora* arrived at the Point Atkinson landing with her much-concerned husband aboard, along with Emma Alexander. Emma, who seemingly had a knack for hearing of every urgent situation the length and breadth of Burrard Inlet, had brought a thick warm blanket for Emily and assembled a crate of supplies for the Erwins, including an assortment of medicines, fresh baking, bottled preserves, tea, coffee and sugar. Chinalset and his companion, having received a handsome payment from Walter Erwin, made ready to head back to Skunk Cove for the canoe.

"They were amazing," Emily said to Emma, as she watched the two men disappear into the woods. "Utterly fearless!"

"The same could be said of you," Emma said admiringly. "What an extraordinary venture! I'm sure that this will be talked about for weeks to come."

"Oh, I highly doubt that," Emily sighed, closing her eyes momentarily.

CHAPTER 19

The Perfect Vacation

As the winter of 1884/85 approached, Emily decided that she would dearly like to have a vacation—not just an occasional afternoon picnic that would more often than not be interrupted by someone in need of medical care—but a proper restorative retreat somewhere far away. Now that she was well into middle age at forty-eight, the obligations of attending childbirths too numerous to count and the seemingly never-ending medical emergencies often left her emotionally and physically exhausted. She knew that her husband had full-time obligations at the mill and would not be able to take on the added role of managing the Patterson household, but Alice, Calvin and Freddie were old enough to look after themselves. Granville did not have a doctor in residence at this time. Dr. Masters had taken ill and died in hospital the previous January, but there were now several practising doctors in New Westminster and road access between the communities was steadily improving. Abbie had given birth to baby Hazel Gertrude on June 28, 1884, and Emily yearned to travel south and spend some quality time in San Francisco and Alameda, visiting with both of her daughters and getting to know the latest addition to the Jordan clan.

Steamer service between Victoria and San Francisco was more frequent and efficient than ever, with new safety standards—the most favourable of which, in Emily's mind, was a simple white line, now painted upon the hull of most sea-going vessels. In 1876, a British parliamentarian by the name of Samuel Plimsoll had been so concerned over the rampant loss of cargo ships due to overloading that he proposed the easiest of solutions. If a horizontal line painted on the exterior of a vessel's hull disappeared beneath the surface of the water during loading, too much cargo had been taken aboard. The Plimsoll Line, although adopted with some reluctance by certain shipping companies, was now in wide use and had clearly made a positive impact by reducing the number of ships lost to overloading.

Emily wrote to Abbie, providing her with full details of her travel itinerary and Abbie had written back that she was "thrilled with the idea and counting the days." The plan was for Emily to spend Christmas at home in Moodyville, followed by a "second Christmas" with the Jordan and Pierce clans in San Francisco. John, however disappointed he was not to be joining her for the trip, wished Emily well as she departed for Victoria aboard the paddle steamer *Princess Louise*.

"Have a wonderful time, my dear!" he said, giving her a hug and kiss. "This will do you good!"

"I'm feeling rather guilty," Emily admitted.

"We will all manage just fine. There are plenty of women with midwifery skills in town now and we can readily telegraph New Westminster to send for a doctor if necessary, so you just go and enjoy yourself!"

"Be sure to try some of Mr. Ghirardelli's chocolates, Mama," Alice spoke up. "They're absolutely heaven!"

The steamer trip south from Victoria was uneventful, but Emily was relieved to finally glide past the San Francisco harbour entrance after a week at sea. Docking procedures had also become more streamlined in the twenty-five years since she had first set foot in the city, and in short order she was able to disembark and reclaim her trunk. Numerous horse-drawn taxicabs waited near the wharf to take passengers to their final destinations of choice. Emily was only mildly surprised that no member of the Jordan or Pierce family was on hand to meet her. Seagoing vessels frequently ran late, especially in winter conditions. She climbed aboard one of the taxis and directed the driver to the Silver State House, a lodging house at the intersection of Mason and Ellis streets in the downtown area. While the driver attended to her trunk she ascended a staircase from the lobby and knocked on the Jordans' door. After there was no answer to repeated knocks she let herself in to find a distraught Abbie Jordan just coming down the entrance hall.

"Oh, Mama, we're having trouble!"

Abbie collapsed into Emily's arms with a volley of tears.

"Abbie!" Emily exclaimed. "What is wrong?"

"The children have scarlet fever . . . every last one of them, except for Hazel. She's only six months old and I'm terrified that she will catch it. So far she's healthy, but I know it's only a matter of time. She's already beginning to crawl about and put things into her mouth and I can't stop her!"

"Where is she now?" Emily asked, abruptly brushing past Abbie into the house.

"In the parlour. I'm trying to keep her in there, away from the others, but it's so hard. . . . I can't keep an eye on her and tend to the children as well! I cannot send her to Beckie's because she's understandably afraid of exposure, and of course our neighbours and friends would feel the same. We cannot have Frederick take us out to sea on the *Belvedere* because that would be cold and unhealthy."

Emily found Hazel in the midst of the comfortably furnished Jordan parlour—a smiling little cherub with rosy cheeks and baby doll eyelashes, chortling and cooing contentedly. Abbie had carefully placed every fragile item—porcelain vases from China, teacups and saucers, crystal decanter and other knick-knacks from her wedding and travels —well out of harm's way.

"She's lovely!" Emily exclaimed, picking her up and giving her a warm squeeze.

Meanwhile, Emily could see that Abbie looked the very picture of exhaustion—her face pale, hair dishevelled and she was clad in a simple housedress that clearly hadn't been laundered recently. Five-year-old Edward, three-year-old Lewis and two-year-old Emily were tucked in bed in the upstairs nursery, all sleeping soundly the last time their mother had checked them.

"I don't know what to do, Mama!" Abbie said in a choked voice, sitting on a velveteen divan and picking up a partially finished knitting project, new socks for Edward. "I'm trying to keep things clean and sanitary, washing my hands and disinfecting the laundry, but it's a downright miracle that Hazel hasn't contracted the disease so far!"

"How long have the children been ill?" Emily asked.

"Just since earlier this week. They all came down within a few hours of each other. They may have been exposed at a party."

"Well then, we will do the only logical thing we can do under the circumstances," Emily said firmly, "and that is to remove Hazel from the scene. I will take her back to Moodyville with me straight away . . . on the next steamer, if possible."

"But Mama . . ." Abbie began.

Emily gave her daughter a gentle hug.

"Now, no quibbling! My mind is made up. Show me where you keep Hazel's things and we'll be packed up and out of here."

The Pacific Northwest winter of 1884/85 was more severe than any in recent memory. By early January, snow lay thick upon the ground throughout the Burrard Inlet region. Lewis's Stagecoach Line normally provided once-a-day carriage service along Douglas Road between New Westminster, Hastings and Granville, but with the heavy snowfall, an open sleigh had been brought into service. Harry Frieze, the driver, did not expect much demand when the weather was inclement and was only too happy to forgo the journey and doze before a warm fire if his services were not required. He was surprised to see Emily show up at the Columbia Street depot one frosty afternoon with a tiny baby bundled in thick layers of blankets clutched in her arms.

"Hello Harry, can you get us over to Granville today?" she asked.

Harry Frieze was a familiar face to all on Burrard Inlet and Emily had ridden with him on a number of occasions previously.

"I dunno, Mrs. Patterson," he said doubtfully. "Got a fresh fall of snow just last night. Might be pretty tough slogging out there. . . . What are you doin' out here on a chill day like this? And who is this little one?"

"My granddaughter, Hazel," Emily said. "We've had a long journey from Victoria, and San Francisco before that, and I'd very much like to get her home. Do you think it will be possible?"

"Well, might need to do some digging out here and there . . . we'd best bring along some extra kerosene," Harry replied, "and I'll scare up some extra blankets."

Emily knew that the sensible thing to do would be to find accommodation in one of the many New Westminster hotels and wait for the snow to melt to a reasonable depth, but that could take days. Her supply of clean diapers was rapidly dwindling, not to mention her finances, carefully stowed in a leather pouch about her waist. She was desperate to get Hazel safely settled in the warmth of the Patterson home in Moodyville, where everything she needed would be easily at hand. She knew that someone from Hastings Mill or Granville would more than likely be happy to ferry her and Hazel across the inlet if the sleigh could make it through to either of those communities.

Bundled up under several warm layers aboard the sleigh, Emily clung to Hazel as Harry Frieze urged two sturdy-looking dray horses up the steep New Westminster hill from the depot barn. Few vehicles had ventured out since the snowstorm, but several local children were joyously careening down nearby slopes aboard bobsleds. The sleigh lurched and swayed precariously as the horses struggled to find their footing in knee-deep drifts. Temperatures were well below freezing and the snow was of powder consistency, fortunately making the going that much easier. Fine white crystals sprayed up from the sled runners, bedazzling the blankets with a sparkly sheen. Harry yarded on the reins this way and that, weaving around dips and gullies, gently coaxing his team all the while. He was a well-experienced and skilled driver and Emily had full confidence in his capabilities. Thankfully, Hazel was a placid baby who slept soundly through the journey, despite Emily frequently checking her fingers and toes for circulation. The sky never seemed to grow fully dark and it was possible to make out the distant snow-covered expanse of a frozen Burnaby Lake midway along the route.

Late in the evening, Harry pointed out the welcoming lights of tiny Hastings, slowly becoming visible through the trees. Before long they pulled to a stop alongside Maxie's hotel. Maximilien Michaud had died in 1882, but the popular old name continued, despite the fact that the old facility was now largely used for CPR offices. Harry climbed down from the driver's seat and rubbed his gloved hands together vigorously.

"Need a hot cup of coffee, ma'am, if we're continuing on to Granville this evening," he told Emily.

Emily felt badly for his discomfort, but still yearned to get over to Moodyville by the quickest available means. As luck would have it, one of the Moodyville mill workers had come across to Hastings by rowboat for an evening of cards, and generously offered a ride back straight away. Harry was clearly pleased with the idea and happily settled himself in at the card table.

"Thank you very much, Harry!" Emily said, before making her way down to the dock with Hazel. Having left her trunk at the Lewis depot, she quickly added, "There's no hurry for the trunk!"

"Anything to oblige." Harry nodded, barely glancing up from his cards.

All was dark and silent at the Patterson household when Emily arrived in the early hours of the morning, jouncing a tearful Hazel, whose appetite had finally got the better of her. The kitchen itself seemed just slightly warmer than outside.

"John!" Emily yelled upstairs, hoping to make her voice intelligible above Hazel's cries. "Come down, please!"

Her bleary-eyed husband soon appeared, shivering slightly despite being clad in his thick woollen long johns.

"Emily?" he croaked, barely half awake. "What the devil are you doing here . . . ?"

"I'll explain later! We have to get Hazel warm and fed!"

Emily was virtually shouting to make her voice heard over Hazel's high-pitched yowls. Shaking off his grogginess, John rushed to the stove and heaped kindling into the firebox. There was a flurry of activity as Alice and Calvin soon emerged, awakened by all the commotion downstairs. Alice hurried outside for a milk can, standing half full in a crate of snow on the porch. The milk was partially frozen and she had to chisel through a layer of ice before being able to pour some of it into a pan.

An hour later, Hazel was sleeping contentedly in a wooden cradle and Emily was able to relate the story of her unexpectedly brief holiday.

"I knew it was foolhardy of me to bring a child on board a steamer who had been exposed to scarlet fever," she sighed. "We stayed in our cabin all the way to Victoria. It's so good to be back home! I must telegram Abbie tomorrow and let her know that we arrived safely."

"Tomorrow is here," John reminded her. "But for the time being, you must get some sleep."

It would be some weeks before the Pattersons received a welcome letter from Abbie, informing them that the Jordan children had fully recovered, and she had booked steamer passage north to collect Hazel. Emily was proud of the way her family had rallied to care for their little niece. Alice, Calvin and even young Freddie shared in the babysitting responsibilities.

"It's too bad you didn't get your holiday, Mama," Alice remarked. "San Francisco is so much fun. It would have been such a perfect vacation!"

"San Francisco may be fun," Emily retorted, "but I prefer seeing happy, healthy children foremost. Perhaps I am just not suited to vacations."

✧

It was back to business as usual, and Emily was all the more at peace for the fact. In the early morning hours of February 11, 1885, there was an urgent and persistent knocking at the Patterson door. Emily opened it to find Angus Fraser, puffing heavily from what had clearly been a very fast run up the hill.

"Mrs. Fraser is about to have her baby!" he told her frantically. "She's asking for you!"

Emily had come to know Angus and Annabella Fraser well over the years. The Frasers, like the Pattersons, could count themselves among the earliest pioneers of Burrard Inlet's south shore, having settled in 1875. They lived with their four daughters in a two-storey house at the northwest corner of Cordova and Carrall streets, not far from Gassy Jack's Deighton House. Sadly, Angus and Annabella's first daughter, Annie Nicholson Fraser, had died in 1879 at two years of age. Deeply aggrieved, Angus Fraser had thrown himself into his passion of boat racing. Together with crewmates John Murray, Alex Johnston and Jim Fraser and coxswain Cum Yee, he purchased a racing sailboat from Moodyville boat builder Tom Maloney. Christened *Annie Fraser*, the vessel and its crew had achieved memorable victories at racing events between Moodyville and Granville, on the Fraser River off New Westminster shores and as far away as Victoria.

Although her thoughts were mostly focused on Annabella Fraser and her imminent delivery, Emily could not help feeling an underlying thrill of excitement, being whisked across the inlet aboard the famed *Annie Fraser*. The craft all but flew over the water, sails billowing, with a speed that would challenge the fastest of steamers. A full thirty-two feet in length, the *Annie Fraser* was of clinker design. Her overlapping hull planks could quite literally bend and flex from stem to stern, enabling her to plow through the surrounding waves with little resistance. Clinker-built vessels dated as far back as Viking times, when the great longboats brought marauding warriors to widespread localities across the northern hemisphere.

"This is wonderful!" Emily exclaimed.

The air was brisk and deliciously fresh—not uncomfortably cold—and morning sunlight dappled the snow-covered heights of the north shore mountains.

Angus Fraser pulled up alongside the city wharf at the north foot of Carrall Street, whereupon Emily hurried to the Fraser household with her midwifery kit, well in time to safely deliver Olive Ruth Fraser into the world.

"A lovely baby daughter!" she told Angus, who had been awaiting word with his friends outside Deighton House. A round of cheers arose.

Hours later, back home in Moodyville, Emily's thoughts reverted to her lost San Francisco holiday. It was strange how the fates twisted and turned. She realized that she would not have been able to attend Olive Fraser's birth, had her trip south gone according to plan. Now the Jordan family was healthy, and the Fraser family was ecstatically happy. She had experienced the joy and exhilaration of a ride aboard the *Annie Fraser*. All in all, it had been a most remarkable winter, perfect vacation or not.

CHAPTER 20

Historic Days

Ongoing construction of the Canadian Pacific Railway dominated the news of the mid-1880s and anticipation mounted up and down Burrard Inlet with the heady realization that a coast-to-coast railway line was nearing completion. By early 1886, Granville had been formally re-named Vancouver, although the popular old nickname of Gastown re-mained in wide use. On April 6, the city was officially incorporated with a small ceremony at the Miller residence. Vancouver's first mayor, Scotsman Malcolm Alexander MacLean, was elected on May 3. Look-ing across Burrard Inlet from her Nob Hill vantage point on any given day, Emily could see a rapidly changing cityscape. Over the past few months, Vancouver had eclipsed Moodyville in growth. New hotels sprouted seemingly overnight, the "New Road"—a more direct route to New Westminster—had been completed, passenger and freight ser-vice via ship and shore was ever expanding and the local population seemed to increase daily.

Demands upon Emily's skills in medical care grew all the more. Past jealousies long forgotten, she was greatly relieved to see more doctors taking up residence among the new arrivals. By early 1886, no less than

Dr. Henri Langis

five trained physicians had established practices on the south shore—Dr. William McGuigan, Dr. Daniel Beckingsale, Dr. Henri Langis, Dr. John Lefevre and Dr. Duncan Bell-Irving. Dr. Langis was particularly impressed with Emily's self-taught capabilities and willingly consented to her assistance. In certain cases he had no option, as longtime Burrard Inlet residents often demanded her presence. Concerned that no formal medical training had previously been offered in the region, Dr. Langis established a small school of anatomy in his Vancouver office—the city's first semblance of an educational facility for medical students.

"An historic day for the city!" he declared.

On the morning of June 13, 1886, Emily and John attended Whitsunday service at St. James Church with their family. Abbie was in town once again with the rest of the Jordan children, as a much-belated christening for Hazel was happening later that month in Nanaimo. While both families returned home to Moodyville after the service, thirteen-year-old Calvin, who was rapidly growing into a young man and feeling the need to assert his independence, lingered behind.

It was yet another hot day for the region—the latest in an unbroken string that had now lasted three weeks. The ground was parched dry, and a massive debris pile leftover from the logging operations on the outskirts of Vancouver lay withered and temporarily abandoned. Logging activity was voracious. Thousand-year-old coastal giants were felled strategically, so that their enormous bulk would bring down smaller trees in proximity as they crashed to the forest floor. Trunks would be stripped of their branches and skidded to the mill, unusable foliage left behind eventually to be burned away. The sight and smell of smoke from clearing fires was constant up and down Burrard Inlet. That is why early in the afternoon of June 13, no one immediately took notice when an abnormally excessive amount of smoke filled the air. Down by the shoreline of False Creek, a clearing fire had lost control and was barrelling northeastward. The massive debris pile lay directly in its path.

The Pattersons finished a light lunch, whereupon Alice went outside to bring in a dessert that had been set to cool on the veranda. In doing so, a southward glance made her jaw drop. End to end, the city was aflame. An enormous, mushroom-shaped cloud of black smoke billowed high above, and Burrard Inlet was a seething mass of whitecaps. Alice turned on her heel and raced back inside.

"Gastown is burning!" she cried.

"Gastown's not burning," Emily retorted, scraping plates into her compost tin.

"Well, you can't see a fire but you can see smoke. Come look. Everyone, come and look!"

Emily and John hurried outside, quickly followed by the others.

"Great Scot!" John gasped.

Emily's face went white as she uttered a single word.

"Calvin!"

Leaving Abbie to mind the children, everyone else raced down to the Moodyville dock, which was already a scene of what could best be described as organized pandemonium. Rescue craft were steadily departing—every available vessel, no matter the size, was being rapidly commandeered for service. A potlatch had been underway at the Mission Reserve and several canoe-loads of native paddlers were visible, already midway across the inlet. Above the roar and crackle of the flames, screams could plainly be heard—shrill cries of distress carrying across the water from the length of the Vancouver foreshore. John raced for one of the steamers about to cast off, with Emily close at his heels.

"Not this time, Emily," he said firmly, grabbing her by the arms. "You are going to be needed here. I'll look for Calvin!"

Even as he spoke, the first craft from the Vancouver side was pulling up to the Moodyville dock. A cluster of soot-smeared, frightened passengers waited to disembark, some clutching small satchels or squirming pets, others with little but the clothes on their backs. Their blackened faces wore expressions ranging from abject panic to dazed shock. Tears flowed freely from old and young.

"All right," Emily said, reluctantly recognizing that there was work at hand. "Find our Calvin."

As more and more fire refugees amassed at the Moodyville dock, stories began to circulate of the fire's astonishing suddenness. What had begun as a thick shroud of smoke had quickly transformed into a wall of flame that bore down upon the city "without a minute of warning." Emily moved quickly among the crowd, visually sorting the most seri-

Calvin Oric Patterson

ously injured of the casualties from those with lesser trauma. There were numerous incidences of burned and blistered feet and hands. Many victims had run down the middle of Alexander Street for Hastings Mill, abandoning the boardwalk as flying embers ignited the wooden slats. Those who underestimated the fire's ferocity or wasted precious minutes trying to save personal effects paid the price dearly. Emily could see that no small amount of ether or morphine would resolve the agony of some. Victims with severe burns would require transport to New Westminster or Victoria for hospital care.

"At the earliest opportunity!" she told herself grimly, realizing that every available vessel on both sides of the water was being put into use for the rescue effort.

Virtually every resident of Moodyville had come to the dock to provide assistance. Before long, there was a steady assembly line from the store, as every available supply of painkiller, bandaging and salves was brought forth. Parched throats were slaked with ample quantities of fresh water and giant urns of coffee were brewed up at the mill cook-house. Alice searched among the crowd, trying to reunite family members that had been separated in the chaos. In doing so, she discovered Calvin, who had made it back across the inlet aboard his Uncle Calvin's steamer, the *Edward James*.

"Calvin, don't you scare us like that again!" Alice scolded, at the same time giving him a hug. "Now you go find Mama straight away and tell her you're safe!"

A distraught Margaret Miller anxiously waited at the Moodyville dock with her children for Mr. Miller—who, at last word, had been attempting to save valuables from the city post office. Sooty and dishevelled Jonathan Miller finally arrived, carefully balancing his blackened spectacles atop the post office cash box.

"Mother, I saved my glasses!" he told her, with a ghost of a smile.

At Emily's urging, Abbie and Alice escorted the entire Miller family to the Patterson home.

"I hope they saved our piano," Ada Miller spoke up, as Emily prepared tea.

"You're all here," she replied. "Let's try to be cheerful."

John Patterson arrived back later in the day, having spent much of the afternoon ferrying fire refugees across the inlet. In doing so, he, like Emily, had been greatly relieved to hear of Calvin's well-being. Homes throughout Moodyville were filled to capacity that same evening, as was the hotel, the Masonic Lodge and the Mission Reserve's church down-inlet at Ustlawn. Alice and Abbie served free meals to fire refugees at the Moodyville Hotel. Returning home at the end of an exhausting shift, they were met at the door by their mother, motioning for them to be quiet. Floor space throughout the Patterson residence had been taken up by exhausted, traumatized refugees—both stranger and friend. Emily had brought out every spare blanket she could find in addition to coats, pillows, empty flour sacks—anything she could use to fashion some semblance of a comfortable bed.

"It's so very pitiful, Mama," Alice whispered.

"We must watch through the night for symptoms of shock," Emily replied. "I'll keep a full kettle on the stove for tea."

✻

It was later estimated that eight lives had been claimed by the fire, although no one was certain of the exact tally. Many individuals who had lived in Vancouver were wayfaring transients, who came and went as they saw fit. Some left immediately after the fire, their whereabouts unaccounted for. Treating fire victims took up much of Emily's time in the days and weeks ahead, as she criss-crossed the inlet regularly to offer her skills wherever they were needed. A city of white canvas sprung up where Vancouver had once stood—government-issued tents, dotting the blackened landscape. A fortunate—some would say miraculous— change in wind direction had caused the fire to abate, sparing most of the structures at Hastings Mill. Relief donations large and small poured in and reconstruction progressed rapidly. Richard Alexander offered up mill lumber free of charge.

While new businesses and homes sprouted within days from the

Great Vancouver Fire aftermath, June 14, 1886.

ashes, less attention was given to sanitation. Thirsty construction work-ers hauled up water from wells that were ash-clogged and contaminated. Outhouses, both public and private, were not given priority and in-dividuals carelessly relieved themselves in random, undesignated loca-tions. Disgusted by their behaviour, Emily vented her displeasure directly to Mayor Malcolm MacLean. The mayor had been a routine sight about town, visiting one construction site after another to encour-age progress and facilitate the distribution of relief funds. Emily raised her voice, in hopes that some of the nearby perpetrators would hear.

"These so-called gentlemen are relieving themselves anywhere and everywhere they see fit! All of this mess will seep into the groundwater and, mark my words, Mayor MacLean, you will see rampant contami-nation all over the city!"

The popularity of Mayor Malcolm MacLean, a Scotsman who nar-rowly defeated Richard Alexander to become Vancouver's first mayor back on May 3, had surged in the days following the fire for his organi-zational and charitable efforts. He acknowledged Emily's concerns and agreed that more needed to be done. Public warnings were issued, but the problem was clearly not to be resolved in the short term. While cer-tain Vancouver businesses were being reconstructed with thought and care, others were completed hastily with one purpose in mind: the un-fettered resumption of alcohol sales. Some hotels resembled little more than clapboard shacks—their main purpose, to facilitate the ever-in-creasing demand for alcohol. Whiskey was often being openly con-sumed on Vancouver streets.

Along with advocating for the speedy reconstruction of outhouses, Emily urged as many Vancouver residents as she could to obtain their drinking water from large cisterns being delivered by scow from Moodyville. But exactly as she had feared, the first cases of typhoid be-gan to emerge within weeks after the fire. Jonathan and Margaret Miller, much to the Pattersons' objections, had returned to Vancouver with their family to live in one of the government-issued tents, while Jonathan Miller supervised the construction of a large new home on Burrard Street. Their daughter Carrie soon came down with the classic typhoid symptoms—high fever, abdominal pains and diarrhea.

"I tried to be so careful!" Margaret Miller said tearfully as Emily called by one afternoon to check on Carrie's condition. "I told Carrie not to drink anything unless it was boiled. I feel as though I've been boiling water twenty-four hours a day!"

"She could have contracted typhoid many ways," Emily replied, dabbing at Carrie's feverish brow with cistern water from a partially full bucket near her bedside. "Eating a piece of fruit or vegetable washed in contaminated water . . . drinking from an unwashed cup. Once typhoid has become established, it is very difficult to eradicate. We must do everything we possibly can to stop this illness from becoming an epidemic."

"What can we do?"

"Advocate for cleanliness!" Emily replied firmly.

As typhoid cases continued to mount, Emily did just that, sharing her advice with any and all who would listen. General care had always been taken in the construction of public outhouses and several crewmen got to work, choosing locations well away from water sources and digging through the ash and soil to create deep cesspools. A small quantity of lime for disinfection was sent over from Moodyville, while a larger supply was ordered from New Westminster.

Mayor Malcolm MacLean

"Soap must be distributed to everyone," Emily directed. "For the interim, fruits and vegetables may not be consumed unless they can be peeled. No lettuce, no beans, no strawberries, no cherries, just to name a few. Cooks, waiters and dishwashers must not be permitted to work if they are showing any signs of illness, no matter how insignificant. Furthermore, those caught relieving themselves where they know they shouldn't be must be penalized with a heavy fine!"

Certain individuals laughed off her recommendations. Some flatly declared, "when you gotta go, you gotta go" and that they would rather "take their chances." Emily's response was simple and matter-of-fact.

"You will suffer the consequences."

✥

Despite the bleak atmosphere on Burrard Inlet during the summer of 1886, an underlying celebratory mood began to emerge as word spread that on July 4, the first through CPR transcontinental train from Montreal was scheduled to arrive in Port Moody. While many members of the Port Moody community were resentful of the fact that Vancouver, with its more suitable deep-water port, had recently been selected as the CPR's western mainland terminus, most others were ecstatic. Captain John Irving, owner of the Victoria-based steamer *Yosemite*, was arranging to celebrate the occasion in fine style. He sent invitations to local dignitaries and dozens of high-society passengers, including adult members of the Patterson family, to join him for a one-day excursion up-inlet to take in the historic spectacle. The *Yosemite* was to leave from Victoria early in the morning on July 4, pick up passengers at Hastings Mill, and then steam to Port Moody for the train's anticipated high noon arrival.

"It will be wonderful!" an enthralled Alice cried. "We must go, Mama. All of us!"

Although seldom prone to getting overly excited about celebratory occasions, Emily had to acknowledge that the arrival of the first CPR train was something she would indeed like to witness. Over the years, she had followed the progress of construction with keen interest. Railway service to Burrard Inlet raised glowing prospects for the future. Settlers would arrive with a wealth of new ideas, skills, energy and determination. A wider selection of products would appear on Moodyville and Granville store shelves. Mail service would be faster and more efficient. Journeys that had once taken months would now be made in two weeks or less. Recalling her own family's circuitous route to arrive on the Pacific shores twenty-six years ago, Emily was quite simply in awe.

"Yes," she responded to Alice. "This is something that I would most definitely like to see."

While many fire and typhoid victims continued to require Emily's care and attention, she zealously guarded the date of July 4 as it approached. To her knowledge, there were no impending baby deliveries. Seasonal influenza was manageable in the warm days of summer. She purchased a new hat and had her seldom-used best dress laundered and pressed by the Chinese washerwomen down at the Rookeries.

On July 1, Dominion Day festivities occurred as they always did at Hastings Mill, attracting celebrants from up and down Burrard Inlet. Having come across to watch Freddie participate in the races, Emily was surprised to encounter Jane Erwin. Looking fresh of face and healthy, Jane, in the later stages of pregnancy, had come across from Point Atkinson to board the *Princess Louise* for Victoria.

"Mr. Erwin says he's perfectly capable of delivering the baby, but I'd prefer to go to Victoria," she remarked, "no matter the expense."

"When is your baby due?" Emily asked.

"Not for another month or so."

"Then that is likely to be an expensive confinement," Emily said, knowing full well that the Erwins subsisted on a meagre government salary. "You might just as well stay with us and I will deliver your baby. The boys can camp outside with their cousins and you can have their room."

Emily continued to insist despite Jane's protestations, until with much reluctance and embarrassment, she finally agreed to the new plan.

"It's so very kind of you, Emily," she said appreciatively. "I know how difficult we made things for you two years ago. We've never forgotten and we never will!"

"No trouble at all." Emily smiled.

><

Something stirred Emily awake in the early morning hours of July 4, well before her alarm was set to go off for the big day in Port Moody.

The sound of a subdued moaning was emerging from the bedroom being occupied by Jane Erwin. Hurrying in, Emily found Jane sitting up in bed, breathing deeply and massaging her stomach.

"I'm afraid I've been having some rather strong contractions," she said in a small voice.

"Are they happening regularly and radiating from your lower back?" Emily asked, as she reached for the stethoscope she had left by the bed for convenience.

Jane shook her head no to both questions.

"Well then, I suspect they may be Braxton Hicks contractions . . . false labour . . . although as you are well along with your third trimester, this little baby could be arriving sooner than expected."

Emily could barely suppress a weary sigh as she said these words, realizing that her long anticipated rendezvous with Canada's first through train was not destined to be.

Alice was equally disappointed that her mother would not be making the journey. Work obligations prevented John Patterson from attending, but Abbie was still in town and eager to go, having arranged for a babysitter. Emily waved her daughters off on an early morning departure of the *Senator* to connect with the *Yosemite* at Hastings Mill.

"I want you to tell me all about it," she said firmly. "Every last detail, do you hear?"

"We will, Mama!" Alice promised.

An hour later, Emily watched from her veranda as the *Yosemite* chugged its way up Burrard Inlet. Jane Erwin's contractions had ceased and she was sound asleep. The strains of music could be heard from a live band on board the vessel.

"Have a good time, everyone," she said with a sigh.

Emily carried on with her day, doing regular household chores, folding the laundry and polishing her silver tea service. Late in the evening, she was surprised to learn that a large crowd had congregated at the Moodyville Mill cookhouse for dinner. A call had circulated among residents that food was in desperate want. The morning breakfast provided by Captain Irving had been voraciously gobbled up by *Yosemite* passengers who had embarked on the excursion from Victoria, and all day long, there had been little or nothing to eat, save a few sandwiches.

"It was so exciting though, Mama!" Alice raved, as she tucked into a steaming bowl of stew. "There was a huge crowd at the station and there were banners and decorations everywhere. You could hear the whistle blowing in the distance and then it became louder and louder. . . . I couldn't decide whether to cheer or listen for the whistle. The only thing to make it more perfect would have been you being there too."

"Ah well," Emily said flatly. "Some little babies announce their impending arrival at awkward times. I guess my trip to Port Moody was not meant to be."

On July 6, Emily delivered Effie Jane, a healthy baby daughter for Jane and Walter Erwin.

CHAPTER 21

Sister Frances

On May 23, 1887, less than a year after the historic day in Port Moody, the first through CPR train from Montreal to Vancouver arrived, pulled by a glistening Engine 374. Crews had been hard at work over the last few months clearing, grading and laying track between the precipitous cliffs of Burnaby Mountain and Burrard Inlet foreshore to the line's final destination: a small wooden station at the north foot of Vancouver's Howe Street. Now their efforts would be rewarded with a celebratory occasion that draws thousands of jubilant spectators from both sides of the inlet. Emily was finally able to join in the pomp and ceremony and found she enjoyed it all immensely. The train was bedecked end-to-end with colourful flags, flowers and bunting. Painted banners touting a variety of mottos adorned the tender, buffer beam and smokestack: "From Ocean to Ocean," "Our National Highway," and "Montreal Greets the Terminal City." A painting of Queen Victoria in honour of her Golden Jubilee was prominently displayed on the front of the loco-motive.

While Emily was delighted with the completion of the railway line, her greatest pleasure was in the post-fire reconstruction of her beloved St. James Anglican Church in Vancouver. The original St. James, which she had supported with so much enthusiasm, had been completely destroyed in the fire. Now there was an opportunity to begin afresh and build a new church that would be twice as large as its predecessor, a much more fitting place of worship for the burgeoning local populace. Father Henry Fiennes-Clinton, who had arrived in Vancouver just months before the fire to take up pastoral duties in the former St. James, spearheaded the project with unbridled vigour. While Sunday services alternated between the still-intact Hastings Mill schoolhouse and the Masonic Lodge at Moodyville, construction steadily progressed on the new St. James.

CPR officials, through the assistance of Western Superintendent Henry Abbott, offered to donate two lots either to the east or west of the city for the new church. After some deliberation, a site was chosen at the northeast corner of Gore and Cordova streets, in a residential

Arrival of the first CPR train in Vancouver, May 23, 1887.

neighbourhood midway between Hastings Mill and the central business district of Vancouver. Repeating their successful effort for the original St. James, Emily and other women parishioners organized a giant bazaar to raise funds and simultaneously celebrate Queen Victoria's Golden Jubilee. After numerous delays and financial setbacks, the new St. James Anglican Church finally opened with a full roster of divine services on Sunday, June 12, 1887—exactly three hundred and sixty-four days after the fire.

"It's beautiful," Emily whispered to John as they entered the spacious sanctuary.

Father Clinton greeted each and every parishioner following the morning service, thanking them for their efforts on behalf of the church. As the Pattersons filtered past, he shook Emily's hand and asked if she would mind meeting with him afterwards "to discuss a proposition."

"Of course." Emily nodded, not at all aware of what he was considering.

"Excellent," Father Clinton replied. "Please join me for tea in my office."

The church rector's office, like the sanctuary, was spacious and new. It smelled of freshly stained wood and was already sumptuously furnished.

"I appreciate your taking the time to meet with me, Mrs. Patterson," Father Clinton began. "As you may or may not have heard, it is my intention to build a hospital next door to the church . . . a good, soundly constructed building that will be used to shelter and treat patients in need of care."

"I think that is a wonderful idea, Father Clinton."

"Now I know that you have an excellent reputation as a lay nurse up and down Burrard Inlet," he continued, "and I was wondering if I could ask a favour of you."

Emily started to wonder if Father Clinton was angling towards offering her a position of employment with the hospital and was about to respond when he carried on, his voice matter-of-fact and distracted.

"I would like to obtain the services of a fully-trained nurse, to assist me with the development and running of the hospital. I'm in the process

New St. James Church, c. 1892.

of drafting a letter to the nursing faculty of the University of Laval in Montreal, and I was wondering if you could offer your suggestions with regard to applicant criteria. Just what might our successful recruit expect to deal with out here on the western frontier? Do you think you would be able to help me out with this?"

Emily immediately felt a mild resurgence of that same old reaction she had fought back upon her first encounter with Dr. Walkem. For all intents and purposes, *she was a nurse*. She knew it, her many friends up and down Burrard Inlet knew it; even some of Vancouver's most re-spected physicians had come to acknowledge it. At the same time, she could not deny the reality that her long years of unconditional service were beginning to take their toll. She was now into her early fifties and at times every muscle in her body seemed to ache. Sitting tall in her chair, Emily drew in her breath, eyes levelled at Father Clinton.

"She must be a strong woman," she said bluntly. "Physically and emotionally. She will be required to lift patients twice her weight or more on regular occasion. She must be at ease with the sight of blood, whether from a minor scratch or an aortal hemorrhage. She must be at ease with death, for she will come face to face with it often. She must be able to cope for hours, sometimes days, with minimal food and little or no sleep. She should be able to ride a horse or walk long distances in all weathers at any time of day or night. She must have no fear of travel in open water or thick forest or of wild creatures such as bears. Some of her patients will be belligerent. They may threaten her or even try to harm her physically. At times . . ."

"Slow down please!" Father Clinton interrupted. He had been scribbling notes frantically as Emily spoke. She smiled demurely and waited.

"I'm afraid we may discourage any potential applicants with requirements such as these," he admitted with a frown.

"Well then," Emily said, "I suggest you strike a balance by listing some of the positive aspects of the position as well as the more demanding ones. De-

Father Henry Fiennes-Clinton

scribe what a unique and interesting challenge it will be to assist with the planning of a new hospital for our rapidly growing city. Tell of our spectacular situation here on the inlet, with its mountain vistas and fertile soil and vessels arriving from international ports of call. Make Vancouver sound as attractive as you can, and I'm sure you will have no shortage of fine young applicants."

One Sunday a few weeks after her discussion with Father Clinton, Emily noticed a new parishioner in attendance at St. James—a woman appearing to be in her early thirties, dressed in the traditional black robes and bonnet of a deaconess. Deaconesses were a sisterhood of women in certain Protestant churches who were trained in public service and dedicated to care of the poor and sick. Father Clinton asked the woman to stand during the service and introduced her to the congregation.

"On behalf of our family in Christ at St. James Anglican Church, I extend a heartfelt welcome to Sister Frances Dalrymple Redmond, nursing graduate of Laval University, Montreal. Sister Frances, I know

Sister Frances of St. Luke's Hospital and St. James Church, 1894.

that you will find friends and fellowship in our little community and I invite you to call upon us at any time, should you require any assistance with your relocation to Vancouver."

There was a lengthy lineup to meet Sister Frances after the service and Emily had to bide her time before being able to step forward and introduce herself.

"How do you do, Sister Frances. My name is Emily Patterson." Emily proffered her gloved hand and much to her surprise, Sister Frances grasped it warmly.

"Emily Patterson!" she exclaimed. "I understand that you have been nursing here for many years. I will be ever so grateful for any advice you can offer!"

"Of course, I will help you any way I can," Emily replied, finding that she had taken an instant liking to Sister Frances's spontaneity and approachable manner. "Did you enjoy your train journey?"

"Very much indeed!" Sister Frances raved. "The Rockies were so breathtakingly beautiful I was tempted to ask if I could ride out on the cowcatcher like Lady Macdonald did."

Emily laughed. Word had travelled far when Lady Agnes Macdonald, wife of Prime Minister Sir John A. Macdonald, successfully begged for the opportunity to sit atop the locomotive cowcatcher to enjoy the magnificent views when she and her husband took their first CPR journey west the previous year.

Over the weeks and months that followed, Emily had to acknowledge that Father Clinton had indeed struck gold in finding Sister Frances. Under the deaconess's watchful guidance, construction soon began in earnest on St. Luke's Hospital—a three-storey wooden structure adjacent to St. James Church on Oppenheimer Street. Meticulously planned, it would be a major improvement upon the CPR Hospital, a small board-and-batten facility that had been hastily erected on Powell Street near Hawkes Avenue, during rail line construction in 1886.

Emily had visited the CPR Hospital on occasion, but found conditions to be so cramped and unsanitary that she had often declared patients would have a better chance of recovery elsewhere. Sister Frances performed whatever task was required of her with youthful energy and

St. Luke's Hospital, c. 1889.

Vancouver's first City Hospital near the corner of Pender & Beatty, c. 1899.

zeal. Through the ever-active St. James Church grapevine, Emily learned that she had been injured while serving as a nurse in the Boer War. There were even rumours that she was a recipient of the legendary Victoria Cross for valour.

"She's an extraordinary woman," Emily admitted to John one evening. "I am humbled by her good works."

"Well then, I would say we are doubly blessed, because we have two extraordinary women on Burrard Inlet!" John said with a smile.

St. Luke's Hospital was officially opened on July 5, 1888. Sister Frances soon began a small school of nursing and worked in close partnership with Moodyville schoolteacher Margaret Thain on a wide variety of activities related to education and charity. The opening of St. Luke's Hospital was quickly followed by that of Vancouver's first official City Hospital, on September 22, 1888. A two-storey, fifty-bed facility, the City Hospital occupied a large lot at the southeast corner of Pender and Cambie streets. Patients "with means" were charged a weekly rate of ten dollars. Patients "without means" were admitted free of charge, providing they obtained a certificate of authorization from the hospital board with the signature of one physician. Emily was somewhat puzzled over the "with means" category.

"I find that very vague!" she commented to Sister Frances one day after church. "There are those of us who are fortunate enough to live comfortably and affordably on Burrard Inlet, but for others, a two-month stay in hospital could be financially devastating."

"Yes, I appreciate that costs could become insurmountable," Sister Frances replied politely. "We must work to ensure that no hospital patient will ever be denied treatment owing to lack of finances."

Emily realized that she had made something of a faux pas. While the City Hospital received government funding to supplement its budgetary needs, St. Luke's, as a private hospital, was utterly dependent upon patient fees and donations. Sister Frances, as a hospital employee, was dependent upon those same funds for her salary and living expenses.

"You are working very hard," Emily added hastily. "I know that everyone here welcomes the work that you do."

Over her long years of providing nursing and midwifery service on

Burrard Inlet, Emily had never demanded, nor expected remuneration. Dr. Langis was so impressed with her capabilities that he sometimes insisted that she receive payment rather than him. More often than not, appreciative patients would present her with a gratuity in the form of fresh baking or homegrown produce or a piece of fancywork. Emily particularly treasured gifts from her friends in the native community—colourful beadworks, wood carvings, exquisite baskets handwoven from cedar or bogland grasses—each item had its own place of honour in the Patterson home.

CHAPTER 22

Outbreak

On April 3, 1890, Emily left home for another attempt at a San Francisco vacation. She had also been faintly musing over the possibility of a trip on the CPR to Montreal, where she could connect with the Grand Trunk Railway line to Portland, Maine, and be within striking distance of a visit with her mother, who still resided in Bath. But Lucy Thornton had insisted many times in her letters that Patterson coffers would best be spent on reunions with Abbie, Beckie and the grandchildren down south—a standpoint that Emily was ultimately compelled to agree with. Recalling that frigid journey home with baby Hazel years previously, Emily decided that she would err on the side of caution and wait for the warmer climes of spring. This time around, the visit went according to plan and she was able to enjoy a much needed respite with the Jordan and Pierce families. Everyone was keenly interested to hear Emily's updates from home. She recounted how seventeen-year-old Calvin excelled in school, being especially adept at history. Freddie, aged fourteen, was rapidly losing his boyishness and enjoyed observing the mill operations—no doubt planning to follow in his father's footsteps.

"But of course the biggest news," Emily told them, her eyes twinkling, "is that our Alice has a steady beau!"

Abbie and Beckie were immediately ecstatic and demanded to know more.

"I don't know very much," Emily admitted, "but I can tell you that his name is Robert Churchill Crakanthorp, born in the parish of Castle Bytham in Lincolnshire, England. He arrived in Vancouver not long after the fire and took up employment at the Moodyville Mill. I do believe Alice is quite taken with him."

"I'm surprised that it has taken her this long!" Abbie retorted.

However much she enjoyed her vacation, Emily was happy to return home. She felt completely settled in Moodyville after nearly twenty years of residence and she delighted in the companionship of her boys and Alice. Emily and Alice had developed a strong mother/daughter bond over the years despite their distinctly contrasting personalities: Emily—perfectionistic, fearless and determined; Alice—leery of individuals outside of her own social circle, but otherwise fun-loving, frivolous and infectiously cheerful. Emily looked forward to nothing better than social evenings at Moodyville's Masonic Lodge, when Alice and her friends would entertain with rousing sing-alongs and recitals. The Patterson house often became an impromptu gathering place when rain spoiled plans for an outdoor picnic. Robert Crakanthorp was frequently in Alice's company, and Emily admitted to John that she had never seen their daughter look happier.

In July of 1891, Moodyville Sawmill and its surrounding lands were sold to a consortium of English aristocrats for an amount rumoured to be in the astonishing range of one million dollars. Never in British Columbia's history had there been such a lucrative deal. The new investors promised a glowing future for the community, with a doubling of the mill's capacity, new industries, a street network, electric railways and improved ferry service. As Moodyville residents looked on, plans for the reorganization of their community progressed at an astonishing speed. A month following the sale of the mill, the North Vancouver Land and Improvement Company applied for incorporation. Along with the management of real estate, the company would have the authority to issue tenders for virtually every attribute of a modern city— sewers, drains, pavements, telegraph and telephone service, hotels, churches, schools and more.

On August 29, 1891, J.P. Phipps, first Reeve of North Vancouver District, and his team of councillors were sworn in. Owners in Moodyville opted out of the district. Nonetheless, the value of Moodyville townsite had burgeoned, although most of its residents, including Emily and John, would see none of the financial gain. The Patterson homestead atop Nob Hill was company-owned, as was the Invermere Big House, the sawmill, store, hotel and virtually every other Moodyville structure. The very existence of Moodyville remained at the whim of its investors. Emily had always recognized that financial hardship could be on the horizon and encouraged her husband all the more to buy up properties to resell as land values increased.

"Anything could happen at any time," she said firmly. "We must be ready."

>‹

By early 1892, to no one's surprise, Alice announced that she and Robert Crakanthorp were engaged to be married.

"We'll have a summertime wedding," she declared. "With fresh flowers in the church and a picnic at Tom Turner's ranch."

A date was set for late July, and Alice began to sew her own wedding gown and write up a bevy of invitations. It would be a wedding and farewell party rolled into one, for Robert Crakanthorp had accepted a position of employment in the sawmilling community of Port Blakely, Washington, directly across Puget Sound from Seattle.

Emily liked the idea of placing an announcement of Alice's upcoming special day in a local newspaper. By 1892, Vancouver had two major dailies in circulation. A bundle of *Vancouver Daily News-Advertisers* was routinely sent over to the Moodyville Store and John Patterson made a habit of purchasing a copy to bring home after work. On the evening of July 8, Emily settled herself in her armchair after dinner to read the latest issue—her thoughts preoccupied with composing an engagement announcement for Alice. It had been a tiring day and her eyes were drooping, but a small headline midway down the fourth page suddenly made her sit up and take notice:

> PRECAUTIONS NECESSARY—The spread of smallpox in Victoria has aroused the civic authorities there to the necessity of taking stringent measures for its suppression. Although they appear to have been some-what tardy in the matter, if common reports as to the presence and spread of the disease are correct, it is satisfactory to believe that they will not allow time to pass without some vigorous action. We trust that the authorities of Vancouver and New Westminster will also be vigilant in regard to this matter.

"This is not good," Emily commented to her husband. "There is no room for tardiness where smallpox is concerned!"

Emily watched carefully for each subsequent report. The next day, the smallpox epidemic had become front page news with word that two cases of the disease had been discovered in Vancouver. A woman named Ella Matson from a house of ill repute at 121 Dupont Street was "very sick and scarcely expected to recover." A Japanese man staying at the Hotel Europe was also suffering. Both the house and hotel had been placed under strict quarantine with guards stationed round-the-clock.

In response to a telegram from Vancouver city officials, Mayor Beaven of Victoria cabled back, confirming that thirty cases of small-pox were now officially confirmed in the capital city. Unofficial reports gave a number of between sixty and seventy. The Vancouver Board of Health took immediate action, establishing a strict quarantine and banning any travellers leaving Victoria from setting foot on Vancouver shores. Mail and freight would be received only if it had been subjected to rigorous disinfection. Similar rules applied in Nanaimo, Seattle and Port Townsend. Victoria, for all intents and purposes, was to be shut off from the rest of the world.

Emily was incensed to see that the Canadian Pacific Navigation Company—despite all public health orders—was continuing to advertise regularly scheduled passenger sailings between Victoria and Vancouver. The SS *Yosemite* was one of a number of vessels in the Canadian Pacific Navigation Company fleet servicing a broad region of the B.C. coast. Now under the command of Captain George Rudlin, the *Yosemite* was a common sight in Vancouver harbour on any given day.

"Those advertisements should be pulled!" Emily fumed. "There will be trouble again, mark my words."

Emily's fears were well founded. Three years earlier, on January 5, 1889, the Canadian Pacific Navigation Company steamship *Premier* arrived in Vancouver from Seattle. Captain O'Brien had already received a clean bill of health for his passengers in Seattle. He decided to bypass the requirement for all ships entering Canadian waters to call at the federally run Albert Head Quarantine Station, located on an isolated peninsula twelve miles west of Victoria. The Albert Head station—a two-storey facility built in 1886—was woefully inadequate. Patients diagnosed with smallpox were committed to dank, airless rooms, devoid of a heating system or place to bathe. There was no bacteriological laboratory or reliable supply of fresh water. Quantities of portable sulphur-dioxide gas used to fumigate ships and luggage were insufficient. Worst of all, there was no wharf of any kind. Arriving vessels had to drop anchor offshore, whereupon it could be a week or more before a tender arrived with a health inspector aboard.

After the *Premier* docked in Vancouver, the city's chief medical officer Dr. Beckingsale came aboard and insisted upon checking over passengers, despite being presented with the vessel's American clearance papers. Much to everyone's dismay, he soon found an active case of smallpox and demanded that the ship depart immediately for Albert Head. Despite his passengers' disgruntlement, Captain O'Brien complied and proceeded to Albert Head, where he dropped anchor and waited. After eight days of languishing upon rolling seas with no appearance of an inshore tender, the fed-up captain ordered a return to Vancouver under full steam. When word reached Vancouver citizens that the *Premier* was headed their way with active smallpox aboard, near pandemonium broke out. Mayor David Oppenheimer deployed a force of police officers armed with fire hoses to stand guard at the CPR quay. Soon they had been joined by a crowd of angry Vancouverites, determined to prevent anyone from landing. A number of passengers tried to rush the gangway, resulting in several injuries.

It now appeared that the entire scenario of 1889 was about to repeat itself. Canadian Pacific Navigation Company officials served notice that they intended to maintain service, despite the smallpox outbreak. Vancouver's Mayor Frederick Cope telegraphed a strongly worded letter to the company's assistant manager, F.W. Vincent. The wording of the mayor's telegram was reprinted in the July 13 issue of the *Vancouver Daily News-Advertiser*:

> Yesterday, a dispatch was sent to the Canadian Pacific Navigation Company at Victoria by the Mayor, stating that passengers would not be allowed to land off the steamer *Yosemite* in the morning under any conditions.

Beneath, the company's hard-line response had also been printed:

> Steamer will leave here tonight at the usual hour after strictly complying with all quarantine regulations now in force. According to law, we have the right to land passengers, mail and cargo. If the landing is refused, application will be made to the Court for a mandatory injunction against the City of Vancouver, who will be held responsible for damages.

The smallpox outbreak had become a frequent topic of discussion in the Patterson household. Emily was furious over the impending arrival of the *Yosemite*.

"I'm afraid city officials are going to have a lot of difficulty with reinforcement," John commented.

"They must reinforce," Emily replied firmly. "I've been told on good authority that there is no vaccine available here at present and I know of many people who have not been vaccinated, despite my best efforts to encourage them. If that Captain Rudlin tries to dock the *Yosemite* tonight, I shall be right there waiting."

"Emily, as you said, there will be trouble," her husband said, frowning. "I don't want you getting caught up in any of that."

As usual, Emily was not to be deterred.

"A good strong show of opposition should put a stop to this nonsense. Yes, John, I promise that I will stay out of the fray if one develops, but in the meantime, I will not idle away my hours over here while someone willfully attempts to break the law."

Word circulated fast on both sides of Burrard Inlet that the *Yosemite* was steaming towards Vancouver in complete defiance of the ban on travellers arriving from Victoria. By the evening of July 13, an angry crowd had gathered at the CPR dock. A group of city police officers stood off to one side of the dock keeping a wary eye, as did several firefighters with hoses readied. Emily, having travelled across-inlet on the *Senator*, wove her way among the throng in search of any familiar face.

"There's upwards of a hundred here," she remarked to a woman whom she did not recognize.

While the majority of the protesters were adult men, there was a scattering of housewives and young people in the crowd, everyone grim-faced and determined.

SS *Yosemite at Vancouver, 1887.*

"No violence!" someone yelled authoritatively as the *Yosemite* came into view, lights blazing, from around Brockton Point. "We are here to peaceably uphold the law."

A small harbour tug, the *Skidegate*, moved to intercept the vessel as it approached. Word soon spread that Vancouver's chief health inspector, Joseph Huntley, was aboard. The *Yosemite* continued to move forward. Minutes later, three long blasts resounded from the *Skidegate*'s whistle. Instantaneously, a dozen or more firemen moved into position at the edge of the wharf with fire hoses aimed.

"That means they're going to try to land," shouted the same man who had called for no violence.

Emily could feel the mood of consternation swelling amidst the onlookers. While everyone watched, the *Yosemite* eased into position alongside an empty mooring buoy about three hundred yards from shore. In the next few minutes, a lifeboat with four men aboard was lowered from the vessel. The woman standing next to Emily had a pair of field glasses.

"Captain Rudlin himself is at the oars," she reported in astonishment. As the lifeboat reached dockside, one of the men aboard identified

himself as the ship's purser and handed over a wad of papers to Vancouver's Police Chief McLaren. Emily elbowed her way forward to listen in on the conversation.

"Bills of health signed by Dr. Milne in Victoria and customs clearance documents," she heard him mention.

Chief McLaren carried on a discussion with other city officials present in low tones. The *Skidegate* pulled up dockside, whereupon health inspector Huntley disembarked and was also shown the papers. After studying them

Captain George Rudlin

for a time, he firmly and loudly announced his verdict.

"Notwithstanding clean bills of health, the *Yosemite*, under no conditions, will be allowed to tie up at the wharf and no one will be allowed to land."

"This is absurd!" Captain Rudlin replied angrily. "I've got a large quantity of freight aboard, mail for the old country and several passengers who want to go directly to the train. Everyone aboard has been vaccinated and furthermore, everyone was examined before being allowed to board."

Huntley patiently but firmly explained that Vancouver City Council had passed a resolution the previous evening to quarantine the *Yosemite* and it was his duty to uphold the law. After much arguing, Captain Rudlin was finally forced to capitulate, although he managed to strike a deal whereby cargo that had been properly disinfected with carbolic acid could be unloaded.

"Clear this dock!" Chief McLaren yelled sternly to the crowd. "Ship's landing but nobody's getting off, so go on home, all of you."

"A very unwise decision," Emily commented angrily as people around her slowly began to disperse.

Sure as fate, as soon as the ropes had secured *Yosemite* dockside, a young male passenger took a running leap from the main deck onto the wharf. Moments later he was wrestled to the ground by waiting police and muscled back aboard.

"Let us get off!" a woman shouted from the deck. "We don't have smallpox!"

"It's for the best!" Emily yelled back, before being gently but firmly steered away by a police officer.

Much to her anger, the following day Emily learned that Captain Rudlin had managed to land all of his passengers at Port Moody, outside of Vancouver jurisdiction.

"He says he landed in Omaha," she retorted. "He seems to think this is all a big joke!"

"Omaha?" John asked. "Why Omaha?"

"There's a vaccine farm in Omaha. Cows are deliberately infected with the cowpox virus and the serum is extracted for shipment when they develop lesions. Captain Rudlin should be ashamed of himself for his conduct!"

By July 23, Chief Provincial Health Officer John Chapman Davie reported nine cases of smallpox in Vancouver. Dr. Langis set up two isolation hospitals for the victims—one on Deadman's Island in Coal Harbour, and the other at Cedar Cove or Khupkhahpay'ay, a small native community located between the future Clark Drive and Nanaimo Street. Yellow quarantine flags were ordered to be placed at the back and front of any home or establishment with a suspected case of smallpox. No one was to enter or leave the premises. Children from infected households were forbidden to play with their friends. Groceries were dropped off outside doors. Men stayed home from work. A sad report circulated of a young man who decided to help Mr. Hanna, the undertaker. In doing so, he contracted the disease and died. It was the custom in Vancouver for stricken patients to be loaded aboard an express wagon with a bell attached. While the bell was being rung repeatedly to warn people away, the unfortunate victims—many of them from the notorious Dupont Street brothels—were driven to the docks for boat transport to the quarantine station on Deadman's Island.

"This is a terrible July!" Alice said tearfully to her mother one evening. "Robert and I were so looking forward to our wedding."

The Patterson/Crakanthorp wedding had long been postponed and Alice was carefully packing away her wedding gown, folding it tidily amidst cotton sheeting in a trunk, with a scattering of mothballs.

"Weddings can wait," Emily replied unsympathetically. "We must all be grateful every day for our good health and work as hard as we can to assist those who have not been so blessed."

CHAPTER 23

Lost Souls

The smallpox epidemic ran its course by summer's end, yellow flags came down, and life gradually returned to normal on Burrard Inlet. Alice Patterson and Robert Crakanthorp were married on December 29, 1892, at St. James Anglican Church. While it was not the summer wedding that Alice had yearned for, the altar at the front of the church looked like a veritable English country garden, festooned with flowers of silk. Alice and her husband left for Port Blakely, Washington, soon after the wedding, amidst tearful expressions of farewell and promises to write.

The glowing promises of Moodyville Sawmill's new owners were short-lived, as a worldwide economic recession took hold in the early 1890s. A series of bank and business failures in the United States triggered a cascade effect that led to panic sell-offs internationally. The sharp decline in timber trade forced the closure of Moodyville Sawmill for a number of months in 1893. Tens of thousands of dollars were either owing to creditors or lost to shareholders. Development on the north shore, as well as in Vancouver, ground to a halt. Houses were boarded up as their occupants departed in search of employment elsewhere in the country.

Members of the Women's Christian Temperance Union and associated churches decided that with the growing number of parentless children in the Burrard Inlet region, an orphanage was desperately needed. A ladies managerial board was formed and the first annual meeting was held in Vancouver on February 9, 1893. The city's first "Children's Home" was a house located on the corner of Homer and Dunsmuir streets. In its first year of operation, the orphanage took in nineteen children. Emma Alexander was deeply involved with the project and Emily would follow its ongoing progress with keen interest.

While there was no similar such facility across the inlet, Moodyville was a tight-knit community, where everyone knew everyone and people looked out for and supported each other in times of trouble. Emily had always been particularly watchful of the Linn family, who for many years resided in a cottage just to the east of Moodyville, near the eastern bank of what would become known as the incorrectly spelled Lynn Creek.

Mary Linn and her Scottish husband John "Jock" Linn—a member of the Royal Engineers—had travelled from New Westminster to Burrard Inlet with their six children in 1869. Jock had received a free grant of a one-hundred-and-fifty-acre parcel of north shore land (Lot 204) under a British Columbia government plan for rewarding soldier settlers. The Linn cottage—comprising a dining room, kitchen, four tiny bedrooms and little else—stood a mere fifty feet from the creek. At the most extreme high tides, Burrard Inlet waters lapped at the veranda. In Emily's opinion, the Linns resided in a perpetually damp and unhealthy environment, but there was little that she could do to change the situation. Jock Linn was crippled and apparently had no interest in relocating to higher, but less accessible ground.

To make matters worse, Jock was allegedly a long-time drunkard, who many people said would "fight at the drop of a hat" outside Mannion's Hotel in Granville. In the early days, before lameness overtook

Mary and John "Jock" Linn, c. 1865.

his once-sturdy physique, witnesses would recall seeing him dash into the forest after an alcohol-fuelled brawl, with his irate wife hot on his heels. Jock Linn died of a paralytic stroke on April 18, 1876, leaving Mary alone to raise her six children.

Emily had great admiration for Mary, a devoutly religious, "no nonsense" woman who would rise to any challenge to keep her children warm and fed. She worked herself to the bone, raising fruit and vegetables, chickens, cattle for market and draft oxen—the latter always in demand for hauling logs to the mill—and keeping the cottage clean and tidy with the help of her daughters. Not far from the cottage, part of the Linn property was converted to a rifle range, and Mary managed a side business providing meals for the visiting sportsmen. When her daughter Allison died of tuberculosis on June 20, 1882, at the age of seventeen, Mary began calling Alice Patterson "Allison," as the girls had been good friends.

The Linn boys, on the other hand, had proved to be a disappointment in everyone's eyes. Neither held down a job and the eldest son, Hugh, was a notorious troublemaker who frequently wound up in the tiny jailhouse at the back of the Moodyville Hotel. Time and again, Mary would pay the fine to George Calbick, Moodyville's policeman and jailkeeper, to have her son released. Emily was familiar with the jail, having been summoned there on many an occasion to doctor up a prisoner's cuts and bruises. One morning she had encountered Mary, while attempting to check on Hugh—incarcerated yet again for drunken and disorderly behaviour in the Moodyville Hotel. This time around, Hugh had suffered a rather deep knife wound to his arm and Emily was not altogether satisfied with the suturing job she had attempted to make. Drunk or sober, Hugh Linn was one of the most uncooperative patients that she had ever experienced.

"Hello, Ma!" Hugh drawled, as George Calbick opened the cell door. "Missus Patterson."

"How are you feeling today, Hugh?" Emily asked politely.

"I should imagine he has a sore head to go along with that sore arm," Mary Linn interrupted gruffly.

Emily adjusted her spectacles.

"I'd like to check your sutures if I may, Hugh. We don't want any infection to set in."

Hugh fidgeted impatiently while Emily examined his arm. She had not asked how he came by a knife wound and suspected that he would not volunteer any information regardless. Satisfied that the sutures would hold, she closed her medical bag. Mary had paid off Mr. Calbick, and her son was cleared to go.

"Now get down on your knees and thank God you are out of here, and take damn good care you don't get in again!" Mary demanded.

Hugh sauntered off without a further word to either of the women.

"He's a bad seed," she sighed. "A lost soul . . . and there's nothing I can do to win him back."

"Will he not attend church?" Emily asked. "Or perhaps get involved in a sport?"

"Church? Gave up on that long ago. As for sport, I think the only one he's interested in is the kind that belongs in the bedroom."

No resident of Moodyville felt safe around Hugh Linn. Even Emily, fearless as she was, deliberately made a habit of distancing herself from the young man whenever she saw him. After a time, he seemed to disappear entirely. When Emily made inquiries of his whereabouts, Mary tossed her head defiantly.

"I threw him out. Discovered that he'd been cohabiting in my house with a native woman while I'd been away travelling. Told him never to come back and tossed all of his belongings into Burrard Inlet."

"Oh . . . I see," Emily sighed.

The punishment seemed somewhat extreme in Emily's mind. Why had Mary Linn not simply told her son to pack his bags and leave? Visions of a disowned young man paddling off into oblivion with a canoe-load of waterlogged possessions filled her with pity. She wondered thereafter about Hugh. Word had it from various sources that he had become an aimless drifter, living the life of a trapper up and down the coast.

Mary's husband, Jock Linn, had left no will when he died and Mary had been compelled to wait until the twenty-first birthday of her youngest child, daughter Maria, on January 24, 1890, before she could claim legal title to the Linn property. On May 5, 1891, Mary sold her land to Edward Mahon for the price of $21,000. Quite literally overnight, the Linn family had become rich beyond their wildest dreams. Mary moved to Vancouver, taking up residence at 907 Howe Street. An inheritance from family members in Scotland further swelled the Linn fortunes.

One July day in 1894, Emily learned that Hugh Linn had been sentenced to hang for murder. The sordid details of Hugh's final crime and subsequent trial were released in the newspaper. On the morning of October 30, 1893, three fishermen by the name of Norman Smith, Dick Lewis and Albert Hanson hauled their boat up on shore at Savary Island—a pristine locale approximately three miles offshore from the coastal community of Lund. Their intention was to purchase supplies at the small Savory store operated by seventy-six-year-old Jack Green. Surprised to find the store locked and seemingly deserted, they tried the living quarters next door where they made an appalling discovery. Jack Green and his business partner, Tom Taylor, lay dead of gunshot wounds in a pool of blood.

It was known that Jack Green had always distrusted banks and, against the advice of many, had kept his entire life savings in an iron cash box. Robbery was clearly the motive for the murder and suspicion quickly settled upon Hugh Linn, who had been seen drinking with Green on October 26 in Lund—the latter paying for the rounds from a thick wad of ten-dollar bills. After a lengthy chase which led to Hugh Linn's capture and mid-July 1894 trial, he was found guilty and sentenced by Mr. Justice Tyrwhitt-Drake to hang at the New Westminster jail yard.

Knowing well the pain of losing a first-born son, Emily was deeply saddened for her friend Mary Linn. She paid a visit to her home late in the afternoon of August 24 with a basket of fruit and baking. Hugh had been hanged that morning but Mary had staunchly refused to exchange any last words with her son or be present at his execution.

"I'm so very sorry, Mary," Emily said softly, giving her a gentle hug.

In her typically gruff fashion, Mary waved off Emily's sympathies.

"They tell me he made a good end," she said. "Ate a breakfast of steak and eggs, smoked a cigar and asked for a pair of carpet slippers to wear to the scaffold."

Emily chose not to linger. Returning home, her mind aimlessly drifting, she came upon John, who had come to find her—telegram in hand from Port Blakely. Alice's newborn son had died that same morning.

CHAPTER 24

Return to Vancouver

It was a rain-soaked Thanksgiving Day on November 22, 1894, but Emily was unperturbed. She had travelled over to Vancouver to witness the official opening of St. Paul's Hospital on Burrard Street. The hospital had been a work-in-progress for many years, all thanks to the unrelenting efforts of the Sisters of Providence, founded by Mother Émilie Gamelin in Montreal in 1843. Under financial sponsorship of the Catholic dioceses, local government and publicly solicited donations, the Sisters of Providence were establishing schools, hospitals, orphanages, homes for the elderly and asylums across Canada. Although not of the Catholic faith, Emily had great admiration for their work and was curious to see this latest addition to Vancouver's expanding health care network. Opening ceremonies were conducted by the hospital's namesake, Bishop Paul Durieu and Mr. L.G. McPhillips, QC—the latter declaring that St. Paul's "would not be run as a sectarian institution, but for all denominations and creeds." Several Vancouver doctors were on hand and gave the twenty-five-bed facility high praise—especially noting the abundance of private rooms, an attribute not to be found in the City Hospital.

"It's wonderful, don't you think?" Emily commented to Dr. Langis, as they followed guests through the corridors.

"Yes," he acknowledged, "and I'm very pleased to hear that one needn't be a Catholic to qualify for care!"

In the grip of the recession, Moodyville Sawmill operations had been shut down repeatedly during 1893 and 1894, sometimes for months at a time. Compounding troubles on the north shore, torrential rains in January of 1895 led to flash floods, which destroyed newly built bridges

St. Paul's Hospital on Burrard Street, c. 1898.

over the Seymour and Capilano creeks. In March of 1896, Emily and John reluctantly joined the steady numbers of families departing from Moodyville, and moved back to Vancouver with Calvin and Fred. Emily was sad to vacate her much-loved Nob Hill home, but the decision was inevitable with the uncertain labour climate at the mill. There was also the reality that John Patterson, now into his early seventies, was struggling to keep up with the physical demands of his position. He had always been an exemplary model of strength and endurance but had developed a chronic cough and complained of aches and pains that seldom seemed to ease to his satisfaction.

The Pattersons took up residence in an apartment block at 415 Gore Avenue, and Emily consoled herself with the fact that her new home was just a short walking distance from St. James Church. Having made frequent visits to Vancouver over the years, she was well aware that the once-humble milltown had evolved—yet she could not help marvelling at the changes. In the years since her 1873 arrival, the clapboard logging community had evolved into a sophisticated city of some 19,000 inhabitants with neatly laid-out streets, electric lighting, tramcar service and piped drinking water. Owned by the CPR, the five-storey, sixty-room Hotel Vancouver graced an extensive lot on Georgia Street. Charlie Woodward had opened a dry-goods store near Main and Hastings. The likes of Vienna-born soprano Emma Juch, violinist Mischa Elman and French actress Sarah Bernhardt performed in the two-thousand-seat Opera House at the corner of Granville and Robson.

Much against Emily's wishes, John took up employment as a night watchman with the Union Steamship Company. Founded in 1889 by New Zealander John Darling, the Union Steamship Company owned a small fleet of vessels that provided passenger and freight service to communities up and down the B.C. coast.

"I've got a few good years left in me and we need the money," John reasoned. "We can't just let our savings dwindle away."

"But working all night long!" Emily objected. "In the dark and cold and rain . . . you're not twenty-one anymore, John, and breathing up all of that sawdust and smoke over the years has done nothing good for your lungs."

"We need the money," he responded simply.

"We can manage!"

But John was not to be deterred. Every evening he kissed Emily goodnight and walked through the cobbled downtown streets to the Union Steamship wharf at the foot of Carrall Street. Emily correctly suspected that her husband had always held a fond regard for his sea-faring days and enjoyed his reconnection with them, however humble the position.

Calvin and Fred Patterson, both in their early twenties, continued to reside with their parents—Calvin being employed at Hastings Sawmill and Fred working as a teamster with the firm Veitch and Berry. While the Pattersons' quality of life had not been severely affected by the recession, it was clear that many other individuals and families on Burrard Inlet were facing hard times. St. James, along with many churches of various denominations that had emerged in Vancouver over the years, began operating soup kitchens to provide hot, nourishing meals for any and all in need. Lineups were long and demand was never-ending. Emily worked regularly and tirelessly at the St. James kitchen. Mounds of unsold vegetables were delivered daily from Vancouver's green grocers, chopped into giant iron crocks and placed atop wood stoves fired with kindling provided free of charge from the sawmill. Dispensing hot soup gave Emily the opportunity to briefly evaluate each grateful recipient that came through her line. They were Vancouver's most destitute—some mere shadows of formerly robust souls, their clothing old and tattered, shoes held together with string or rags. Devoid of umbrellas, they were often rain-drenched, and Emily placed mug after mug of soup into hands that were shaking with cold.

One fall morning a truly frightened young woman elbowed her way to the front of the soup line demanding to see Emily. She had a little girl clutched in her arms—a pretty, blond cherub little more than two years old. Emily instantly recognized them both, having treated the child for croup not so long ago. She was concerned to see that both mother and daughter were crying uncontrollably.

"Dora!" she exclaimed. "What's the matter?"

"Christine has eaten a mushroom!" Dora told her frantically. "We'd gone to Stanley Park for a walk in the forest and I saw that she was chewing on something. I grabbed it out of her hand but I could see that she had already swallowed some of it."

"Do you have the piece of leftover mushroom?" Emily asked, quickly replacing her ladle into a steaming pot of soup and wiping her hands on her apron.

"No," Dora said ashamedly. "I threw it away, picked up Christine and ran out of the park to find a taxi. She already seems to be feeling poorly. I'm so afraid she's been poisoned. My only thought was to find you as soon as I could."

"We have syrup of ipecac in the church," Emily told her. "We'll give Christine a dose straight away and then take her to the hospital so that she can be watched over. Then you and I will go back to Stanley Park to try and identify that mushroom."

In the back office of St. James Church, Sister Frances maintained a small dispensary of medicinal items for immediate use as required. Rummaging within a cupboard, Emily quickly brought out a small bottle of syrup of ipecac and a teaspoon. While Dora had managed to calm down somewhat, Christine continued to cry. After pouring out a carefully measured dose of brown-coloured liquid, Emily added a very small pinch of sugar.

"I'm afraid this is not going to be very pleasant for Christine," she told Dora in a voice just loud enough to be heard over the crying. "But we must do what we must."

Gently cradling Christine's head, she tilted it back in the crook of her arm, forced open the little girl's mouth with her free hand and emptied the contents of the spoon well into the back of her mouth. Quick as a flash she placed both hands over Christine's upper and lower jaw, clamping her mouth tightly shut.

"Swallow, sweetheart," she urged softly. "That's a good girl."

Within ten minutes, the syrup of ipecac produced its desired effect. Christine was retching violently into a porcelain bowl. Emily cuddled her after each episode murmuring gentle words of praise.

"There's a good girl . . . you will feel better soon."

By early afternoon, having settled a still sickly Christine with the care of nurses at St. Luke's Hospital, Emily and Dora made their way to Stanley Park, again by horse-drawn taxi. Their vehicle clattered over the wooden bridge at the park entrance. An incoming tide was just beginning to refill the broad, shallow bay to the west. Dora claimed to know exactly where she had found her daughter picking mushrooms. They veered left under her direction, following a well-travelled bridle path that passed the home of park ranger Henry Avison.

"This is it!" Dora called out presently. "I'm sure of it!"

The cab driver pulled to a stop in a shaded area not far beyond the Avison house. Requesting that he wait, Emily followed Dora into the trees. It was not long before they came across a rotten log, from which sprouted several clusters of white mushrooms.

"Look!" said Dora, pointing to the ground. "There's the piece I grabbed away from her."

Emily picked up the broken bit of mushroom and examined it. An expression of relief quickly spread across her face.

"These," she said with a smile, "are oyster mushrooms. See how much they look like oysters? They make wonderful eating, fried up with butter. We used to pick them often around Moodyville."

"Are you certain?" Dora asked doubtfully.

"I am absolutely certain," Emily reassured her. "They really should not be eaten raw and may have indeed given Christine a bit of a tummy upset, but they are most definitely not poisonous."

She gave Dora a warm hug as the young mother shed tears afresh.

Despite her more fortunate circumstances in life, Emily felt a certain kinship with the regular habitués of the St. James Church soup line. She had seen abject poverty on many an occasion and had often spent long hours attending patients in what she could well term "the most primitive of situations." There were times when she herself would have welcomed a rejuvenating hot meal or a warm blanket to throw around her shoulders when there was none to offer. Out of habit she chose to wear simple dresses, designed for practicality rather than being fashionable. Having long ago recognized that elegant hairstyles were not suited to her busy and demanding lifestyle, she routinely gathered her formerly thick, dark tresses into a tight bun. While not the most flattering, it was a quick and easy, low-maintenance style that kept annoying stray locks well out of sight and enabled her to go about her tasks with less distraction. She seldom, if ever, wore jewels or perfume—indulgences for which she had little interest.

Along with her faith, Emily's abiding joy had always been in her family. Having steadfastly maintained contact with her mother over the course of years with lengthy letters and family photographs, great was her sorrow upon learning that Lucy Thornton had died on October 20, 1897, in Bath, at the age of eighty-one.

Lucy Branscombe Thornton, c. 1896.

212 / Emily Patterson

"She was so beautiful!" Emily commented sadly to John, looking over the portrait photograph that her mother had sent only recently. "With lace about her throat and earrings . . . how I wish that I had seen her one more time!"

Letters from Port Blakely only compounded Emily's sense of loss, for it was clear that Alice was exceedingly homesick. She spoke candidly of her dislike for Port Blakely and her yearning to be back in her old familiar realms. A healthy baby daughter, Muriel Dorothy, had been born to the Crakanthorps on October 20, 1895, and Alice desperately wanted her to meet her grandparents and uncles. Emily urged Calvin to travel down to Port Blakely for a visit, with instructions to make "subtle inquiries" into the possibility of the family returning to Vancouver.

"I do not want Alice to feel obligated under any circumstances," she warned. "But if she is as unhappy as she sounds, I want them to come home."

Calvin's visit had the desired effect. Much to Emily's pleasure, Alice returned to Vancouver in 1898 with her husband and young Muriel, a bright-eyed and robust little girl who would become the delight of her doting grandparents. The Crakanthorps took up residence around the corner from the Pattersons, at 334 East Hastings Street. Robert Crakanthorp obtained a position as tallyman at Hastings Sawmill.

"It's so good to be back, Mama!"

Alice spoke time and time again of her great joy in returning home. The general mood throughout Vancouver had taken an upward surge, coinciding with the heady discovery of gold in the Klondike. Ever since the steamer *Excelsior* had landed at San Francisco on July 17, 1897, with half a million dollars in gold, followed by *Portland*—docking three days later in Seattle with more than a ton of nuggets—population centres up and down the Pacific Coast were reaping the financial gains. Stampeders surged through the Klondike supply stores that had proliferated, snapping up everything from whip saws to leather boots to coffee pots, before booking northward passage to Skagway, Alaska.

One public figure who rose to prominence nationwide during the gold rush was Ishbel Maria Gordon, Marchioness of Aberdeen and Temair, otherwise known as Lady Aberdeen. The wife of Canada's Governor General John Campbell Gordon, 1st Marquess of Aberdeen and Temair, Lady Aberdeen was a woman of boundless energy and conviction. She had been instrumental in founding the National Council of Women of Canada in 1893 and, more recently, had established the Victorian Order of Nurses—a non-profit organization dedicated to providing desperately needed home nursing services in Canada's remotest communities. Emily followed Lady Aberdeen's activities with great fascination and on April 25, 1898, joined a delegation from the Vancouver Women's Council to welcome four young VON nurses arriving in Vancouver aboard a CPR Express train. The nurses had bravely stepped forward to offer their services in the

Lady Aberdeen

Klondike goldfields—a wild and remote destination in the Yukon Territory, currently in dire need of medical professionals.

Smartly attired in VON navy blue uniforms, Miss Georgia Powell of New Brunswick, Miss Rachel Hanna of Toronto, Miss Amy Scott of London, England, and Miss Margaret Payson of Weymouth, Nova Scotia, alighted from their coach to a bevy of curious onlookers and crush of reporters. Emily waited patiently for her opportunity to have a brief word with any member of the group—each of whom seemed to have her own disposition. Miss Hanna's mouth appeared ready to curve into a smile at the slightest provocation. Miss Payson was tall and dark with a grave, almost sad expression. Miss Scott was shy and demure. Georgia Powell, lieutenant of the group, had a stately appearance with a sweet but strong face.

"I'm in awe of what you are doing!" Emily said quickly to the latter as she passed nearby. Much to her pleasure, Lieutenant Powell stopped and smiled.

Nurses in front of Vancouver City Hospital, 530 Cambie Street, 1902.

"Thank you!" she replied. "It certainly has been an adventure so far!"

Over the next few days, the VON nurses would become the media darlings of Vancouver, their itinerary packed with receptions and benefit concerts and a driving tour of Stanley Park. From Vancouver, they travelled to Victoria for a lavish dinner with British Columbia's Lieutenant-Governor, Thomas Robert McInnes, and his wife at Government House before their departure for the north.

With the new influx of Klondike gold-fuelled commerce, publicly funded projects steadily began to make their reappearance in Vancouver. Emily was pleased when the Vancouver City Hospital Training School for Nurses admitted its first students in 1899—eight girls—very much looking the part in their new uniforms of ankle-length blue cotton dresses with five-inch linen cuffs, high "bishop's collars" and long bibbed aprons. Emily and Alice walked past the facility from time to time with Muriel in the perambulator, often noting the trainees bustling back and forth with armloads of books and papers.

"Do you wish you'd had a uniform like that?" Alice asked her mother.

"Oh, I suppose I had dreams of looking like that at one time," Emily acknowledged, "but there is so much more to nursing than how one appears. I do envy those young ladies, for they have so much more to work with now than I could ever have dreamed of . . . X-ray machines, antitoxins for diphtheria and typhoid and tetanus . . . new fever-reducing medicine. One can only imagine what lies ahead in medical study!"

CHAPTER 25

Ustlawn

The Mission Reserve, also known as Ustlawn, home to so many of the families that Emily provided medical care for, had evolved under the watchful eye of Oblate priests, presided over by Father Paul Durieu. Born in France, Father Durieu had entered the Oblate order in 1848 and was ordained as a priest six years later. Oblates were dedicated to serving God through strict adherence to rules and rituals, not unlike those of a Catholic monk or nun. After several years of service in Washington, Father Durieu had travelled north, delivering his doctrine to native communities in Esquimalt, Sechelt, Kamloops and New Westminster. In 1867, he took over the running of St. Mary's Mission in the Fraser Valley. Under Durieu, many members of British Columbia's native population were converted to Christianity.

The "Durieu system," as it came to be known, was based upon consolidating native residents within a village of modern-style houses, with a central, predominant church. To obtain the right to live in the village, prospective occupants were told that they must forsake non-Christian beliefs and adopt a European lifestyle. Ustlawn and other native communities throughout the province evolved into typical examples of Father Durieu's vision. Gone were the cedar longhouses, richly painted with symbols and figures of deep cultural significance. Forbidden were the traditional masks and ceremonial regalia. Organizers of potlatch gatherings, which had been outlawed by the federal government in 1884, were subject to punishment by jail term if they were caught trying to resurrect the practice.

On the surface of it, Ustlawn was a textbook Durieu community of tidy, whitewashed row houses, its residents attired in western-style clothing of cotton and linen trousers, shirts and dresses. But despite the best efforts of Oblate missionaries throughout the country and the tidal wave of European influence in general, native communities had proved to be reluctant in forsaking age-old traditions. It was now widely believed by church and state that the best way to influence change was through the complete segregation of native children.

Under direction of the Oblates, the four-storey, government-funded St. Paul's Indian Residential School was constructed in 1899 on West Keith Road. Students as young as four years old were willingly or

Mission Reserve at Ustlawn, 1886.

forcibly required to live at the school. Most came from the local Mission, Musqueam and Tsleil-Waututh reserves, although some had travelled from places much further afield like Howe Sound, the Squamish River valley and Mount Currie. Emily had heard that the typical school day began at 6 a.m. with prayers and religious studies, followed by lessons in spelling, mathematics, science, geography, history and Latin. After class, everyone was required to help with daily chores—washing and waxing the extensive hallways and dormitories, cooking and doing laundry. The boys helped to cultivate a kitchen garden on the grounds, which kept the school supplied with fresh fruits and vegetables. Girls were taught how to darn, knit, crochet and sew.

Emily missed her friends on the north shore and often thought about "her other babies," the many native children that she had brought into the world and cared for at Ustlawn. She was curious to see the residential school and decided to make arrangements through the clergy for a visit. Travelling across-inlet was now easier than ever, thanks to a sleek and modern passenger ferry, SS *North Vancouver*, which began regularly scheduled service between Vancouver and the developing north shore townsite of Lonsdale on May 12, 1900. The SS *North Vancouver* (soon popularly shortened to *Norvan*) had a passenger capacity which far surpassed that of the aging *Senator* and *Leonora*.

It was just a short carriage ride from the Lonsdale dock up to Keith Road, where the residential school stood prominently in a wide clearing. Walking through the lengthy halls with one of the school matrons, Emily was impressed with how spotlessly clean everything was. However, she could not help noticing the overall sombre atmosphere. Children whom she had recalled from their very early years of laughing and playing outside their Ustlawn homes passed her by wordlessly, their eyes sunken, expressions hollow. She could hear the sound of coughing from the dormitories but was politely advised not to enter.

"Are the children up-to-date with their immunizations?" she asked.

"Of course they are," the matron replied. "We do have outbreaks of influenza from time to time and it is difficult to hold contagions at bay with so many children in our care. If we have a severe outbreak, one or more of the dormitories can be converted to an isolation ward."

St. Paul's Indian Residential School

Emily was troubled by what she saw and heard. St. Paul's Indian Residential School somehow did not measure up to what she had expected. Taking tea with Emma Alexander a few days after the visit, she quietly confided her impressions.

"I can appreciate what the staff of the school is trying to do," she said. "I'm just not at all certain that they are going about it in the right way."

"Children died at Ustlawn years ago," Emma reminded her friend gently. "I believe the purpose of the residential schools is to give them better health care, as well as an education, is it not?"

"Yes, and children of all racial backgrounds have died through the years, including my Frank and Addie. But why should children be segregated from their parents just because they happen to be Indian?"

Emma's face coloured. Emily had not intended to cause her most trusted friend discomfort and quickly apologized.

"No offence taken," Emma said firmly. "Years ago as you recall, we employed an Indian man named William as a servant. One morning William came to our home looking very poorly indeed. I asked him what was the matter and he replied that he had met an old native woman on the trail from the rancherie who had 'clawed out his soul.' I tried to reason with him, telling him that a soul could not possibly be 'clawed out.' I reminded him that he was a Catholic and suggested that he talk to the priest. He claimed to agree with me, but he continued to look miserable, gradually becoming sicker and sicker. Finally, as I understand it, his family called in a native witch doctor to try and undo the damage. I have no idea what sort of ritual or treatment the witch doctor offered, but much to my amazement, William was back to his old cheerful self within days. I've never forgotten that, and I never will. It was really quite astonishing!"

"Then perhaps there really is something to be said for their ways of faith," Emily said thoughtfully. "What may seem pagan and savage in our eyes has been a fundamental part of their culture for thousands of years. I'm beginning to suspect that our interference, however well-intended, will have grave consequences for these dear people."

Emily made no further visits to the St. Paul's Indian Residential School and made little mention of it. Initially she thought about reporting on what she had seen and heard to higher authorities but who would listen to the rantings of an elderly lady? She remained quietly troubled. If anyone asked about her visit, she merely stated that she had found the building and atmosphere "rather unpleasant" and left it at that.

CHAPTER 26

Taking Responsibility

One hundred and twenty-eight people were dead and Abbie's husband was being blamed for their loss. In the early morning hours of February 22, 1901, Pilot Frederick Jordan came aboard the Pacific Main Steamship Company's iron-clad passenger steamer SS *City of Rio de Janeiro*, inbound for San Francisco from Hong Kong. The vessel had dropped anchor just outside the Golden Gate harbour entrance and it was Jordan's task to take over the wheel for final docking. A heavy fog had settled upon the bay, severely hampering visibility.

Captain William Ward gave the order to proceed and Jordan complied with his instructions, despite sailing virtually blind against a strong current running out to sea. At 5:40 a.m. the *Rio* collided full force upon the rocks near Land's End and Fort Point. The ship had no watertight bulkheads and seawater gushed freely into the engine room and cargo hold. In less than ten minutes, the *Rio* sank in 320 feet of water, taking 128 passengers and crew to a watery grave. Eighty-five

SS City of Rio de Janeiro

survivors—many clinging to pieces of floating wreckage—were pulled from the frigid waters, including an injured Jordan. Captain Ward had last been witnessed entering his cabin and closing the door to go down with his ship.

Through much newspaper coverage of the *Rio's* loss in the days ahead, Emily was stunned to learn that her son-in-law was being considered solely responsible for the shipwreck. Abbie sent a brief telegram, stating that her husband was recovering well in hospital. Emily immediately sent a telegram back, urging her daughter to provide more information. An angry San Francisco public, hell-bent on retribution, was pointing an accusatory finger directly at Frederick Jordan.

"It must be horrible for our family!" Emily said to her husband.

"I suspect that the Pacific Mail Steamship Company has a long-standing order prohibiting ship's captains from entering or leaving a harbour in a fog," John replied flatly. "The final responsibility lies with the captain. If Ward chose to ignore that ruling and ordered our Frederick to proceed, it's his own damn fault and he deserved to go down with that ship!"

Emily fumed with indignation and worry as the days passed. A letter from Abbie finally arrived, confirming her worst fears:

Words cannot describe our sorrow. So many victims of the disaster were women and children, unable to save themselves in the deep waters. Frederick has been discharged from service and we are facing a number of lawsuits. A special commission has been formed to decide who was at fault—the ship's captain, or the ship's pilot. I fear that the process may continue on for weeks. Some of our friends are no longer friends and I imagine looks of anger and hatred from utter strangers as we walk the streets. Thankfully there are also those who stand by us and for that we are eternally grateful.

The Jordan family now lived in San Francisco's upscale neighbourhood of Haight Ashbury, and Abbie, now forty years of age, had given birth to Sarah Fuller Jordan in January of 1900. Emily knew that, compounding the stress already at hand, Abbie would be chasing around after a toddler. To worsen matters, San Francisco was also dealing with outbreaks of bubonic plague, centred mainly in the city's Chinatown district—mere blocks from Frederick Jordan's company office on Battery Street.

"We must send them some money," Emily said determinedly. "Perhaps they will go to stay with the Pierces until this has all been settled."

The commission of inquiry into the sinking of the *Rio* did not reach its final verdict until April 10, 1901. Abbie summed up the decision with a one-word telegram that arrived the next day: "ABSOLVED." Glasses were raised around the Patterson dining table that same evening in celebration.

"To the commission!" John said triumphantly. "May they be congratulated in sparing our son-in-law from a reprehensible miscarriage of justice!"

As she took a tiny sip of wine, Emily inwardly acknowledged that she had no clue as to who was ultimately responsible for the *Rio* disaster. She had given much thought to the matter over the past few months and had secretly concluded that she would have personally declared mutiny rather than sail into a blinding fog. There was little doubt that Frederick Jordan would have saved lives if he had resisted Captain Ward's orders. But her family would be spared further emotional trauma and at the end of the day, it seemed that was all that mattered.

"To our dear family," she added quietly.

Moodyville Mill was unceremoniously closed in December of 1901, following a number of years of financial mismanagement. The mill and its surrounding lands were purchased by Vancouver lumber magnate John Hendry, who had owned Hastings Sawmill since 1889. Moodyville residents had long since dispersed, and to Emily's sorrow, most of the households including her own—once so full of life with parties and human interaction—stood empty and derelict. Hendry's plan was to retain the Moodyville site for the interim, while he formulated his grand scheme of developing a railway line far into the resource-rich northern B.C. interior. Meanwhile, the once richly forested expanses throughout the Burrard Inlet region continued to be transformed. Lots were subdivided and cleared, new homes were constructed and an ever-widening network of roads and streetcar lines connected far-flung homesteaders with all the accoutrements of modern-day living.

Emily took an active interest in the Women's Auxiliary, formed in 1902 to provide charitable assistance to the newly renamed Vancouver General Hospital. With Vancouver's rapid expansion, it was decided that the hospital was in dire need of improved ambulance service. Thomas Lobb, who ran a blacksmith business at the junction of Westminster Road (future Kingsway) and Westminster Avenue (future Main Street), had been commissioned to build Vancouver's first city ambulance some three or four years previously. Lobb constructed a wagon that very much fit the bill in appearance with its stem-to-stern coat of white paint and red crosses prominently emblazoned upon the carriage. But for all his good intentions, Lobb's creation was quietly pronounced "inadequate." There were no windows to open for fresh air or provide the ambulance attendant with extra light while administering treatment to casualties. The carriage had been built on such a narrow frame that working space for the attendant was virtually non-existent. No form of canopy or shelter was provided for the driver, rendering him exposed to whatever foul weather was occurring on any given day.

To raise money for a new ambulance, the ladies of the Auxiliary organized fundraising balls and "tag days," during which everyone who made a monetary donation was given a lapel ribbon to wear. Emily and Alice embraced the charitable efforts, with Alice being particularly supportive of the fundraiser dances, for dancing continued to remain her passion. Funds steadily poured in and work began in earnest on the new ambulance. The result was a sturdy and handsome vehicle, complete with large windows for daylight and blinds to close for privacy as need dictated. Tall double doors at the rear allowed for easy loading and unloading of stretchers. A built-in overhang provided the driver with a comfortable degree of shelter. The ambulance was housed at the Fashion Stables on East Hastings Street, and stable employee Mr. Findlay Rose was commissioned to be the driver. City Council negotiated an agreement whereby Mr. Rose would receive $2.50 for each call-out he attended to. Users with means would be billed for their transport, while the city treasury would cover the charge for those unable to pay. A special team of horses was designated for ambulance purposes alone and put through daily training exercises. Everyone pronounced the new ambulance a fine and welcome addition to Vancouver's growing list of health care amenities.

But debate soon arose among Vancouver city officials over when and how the ambulance should be used. If the ambulance was dispatched for a situation that ultimately proved to be non-urgent, would the well-being of individuals truly in need of emergency transport be compromised? Then there was the drain on city finances to be considered. Mr.

First ambulance built by Thomas Lobb in front of his blacksmith business on Westminster Road, c. 1897.

The much-improved Vancouver General Hospital ambulance, 1902.

Rose's bills for payment from the city were mounting up. City officials decided that the best way to regulate ambulance usage was to short-list the locations from which ambulance calls would be accepted: City Hall, the Police Station, the Medical Health Officer, Health Inspector or City Hospital. All other calls would be considered "unauthorized" and subject to the discretion of the ambulance driver.

Emily was shocked upon learning of the city's new policy. On October 9, 1902, her shock was compounded by the terrible news that Louis Springer, son of her dear friend Fanny Springer, had died after falling down an elevator shaft at the Pacific Bottling Works. That very same Louis, who had become everyone's baby at Hastings Sawmill so many years ago while his mother taught lessons at the mill schoolhouse, had just celebrated his thirtieth birthday two days prior to his death. Louis Springer was a healthy, strapping young man who had excelled at rowing and distance running. His ever-decreasing times for the mile had made him the envy of many a local athlete. A well-loved and respected Vancouver citizen, he had just embarked on a promising career in stock brokerage.

Calvin, the same age as Louis less a few weeks, took the news particularly hard. He and Louis had played together as children in Moodyville and had remained good friends.

"Listen to this, Mama!" he said angrily, while reading the story on the front page of the *Vancouver Daily Province* newspaper. "For twenty-five minutes yesterday morning the body of Mr. Louis Springer lay on the floor of the warehouse of the Pacific Bottling Works, while the friends of the injured man tried in vain to get the city ambulance."

"That's surely a misprint!" Emily exclaimed. "The ambulance is parked only four blocks away from the Bottling Works!"

"No, it is not a misprint," Calvin replied, as he continued to read. "Mr. Rose was told to hurry as a man was badly hurt. They waited ten minutes, there was no ambulance, so they called again. Then they were told to go to the Police Station and get a permit. . . . It took another fifteen minutes before the ambulance finally arrived. Louis Springer died in the early morning hours of October 9, having never regained consciousness after his fall."

Emily slammed down a sock-darning she had been working on, her eyes levelled upon Calvin.

"Of all the audacity!"

As Emily suspected, the ladies of the Women's Auxiliary were equally outraged by the newspaper report. Several members converged at Fashion Stables the day following the accident, venting their displeasure at a beleaguered Findlay Rose. Emily joined them, more than curious to hear his side of the story.

"Look," he said plaintively. "My hands have been tied by the city. I am ready and willing, horses hitched, to respond to call-outs, but I have been directed to wait for the proper authority. I tell the ambulance hunter to contact the Police Station or the City Hall. The folks at City Hall will recommend the hospital if the City Clerk is not available. The City Hospital people don't know . . . they suggest contacting the Medical Health Officer, who has absolute authority, but he is not in his office. What am I to do?"

"This is a very poor system!" Emily said angrily. "Someone has to take responsibility!"

While arguments raged, there was still the matter of Louis's funeral, and Emily knew that it would be well attended. After resigning as manager of the Moodyville Mill in 1890, Louis's stepfather Benjamin Springer and his family had moved to Vancouver, where he remained a prominent businessman. Springer died of heart failure in 1898 and Fanny, unable to bear the memories, relocated with her family from their elegant Burrard Street home to a new abode at Denman and Haro. Louis Springer's funeral cortège travelled through the Vancouver streets to the resplendent Christ Church for a sombre afternoon service before a packed congregation on October 10. Following the service, Emily grasped the hands of a tearful Fanny Springer.

"I'm so very sorry, my dear," she said softly. "We all have wonderful memories of Louis."

"All this fuss about the ambulance," Fanny replied, much to Emily's surprise. "They tell me that Louis would never have survived his injuries, even if he had been brought to hospital faster. The real problem lies in that wretched elevator shaft!"

Emily had been so consumed with thoughts of the tardy ambulance that she had failed to consider the root cause for Louis's death—an apparently blatant lack of regard for safety at the Pacific Bottling Works.

"There will be a full investigation, I am certain!" she said firmly. "Measures will be taken to ensure that this never happens again. I will see to that, I promise you, Fanny!"

Emily made good on her promise that weekend, seeking out Dr. William McGuigan, who also served as City Coroner and would be chairing the official inquiry into the tragedy on the morning of October 11. She had known Dr. McGuigan for many years and fully respected his judgment in such matters.

"A safety barrier has already been installed, Mrs. Patterson," he assured her. "This terrible accident will not happen again."

Full details of the inquiry were published in the October 11 *Vancouver Daily Province*, and once again Calvin shared them aloud.

"Dr. McGuigan confirmed that Pacific Bottling Works had indeed been remiss in not installing a safety barrier," he read.

"Very good." Emily nodded approvingly.

Calvin continued to read.

"Health Inspector Marrion said there was a verbal agreement between the committee and Mr. Rose, that Rose was to send for the ambulance immediately, without waiting for authority, in cases of accident. Rose denied that agreement ever existed, saying 'It's a very poor system.'"

"That's exactly what I told him," Emily said triumphantly. "I'm glad he repeated it."

"Well," Calvin replied, "it appears that Dr. McGuigan wasn't impressed. He told Rose, 'It's facts we're after, so keep your opinions to yourself!'"

"Mr. Rose is perfectly entitled to his opinion." Emily frowned.

One last follow-up to the tragedy appeared in the October 14 *Vancouver Daily Province*.

"Mayor Thomas Neelands had the final say," Calvin reported. "There is to be no more red tape, Mr. Rose is to go promptly to emergency calls and he is to stop trying to shift the responsibility to other's shoulders."

John Patterson, lounging in his armchair before heading off to work, chuckled at Calvin's last comment.

"You know," he mused, "this whole sorry affair reminds me a little of the sinking of the *Rio*. So much indecision over who was ultimately responsible for tragedy. Perhaps City Council may have a point or two about when and how the ambulance is used."

"Your point being . . . ?" Emily asked irritably.

"Well, does a notorious drunkard who happens to be sleeping off his libations in a public doorway constitute an emergency call-out? What of an ankle sprain or a fainting spell? You know as well as I do, Emily, that plenty of illnesses are readily treatable at home, no matter how alarmingly they present themselves . . . like childhood croup, for instance. My point being, if the ambulance is sent for each and every perceived emergency, the city treasury could be drained very quickly."

Emily and Calvin exchanged glances.

"He does have a point, you know," Calvin acknowledged carefully.

Frowning, Emily resumed her sock darning. "Then I suppose we must see to it that the city treasury is never empty," she muttered, half to herself.

CHAPTER 27

Tragedy in Two Cities

Vancouver's growth in the early years of the twentieth century could readily be likened to that of any major port of call on the Pacific Northwest Coast. Although the Klondike gold rush had long ceased, the pace of development in the city continued to surge. By 1905, solidly built brick and granite buildings stood proud and prominent among the wood structures of old. Streets formerly awash in mud and manure had been paved with asphalt or wooden blocks embedded in concrete. A network of electric street lights came on each evening as darkness fell. The city sewer system was of modern design, complete with new tanks to treat raw sewage before its discharge into salt water. In the wake of much lobbying from Vancouver city and public health officials, the provincial government had formally established a watershed reserve on all Crown lands in the Capilano Creek region, thereby ensuring an ongoing supply of safe, clean drinking water.

Among the vast array of businesses to be found in the city, those in

Vancouver General Hospital, 1905.

the field of health care had greatly proliferated over the years. Vancouver now had forty practising physicians and surgeons, nineteen dentists, a dozen or more druggists and six opticians. Accident, fire and health insurance companies by the score touted their policy offerings to an ever-increasing clientele. Three hospitals and a Burrard Street sanitarium were in full service and a large new Vancouver General Hospital was slowly taking shape high up on the city's Fairview slopes. There had been some objection to the new site, with certain individuals questioning the logic of building a new hospital in an area that was "practically a wilderness and too distant from the centre of population." Others, however, recognized that the city was transforming, that the new million-dollar granite facility with its adjoining nurse's home, pathological laboratory and a wealth of other amenities would be a shining example of progress when complete.

With so many medical professionals serving the city, Emily now felt utterly at ease in further scaling back her services. While midwifery was still a popular option, more and more women were choosing to have their babies in hospital. She decided that it was time for another holiday, this time with the companionship of Alice and nine-year-old Muriel.

"I can't believe we're going to San Francisco!"

A wide-eyed Muriel stood on the passenger deck of the SS *Umatilla* with her mother and grandmother, watching the passing scenery in awe as their vessel eased its way out of Victoria's inner harbour. It was early July 1905 and the three were on their way south for a family visit with the Jordan and Pierce families, as well as a celebration of Emily's sixty-ninth birthday.

"I might as well see out my sixties in grand fashion," she had laughed, while plans for the trip were being finalized.

San Francisco of 1905 was a city to marvel at. Over four hundred thousand residents lived in the Bay Area. Market Street hummed with every kind of transport that Emily had ever imagined—omnibuses, cable cars, horse-drawn wagons and an astonishing number of automobiles, the latter still a relatively rare phenomenon in Vancouver. Multistorey hotels, office towers and apartments spread over several blocks of the city's downtown business district. The Jordan family home at 1719 Fell Street stood opposite a pleasant arboretum known as "the Panhandle," which adjoined San Francisco's famed Golden Gate Park. It was an ideal neighbourhood for Abbie to raise her family, far enough away from the noise and congestion of the city to be restful but close enough to allow for shopping trips and other amenities.

Abbie was familiar with the surroundings and greatly enjoyed playing tour guide, taking Emily, Alice and Muriel on visits to Golden Gate Park's Japanese Tea Garden and the extraordinarily beautiful Conservatory of Flowers. But it was the Panhandle arboretum that captured Emily's imagination the most, especially after Abbie pointed out the blue gum eucalyptus trees that had been planted there years ago.

"Eucalyptus," Emily breathed. "You can just smell the fragrance. The very thing to ease a congested throat. Your papa told me about its medicinal properties years ago. You crumble the dried leaves into olive oil and allow them to distill. . . ."

"Oh, Mama!" Abbie laughed. "We can buy ready-made eucalyptus oil here in San Francisco, and just about any other cough remedy you can name, for that matter!"

"Yes, I suppose you can," Emily sighed. "In the old days we had to be very self-sufficient."

Emily always enjoyed her visits to the Bay Area, but adamantly resisted Abbie and Beckie's ongoing pleas to consider relocating there permanently—however achy her bones and joints were becoming.

"Your papa is quite happy with his Union Steamship position," she said firmly. "Retirement is not in the cards for him any time soon and, quite frankly, we would miss Vancouver. We have so many friends there, the summers are lovely and our dear Addie is not far away. We can take the Central Park interurban line to visit her whenever we wish."

Abbie smiled. She knew that her mother often talked about little Addie as if she were alive and well, still very much a part of their lives.

"Vancouver has become much more civilized over the years, hasn't it," she remarked.

Emily could only laugh. "I would never have begun to imagine . . . but I doubt that it will ever reach the eminence of San Francisco."

Emily, Alice and Muriel enjoyed their holiday but were just as happy to return home to the refreshingly cooler, less frenetic environment to which they were accustomed. In the morning hours of April 18, 1906, Emily and Alice strolled down to the Woodward's Department Store at Hastings and Abbott streets. Opened for business in 1903, Woodward's was a larger version of the original Vancouver store, founded by retailer Charles Woodward in 1892 on Westminster Avenue. The new Woodward's had become a hugely popular Vancouver success story—not only as a one-stop shopping location for everything from groceries to men's and ladies' fashions to household goods, but as a favourite gathering place for city residents to see and be seen. Woodward's, on any given day, was alive with conversation, but this particular morning it seemed that virtually every customer wore a sombre expression.

"Have you heard?"

One of Alice's friends stopped both women almost immediately upon their entry.

"Word has it that San Francisco has had a terrible earthquake! The entire city is on fire as we speak!"

Emily imagined that her own face had turned as white as Alice's. To be sure, all through the department, people were gathered in small groups discussing what they knew. Brief descriptions were audible everywhere . . . "happened a few hours ago" . . . "early morning" . . . "fires raging." A few women were unabashedly shedding tears.

"What can we do, Mama?" Alice asked, her own voice beginning to falter.

Emily glanced out of the store's main entrance onto Hastings Street, where there appeared to be an abnormally busy volume of pedestrian and vehicular traffic.

"We'll go to the telegraph office and see what more we can learn," she said determinedly.

Vancouver's three major telegraph companies, the CPR, Great North Western and Western Union were all situated in the 400-block of Hastings, not far from Woodward's. Emily and Alice hurried up the street, only to find that a small throng had gathered outside the telegraph offices, all clamouring for any news. The repeated word was bleak—all communication services with San Francisco and the Bay Area had been severed. Initial word of the quake had been relayed by ships in the vicinity but there were no tangible details on the extent of the damage.

"Keep an eye on the papers," a man told Emily and Alice matter-of-factly, as if he were discussing the weather. "We should know more tomorrow."

Headlines the following morning confirmed everyone's worst fears: "San Francisco Riven by Earthquake and Swept by Flame." Reported to be two minutes in duration, the earthquake shock had razed the entire business centre of the city and the ensuing fire was still burning fiercely. Damage was estimated at a hundred million dollars and loss of life was "incapable as yet of approximation."

"I feel so utterly helpless!" Alice fumed.

She had brought Muriel over to the Patterson residence to stay until there was any word from down south. Seated around the dining table with steaming cups of coffee, the family discussed options.

"There is sure to be a public relief campaign," Emily told her, "and we must all be a part of it."

San Francisco earthquake and fire of 1906.

True to her word, bundled up warmly against the April morning chill, Emily was soon standing on a street corner soliciting donations with a tin labelled "Frisco Relief." A massive relief effort was quickly spreading across the city, for many Vancouverites had family and friends either visiting or living in the San Francisco area. Those having clothing, shoes or any useful household items that they did not need were directed to bring them to offices formerly occupied by the Rand Brothers and Leonard's Coffee House on Granville Street. Cash donations were being accepted at Vancouver's three daily newspapers, as well as City Hall, all local places of worship and the elite Hundred Thousand Club. A relief ship, the SS *Amur*, was being made ready for departure, loaded with food and supplies. Mayor Frederick Buscombe announced his intention to join the voyage south, accompanied by the city medical health officer Dr. F.T. Underhill and two fully trained nurses.

Piecing together newspaper reports in the days ahead brought Emily and her family some sense of hope. It appeared that the Haight Ashbury neighbourhood had been spared the worst of the fire, although the downtown region, including the offices of the Pacific Mail Steamship Company, was completely destroyed. Massive relief camps had been set up in Golden Gate Park, as well as in Alameda. It was an agonizing wait, but after several days, the Patterson and Crakanthorp families finally received a welcome but briefly worded telegram from Abbie to say that everyone was safe. John Patterson silently slipped away to the bedroom upon hearing the news. Emily followed and lay down beside him, gently squeezing his hand.

"All is well, my dear," she said softly. "Are you all right?"

"I'm just tired," he replied. "So tired."

Emily could not help worrying over her husband. At eighty years of age, John Patterson still insisted upon making his way to the Union Steamship dockyards by foot each evening to take up his night watchman duties. She insisted that he bundle up in several layers to ward off the chill and occasionally even joined him at the break of dawn for the walk home with hot coffee carefully sealed in a tin and wrapped with towels. There was great comradery among Union Steamship employees, and Emily could not help feeling that John retained his position merely for the pleasure of socializing as opposed to family finances. He was ever fascinated with the steady growth and broadening service range of the Union fleet. By 1906, eleven vessels operated under the Union banner. The early *Leonora*, *Senator* and *Skidegate* steamers were the oldest of the lot and had soon been followed by a lengthy line of vessels all christened after British Columbia locales beginning with the letter "C"—the *Clutch*, *Comox*, *Capilano*, *Coquitlam*, *Chehalis*, *Cassiar*, *Coulti* and most recently, the *Camosun*.

"I think they'll soon be running out of Cs!" John Patterson would often chuckle.

The date of Saturday, July 21, 1906, was going to be a merry one for the Pattersons. John had the weekend off and Emily had made plans for everyone to celebrate her seventieth birthday at the Hotel North Vancouver, advertised as the "Newest and Best Summer Resort" in the

1906 Henderson's Directory. Among other offerings, hotel services included rig and saddle horse excursions to the spectacular Capilano Canyon Suspension Bridge—a place that Emily had long dreamed of visiting.

Originally constructed in 1889 by Scottish civil engineer and land developer George Grant Mackay to access his six-thousand-acre purchase of dense forest spanning both sides of the Capilano Creek, the bridge had become a popular attraction over the years for locals and tourists alike. The hemp rope used in the bridge's original structure had been replaced in 1903 by sturdy wire cables—more to the liking of those who dared to venture across the 230-foot span. Emily had made arrangements for herself, Alice and Muriel to visit the bridge via carriage and then rendezvous with the menfolk later back at the hotel for a special meal. Her actual birthday would be celebrated the next day with a luncheon at St. James Church following Sunday service.

>‹

"Keep going, Grandma," Muriel giggled, just a tad nervously, as she, her mother and Emily edged their way across the bridge in the early afternoon sunshine.

"I'm enjoying the view," Emily protested, gazing out over the trees and the gentle splash of the Capilano Creek far below. She had brought along her cane to steady herself but kept a tight grip with her other hand upon the metal handrail—more concerned about maintaining her balance than the loftiness of their perch. "It's glorious, don't you think?"

It was late afternoon when the trio arrived back at the North Vancouver Hotel. They soon met up with Calvin, Fred and Robert Crakanthorp, seated at a picnic table on the hotel grounds. There was no sign of John and the men seemed uncharacteristically subdued.

"Hello!" Emily said brightly, still basking in the afterglow of her bridge experience. "Where's Papa?"

"He stayed on the other side," Calvin said quietly. "I'm afraid there's been a terrible accident involving a Union vessel. We don't know all of the details yet."

Emily immediately took a seat beside her son. "Is Papa all right?" she asked.

"Yes, he's fine, but something very bad has happened out on the inlet."

Emily's birthday dinner plans cast aside, the group set their sights on returning home aboard the next ferry. Several passengers had field glasses trained down-inlet towards Stanley Park, where it was plain to see that a major recovery operation was underway. A large flotilla of vessels had dropped anchor off Brockton Point.

The wreck of the Union Steamship Company tug *Chehalis* was the worst tragedy to befall Vancouver since the Great Fire. The next day, full details of the accident were headlined in all of the city's major daily newspapers. After departing North Vancouver en route to Blunden Harbour upcoast, the *Chehalis*, with fifteen passengers and crew aboard, had been caught in a riptide at the Narrows—propelling it directly into the path of the oncoming CPR steamer *Princess Victoria*. The resulting collision virtually cut the *Chehalis* in half, sending it to the bottom mere seconds later. While seven people were rescued, eight were unaccounted

SS Chehalis

for. John Patterson, having learned of the incident while preparing to attend Emily's birthday celebration, had gone immediately to the Union Steamship dock to see if he could be of any help. There Emily had found him later in the day, clustered together with a disconsolate group of Union employees.

"Percy Chick's gone," he told her, his eyes moist.

"Oh no," Emily said softly. "Not dear Percy."

Percy Chick had been a well-known and well-loved former member of the Union Steamship family. He had served as purser aboard the *Camosun* before being laid low with a severe bout of pneumonia in recent weeks. Percy proved to be a fighter and battled back from his illness, but on the advice of his doctor, he had reluctantly resigned his position and had been considering new employment opportunities in the B.C. interior. He had gone on board the *Chehalis*, planning to view oyster beds at Blunden Harbour as secretary/treasurer of the British Columbia Native Oyster Company.

St. James Church was full to capacity on Sunday, July 22—Emily's seventieth birthday—but many in the crowd wore black and their heads hung low in mourning. One of the *Chehalis* victims was a nine-year-old boy, Charles Barnett Benwell, whose father had been unable to rescue him. Another was Mamie Louise Bryce, head of the millinery department at Drysdale Stevenson Limited on West Hastings Street. Mrs. Bryce had outfitted many a Vancouver woman, including Emily and Alice, with fashionable hats. A physician, Dr. William Hutton, had served at logging camps up and down the B.C. coast. Mr. William Harrison Crawford, as well as two Japanese firemen named Morishima and Yama, and a Chinese cook, named Mah Hing, had also perished.

Father Clinton spoke eloquently of the *Chehalis* disaster: "If it had happened many miles away, it would have affected us but little, but it happened, so to speak, at our very doors and we could not help but feel it very deeply."

Seated with her family in the pews, Emily felt her eyes lowering.

"Are you all right, Mama?" Alice asked gently.

"Yes," she whispered. "But I feel that I must do something more."

In the days ahead, Emily left letters of condolence on the doorsteps of every bereaved family or individual that she could track down, along with tins of freshly baked bread. She made frequent trips to the Union Steamship office to pour hot coffee for employees and encouraged them to share their memories of Percy Chick. When one young employee became particularly distraught, she unabashedly put her arms around him.

"We will never forget them," she said softly. "Never."

CHAPTER 28

"He Was a Sea Captain"

Staying true to their earlier years of wanderlust, the Pattersons made frequent relocations in Vancouver. Though conveniently situated just two blocks from St. James Church, their Gore Avenue apartment building bordered on seedy Dupont Street, which continued to be an enclave for prostitution and other illicit activities. At Emily's urging, a move was made to more upscale lodgings at the corner of Powell and Dunlevy. By 1907, having pooled their financial resources with the Crakanthorps, Emily and John were able to purchase two side-by-side lots at 412 and 416 Cordova Street East, between Dunlevy and Jackson streets. Two identical houses were constructed on the lots, relatively small in comparison with others on the block, but the location was ideal for many purposes. The Powell Street streetcar line was within easy walking distance for John if he chose to use it for commuting to work. Calvin was employed in the tobacconist shop of the nearby Hotel Astor, at 147 West Hastings. Hastings Sawmill was in close proximity for

Fred, who was employed at the lumber yard. Muriel could attend nearby Lord Strathcona Elementary School.

But most convenient and pleasing of all was the fact that the Pattersons and Crakanthorps lived directly across the street from Oppenheimer Park. Formerly known as the Powell Street Grounds, Oppenheimer Park had been renamed in honour of Vancouver's second mayor, David Oppenheimer, in 1902. While by no means comparable to Stanley Park, with its many miles of scenic carriageways and forested trails, Oppenheimer Park had become a magnet for local sports followers. From the front parlour windows of homes all along the 400-block of Cordova, residents had an unobstructed view of baseball and soccer games regularly being played in the park. Baseball was hugely popular, particularly among the many Japanese families who had gravitated to the neighbourhood.

Vancouver's Japantown was roughly surrounded by the CPR rail line along the Burrard Inlet waterfront, Main, Hastings and Jackson streets. A large number of Japanese-owned businesses lined busy Powell Street: Japanese grocery and dry-good stores, tailors and laundry services among them. Emily liked her Japanese neighbours, full of admiration for their scrupulous attention to cleanliness and their hard-working demeanour. Finding her fingers less capable than in years previous, she would often call in at the local tailors for assistance with her various sewing projects. She also purchased quantities of rice to cook for her husband, noting that he found it kinder to his increasingly fragile digestive system.

John Patterson was deteriorating in health. In recent years, he had been suffering from chronic respiratory infection—a condition Emily felt was no doubt exacerbated by his lengthy late-night walks to and from the Union Steamships dockyard in the dank, fog-shrouded streets of Vancouver. By late summer of 1907, it was clear that his working days were through. He slept for long hours in the parlour, where Emily and Alice arranged a comfortable bed with propped-up pillows so that he could watch the sporting events in Oppenheimer Park. Emily was concerned for her husband but no amount of her medical knowledge could halt the ravages of time.

In the pre-dawn hours of September 8, 1907, Emily awoke to the distant sound of breaking glass. Instantly thinking that John had gotten out of bed and knocked over a piece of crockery, she quickly slipped on her dressing gown, lit the bedside lantern and hurried downstairs. Her husband was sleeping fitfully in the parlour, but out on the street she could hear a clamour of human voices—some shouting in anger, others unmistakably crying in fear. Opening the front door, she discovered that a noisy throng had congregated in Oppenheimer Park. Dozens of men raced about the playing field, many carrying what appeared to be baseball bats or long-handled shovels. Profanities pierced the air, and by the light of numerous lanterns, Emily could make out crudely worded banners being waved aloft in a sort of mad jubilation. She was so momentarily groggy and surprised that she did not notice her son-in-law Robert standing on his porch next door, baseball bat in hand.

"Go inside, Mum!" he called over to her. "It's not safe out here to-night!"

Anti-Asian riot aftermath, 1907.

"What is going on?" Emily exclaimed.

"Rioters . . . lots of them, protesting over the Asians."

Emily knew straight away what was happening. Over a lengthy period, many of Vancouver's white working-class men had become disenchanted with Asian workers routinely being employed for lower salaries. For weeks, anti-Asian sentiment had been festering in the city. In June, the Vancouver Trades and Labour Council had organized the Asiatic Exclusion League, only two days prior to the arrival of the steamer *Kumeric* from Honolulu with 1,177 Japanese immigrants aboard.

On the afternoon of September 7, an Exclusion League rally had taken place at the Cambie Street Grounds, attracting thousands of supporters. The original plan was for participants to disband following the parade and speeches. However, a large contingent organized an impromptu march to City Hall near Main and Hastings, where British Columbia's former premier and current Lieutenant-Governor, James Dunsmuir, well known for his anti-union, pro-immigration stance, was burned in effigy to the delight of the cheering crowd. Calvin and Fred, curious about all the noise and commotion, had wandered over earlier in the evening to investigate, but had returned home unimpressed. It had been over twenty years since his escape from the Great Fire, but the events of that day lingered in Calvin's mind and he had retained a quiet appreciation for just how devastating a single burning flame could become.

"Go inside, Mum!" Robert repeated. "I'll see to it that nobody bothers us!"

Dozens of shadowy figures were running back and forth in Oppenheimer Park, amidst wild shouts of hilarity.

"The nerve of them!" Emily spoke up angrily. "The absolute nerve!"

Furious that the rioters might awaken her husband or frighten young Muriel, Emily quickly thrust her feet into a pair of carpet slippers, took up her cane and went down into the street.

"How dare you!" she shouted as a group of men ran past. Robert Crakanthorp came directly behind, attempting to grab her raised arm, but she staunchly brushed him off.

"Shame on you! Shame on the lot of you!" she continued to yell into the night, although her reprimands had little effect on the perpetrators. The sound of breaking glass could clearly be heard in the distance, punctuated by screams, angry shouts of "*banzaii*!" and the occasional heartrending cries of frightened children. As one youthful-looking figure came running past her, Emily found herself spontaneously shaking her cane.

"Ruffian!" she shouted.

The young lad glanced back at her as he ran past. In the next instant, he had tripped to the ground in a heap. By the light of the street lamp, she could see that he had torn a hole in his jeans at the knee and a trickle of blood was oozing through the denim.

"Leave me alone!" he exclaimed angrily, slowly rising to his feet as Emily sought to examine his wound. "I wasn't doin' anything."

"A likely story," Emily replied.

She could see that he was perhaps all of thirteen, waif-thin and shabbily dressed. Feeling a small degree of sympathy, she suggested he come into her house by the back kitchen door so that she could tend to the bleeding. After some reluctance he complied.

"Don't you think you should be home in bed at this hour?" she remarked, gently staunching his wound with water and a cotton pad while he sat with a sullen look. "Your parents will be worried about you."

"My ma's dead. My pa doesn't care, he just gets drunk. He can't find work and it's all because of the Asians!"

"I see," Emily nodded, without raising an eyebrow. "Did your pa tell you this?"

"Everybody knows it. My pa used to have his own steamboat, but he had to sell it so he could put food on the table. He was a sea captain, but now he's just a nobody."

"What is your name?" Emily asked.

"Rupert."

"Well Rupert," Emily said quietly, while she applied a bandage to his graze, "let me tell you this. You have every right to be angry. Your world is difficult and that must be very hard for you. But please remember, there is no such thing as a 'nobody.' Everybody on God's green earth is a 'somebody' and every last one of us is very capable of doing something great. Breaking windows and frightening young children is no way to get your point across, no matter how angry you feel."

There was so much more that Emily wanted to discuss with Rupert, including the possibility of getting him into an orphanage, but her husband was calling from the parlour. By the time she returned after giving him a much-toned-down explanation for the noise outside, gently propping his pillows and giving him a sip of water, the lad had gone. Robert Crakanthorp came in to report that the city police were slowly getting the upper hand, together with many irate Japanese business owners who had refused to succumb to the onslaught.

In the days ahead, Vancouver's newspapers were full of sordid details about the rioting as sporadic outbreaks of violence continued. All down Dupont, Carrall and Columbia streets, as well as both sides of Canton and Shanghai alleys, not a single Chinese-owned business window had escaped damage. The mob participants had done their work systematically. Along Westminster Avenue, where white and Asian businesses intermingled, those of white owners were carefully spared while those of Asians bore shattered glass and splintered signage. There was wide demand for revolvers in Vancouver's gun shops. Many city restaurant owners had been forced to close their doors due to lack of staff. Hundreds of Chinese hospitality workers—dishwashers, cooks and launderers—had pulled their services in angry retaliation over the events of the night. Most concerning of all was the news that a deliberate attempt had been made to burn down the wooden Japanese Language School on Alexander Street. Burning cotton waste, saturated with kerosene and machine oil, had been stowed in an aperture under the school's ground floor. Luckily, it had been discovered before any major damage occurred.

Emily yearned to talk about the politics of the riot with her husband, but she knew that it would be better not to worry him. As the weeks wore on, John Patterson gradually declined in health.

"I believe your papa will soon be leaving us," Emily matter-of-factly wrote to Abbie and Beckie. She declined their offers to come up to Van-

John Peabody Patterson, c. 1890s.

couver, insisting that they were more needed in their own homes with their own children. Alice, Calvin and Fred took their turns in caring for their father—saddened to see the robust, stalwart figure that they had once known withering into a frail and helpless soul before their eyes.

On December 5, 1907, John Patterson died of senility and related complications under the palliative care of Dr. Donald Mackay. Dr. Mackay lived on the same block of East Cordova Street as the Pattersons and Crakanthorps and had regularly made house calls to both families. As was typically the case with Vancouver physicians, he was a busy professional with little time to share more than brief pleasantries during his visits. Shortly after John's passing, he produced an official government death registration form and politely asked Emily if she could provide a few details about her husband's background.

"Of course," Emily replied, well familiar with the protocols. "I would like my daughters in California to have copies of the registration."

In response to Dr. Mackay's queries, she informed him that her husband's full name was John Peabody Patterson, he had been born in the United States, was affiliated with the Church of England and was eighty-one years and six months of age.

"A very good age!" Dr. Mackay responded. "Has an undertaker been selected?"

"Yes . . . Mr. Clegg."

"Excellent. Now just one item more . . . his former profession."

Emily was about to say "night watchman" when she found her mind wandering as it so often did these days. She thought of the John Patterson that she had known so long ago, right from that very early afternoon of their first meeting in the Sagadahock House tea room in faraway Maine. Through her tears a smile played upon her lips.

"He was a sea captain," she replied.

CHAPTER 29

The Heroine of Moodyville

Following the funeral at St. James Church, John Patterson was laid to rest in an unmarked plot at Mountain View Cemetery. Emily declined to order a headstone, staunchly declaring that "the money would better be spent on the living."

"We will always remember Papa," she told a saddened Alice. "You must see to it that Muriel will know who he was . . . who we all were and what life was like, for the pioneering days of Vancouver and Moodyville have long gone by the wayside."

"I'll tell her, Mama." Alice nodded.

Emily soldiered on as best she could, but her own health was in decline. Although her nursing services were no longer in demand thanks to the large number of professionally trained young women now working in Vancouver, she continued to pay calls upon neighbours and friends in time of need offering her own simpler brand of care—that of encouraging words, a loaf of freshly baked bread, a bouquet of flowers, anything to lift a troubled spirit, if only for a brief time. The early pioneers of Burrard Inlet were steadily being called by death but many of her dear friends remained, continuing to make their own personal stamp upon the city.

Vancouver was evolving into a heady place with passersby constantly on the go with looks of distraction and determination. Calvin and Fred had matured into handsome young men, steadily forging their own livelihoods—Calvin as a tobacconist and Fred as a boom man at Hastings Sawmill. In the summer of 1909, aged thirty-seven and thirty-three respectively, they both married—Calvin to Mary Adda Smith and Fred to Lucy Mabel Brown. Lucy had a seven-year-old daughter named Beatrice from a previous marriage. Recollecting her own early experiences as a step-parent to Edward, Emily could not resist giving Fred some parenting advice.

Frederick Jordan Patterson

"You must be a friend first, father second," she told him. "Do not expect to be a replacement for what Beatrice has lost."

Emily had always loved to walk, but when walking became too physically demanding, she took to travelling by horse-drawn hansom cab. Horse-drawn vehicles were in rapid decline with the advent of the streetcar system and an ever-increasing number of automobiles, but a few of the old hansom relics continued to be seen on Vancouver streets. Emily and Alice were short enough in height that they could comfortably settle themselves into the two-passenger cab with Muriel nestled snugly in between. Folding wooden doors and a sliding glass window front and back ensured that all three would be well sheltered from the rain and cold while Alice directed the driver to take them to Woodward's or Stanley Park or occasionally for a random drive with no particular destination in mind. Emily could never stop marvelling at how much the city had transformed since the early days.

"Look at that!" she exclaimed to Muriel, while they passed the thirteen-storey Dominion Trust Building, nearing completion at the corner of Hastings and Cambie. "I remember when that was forest—all just forest."

"And not so very long ago," Alice added with a smile. "They say that building will be the tallest in the British Empire!"

By early fall, Emily took to her bed, telling everyone that she was "too tired" to venture out any more. The nature of her illness was summed up, in Dr. Mackay's words, as that of an elderly woman whose body was simply wearing out. Callers visited regularly but did not linger, for she often drifted off to sleep mid-conversation. Bouquets of flowers and baskets of fruit filled the dining and coffee tables. Cards with words of encouragement and affection lined the fireplace mantel. At St. James Church, Reverend Clinton urged all to "pray for our dear and beloved sister in Christ, Emily Patterson."

On November 12, 1909, Emily passed away in the care of Dr. Mackay. Her cause of death was officially recorded as "Senility for a duration of twelve weeks." An obituary appeared in the November 13 issue of the *Vancouver World* newspaper:

Very widespread and very keen will be the sorrow over the passing of Mrs. J. Patterson, relict of the late John P. Patterson, for many years a familiar figure on the waterfront. Mr. and Mrs. Patterson came to Vancouver in April, 36 years ago, when there were only two white families living here, those of Messrs. R.H. Alexander and Jonathan Miller. Mrs. Patterson was a woman of most kindly disposition and she also had that peculiar personality that soothes and cheers a sufferer, and in early days and in later days too, the services of Mrs. Patterson where there was sickness were prized beyond measure. She was ever the ministering angel—when news of suffering reached her and her self-sacrifices and loving kindness endeared her to many. Mrs. Patterson had been ailing for two years, since the death of Mr. Patterson in fact, but she had been confined to bed only three months. Her illness was borne with Christian fortitude, and even in her hours of suffering she had a sympathetic word at all times to say about any whom she heard of having sickness or trouble. The immediate family who will mourn Mrs. Patterson's demise consists of two sons and three daughters—Mrs. Crakenthorpe, of this city; Mrs. Capt. Jordan of San Francisco, and Mrs. Capt. Pierce of Alameda, and Messrs. Calvin O. and Frederick J. Patterson of Vancouver. Outside the friends she won and held through her own goodness and the members of her family the departure of Mrs. Patterson will be deeply regretted by the congregation of St. James, among the first to join which was Mrs. Patterson, and up to the time of her prostration by illness she was always an ardent and consistent church worker.

Emily was laid to rest according to her wishes—alongside her husband in an unmarked grave in the Horne Section of Mountain View Cemetery. The burial plot was in a pleasant location on a gentle, north-facing slope with a sweeping view of the north shore mountains in all their seasonal splendor. Tributes poured in for Emily from the many individuals who had experienced her unique qualities of gentle and unconditional care.

><

True to her word, in the years ahead, Alice shared her memories of the early pioneering days on Burrard Inlet with Muriel and also with Vancouver City Archivist Major James Skitt Matthews. A native of Newtown, Wales, the major had immigrated to Vancouver in 1898 and by the early 1930s had settled in to what would become his life's passion—amassing and recording an extensive archive of early pioneer and Indigenous recollections of life on Burrard Inlet. The meticulous Major Matthews found kindred spirits in Alice and Muriel—women whose vivid recollections were noted in detail during many a meeting between the three of them. Much to Matthews's fascination, a clear and unmistakable picture of Emily Patterson began to emerge. Muriel, a stenographer by profession, embraced the cause with much enthusiasm, sending out letters of inquiry to various individuals who had known her grandmother well. She particularly treasured a reply from Doctor Henri Langis, dated April 8, 1935, which summed up his thoughts on Emily's nursing expertise:

Now about your grandmother, Mrs. Patterson of Moodyville. She was the first woman that did any nursing for us. She was quite efficient and really did wonderfully well, though she never had any training, but she had the experience and took advantage of her anterior observations. She was neat, quick and capable at her work day and night. Never spared herself for her patients and I think that even today she would give good advice to some of the hospital-trained nurses. I am glad to be able to tell you that, because I appreciated her work very much.

In 1936, Nora Duncan of the Vancouver Poetry Society contacted Major Matthews, explaining that she had learned brief details of Emily's heroic journey to Point Atkinson Lighthouse and wanted to know more, "perhaps with a view to writing a poem." The major contacted Muriel and asked if she could have a chat with her mother about that amazing feat and write up a detailed summation. Alice's recollections

Emily Patterson studio portrait, c. 1890s.

were very clear and it was not difficult for Nora Duncan to imagine a stubborn and stoic Emily, fearlessly gripping Chinalset's canoe as it plunged through the swells on that stormy November night in 1883. Duncan's poem, "The Heroine of Moodyville," was published in the 1936 *Vancouver General Nurses Annual* and in the June issue of *Chatelaine Magazine* that same year.

Alice loved reading "The Heroine of Moodyville" and often brought it out to recite to her growing legion of nieces and nephews. The Crakanthorps eventually settled in a home on East 59th Avenue, along with Fred, his wife and their three children. Abbie, Beckie and Calvin continued to make regular visits with their respective families.

"That was your Grandmother Patterson!" Alice told them all proudly, each and every time she recited Nora Duncan's poem.

"You'd think she would have been scared," Fred's daughter Charlotte spoke up one time after she had listened to it.

"Grandmother Patterson? Well, I think I can truthfully say . . . she was afraid of nothing!"

APPENDIX 1

Emily's Family

→ EDWARD

No further records have been found to confirm the whereabouts of Edward Everett Patterson after the family's departure from Butteville, Oregon.

→ ABBIE AND BECKIE

Abbie Lowell Patterson Jordan and Rebecca (Beckie) Park Patterson Pierce lived the remainder of their days in San Francisco and Alameda, respectfully. Though little more is known about these two women, it is said that they were strong of character and dedicated to family. Abbie died on December 27, 1946, at the age of eighty-seven. Her grave is located in Cypress Lawn Memorial Park, Colma, San Mateo County, California. Abbie's surviving children at the time of her death included Edward Burrard Jordan, Emily Belvedere Jordan Martin, Hazel Gertrude Jordan Neumann and Sarah Fuller Jordan Crow. A son, Lewis Sidney Jordan, died as a result of an accident aboard the USS *Undaunted* on March 14, 1918.

Beckie died on September 7, 1948, at the age of eighty-six and was also interred at Cypress Lawn. Beckie's surviving children at the time of her death included Claude Cecil Otis Pierce, David Henry Pierce, Alice Emily Pierce Martin and John Patterson Pierce. Descendants of the Jordan and Pierce families continue to reside in Washington, Oregon and northern California.

→ CALVIN

Calvin Oric Patterson lived in Vancouver for the remainder of his days. He was well known as a tobacconist at two iconic Vancouver hotels, first in the old Hotel Vancouver from 1918 to 1927 and then at the Hotel Georgia until his retirement in 1945. For many years, Calvin and his wife Mary and family resided at 1041 Harwood Street in Vancouver's West End. Calvin died on June 6, 1959, at the age of eighty-six and was cremated following a funeral service at St. Paul's Anglican Church. Calvin's surviving children included John Noel Patterson, Edith Muriel Patterson Caster of Oklahoma City and Charlotte Alice Mary Patterson Matheson of Concord, Massachusetts. No further family records from Calvin Patterson's lineage have been located to date.

→ FRED

Frederick Jordan Patterson also remained in Vancouver and was employed for many years as a boom man at Hastings Sawmill. Fred, his wife Lucy, stepdaughter Beatrice, son Robert John Patterson and daughter Alice Margaret Emily Patterson lived with the Crakanthorp family at 1622 Charles Street in the neighbourhood of Vancouver Grandview.

Fred and Lucy's daughter Alice studied at the Royal Columbian Hospital School of Nursing, graduating in 1930. Alice married Thomas Laing Heads in 1934, and in 1935 the couple had a daughter, Mary Elizabeth Heads. This same year, Fred apparently took early retirement from his boom man profession, perhaps due to injury or illness. He and Lucy relocated with Alice and Muriel Crakanthorp to 586 East 59th Avenue in 1937. Fred died on March 1, 1940, eleven days short of his sixty-fourth birthday.

Although Alice Heads never knew her grandmother, she clearly shared Emily's passion for caring for the sick and injured. Alice was extensively involved with nursing supervision at facilities in Vancouver and Burnaby. Her daughter Mary also became a nurse, graduating from Royal Columbian in 1957. Mary worked as a nurse in Mississippi, Alaska and New York before taking up a long career at

Alice Margaret Emily Patterson, daughter of Fred Patterson, 1930.

Riverview Psychiatric Hospital from 1961 until her retirement in 1995. Descendants of Fred Patterson continue to reside in the Lower Mainland and Vancouver Island region.

✦ ALICE AND MURIEL

Alice Frances Patterson Crakanthorp was well known in Vancouver social circles and lived a life of youthful vigour and zest. Her passion for dancing and parties remained as strong as it had been during her early years in Moodyville. Robert Crakanthorp held a supervisory position with the Pacific Lumber Inspection Bureau, and the Crakanthorps were popular fixtures at many a Vancouver after-hours soiree. Alice was deeply saddened by the passing of her husband on December 6, 1926, at sixty-six years of age, although she would have a constant companion in her daughter Muriel, who never married or left home.

Alice, with all of her historic firsts, became something of a local celebrity as the years went by. She laid claim to being the first white girl born on the west coast of Vancouver Island. She was the sole surviving pupil of the first class in Vancouver's first school. She had attended the first wedding performed at Hastings Mill. She had witnessed the first CPR through trains to arrive in Port Moody and Vancouver. She had been a member of the first confirmation class in the rebuilt St. James Anglican Church. Most intriguing of all was the fact that she had witnessed Vancouver in its infancy, when the future city was little more than a sparsely populated backwater milltown.

Captivated by Alice's upbringing and her ever-present charm, Vancouver City Archivist Major James Skitt Matthews often invited her and Muriel to afternoon tea time. Page after page of Alice's recollections were painstakingly recorded and typed by the major's office staff, complemented by an ever-growing "Crakanthorp file" of newspaper clippings and photographs. When Lady Victoria Alexandra Braithwaite, daughter of Lord and Lady Dufferin, visited Vancouver with her husband in October of 1937, Alice was invited to join them for afternoon tea in their suite at the Hotel Vancouver. Alice found herself in demand to officiate at many a ceremonial occasion, be it distributing diplomas to the Class of 1938 from King Edward High School or cutting the ribbon to officially open Port Alberni's new city hall on May 20, 1959.

Often asked for her secret to a long and healthy life, Alice would reply, "Live it up and you'll live longer!" Dancing at a Vancouver night club to celebrate her 95th birthday, she staunchly declared, "I don't feel half as old as I am and can go around faster than a lot of these young folks. You bet I can!"

Alice (Patterson) Crakanthorp, c. 1955.

Alice and Muriel had lived at various addresses in Vancouver but as the years went by Alice found herself yearning for a more rural setting. Her niece and nephew-in-law Alice and Thomas Heads had purchased property near the Alouette River in Maple Ridge back in 1937 with plans to build a house. Sadly, Thomas had died in 1944, but Alice Heads eventually realized her dream of constructing a house on the property for her retirement years. Visits to her niece's idyllic home in the countryside fuelled Alice's longing for the wide open spaces of her childhood years. She and Muriel also made the move to Maple Ridge in 1960, taking up residence at 12276 11th Avenue.

On February 25, 1961, CBC Radio producer Imbert Orchard sat

down with Alice and Muriel for an hour-long recording session, during which a somewhat quavery-voiced Alice spoke about the early years of her lifetime. While requiring the occasional prompting from Muriel, she answered most of Mr. Orchard's questions with great lucidity and enthusiasm—especially if the subject broached upon dancing.

"Oh yes!" she replied, when asked if she recollected the grand ball at the opening of the first Hotel Vancouver. (Alice's much beloved dancing shoes, worn that night, remain in the collection of the Museum of Vancouver.)

On October 9, 1961, Alice died peacefully in her home at the age of ninety-seven. Muriel received heartfelt expressions of sympathy from friends near and far, including a message via telegram from Major Matthews:

"ALL VANCOUVER MOURNS WITH YOU."

Muriel continued to reside in Maple Ridge until her death on February 10, 1978, at eighty-two years of age.

In Emily's Footsteps

↳ BATH

Currently home to over eight thousand residents, Bath, Maine, the "City of Ships," continues a longtime tradition as one of the U.S. nation's most notable shipbuilding centres. The massive Bath Iron Works shipbuilding complex now presides over the Kennebec riverfront area formerly occupied by the shipyards of Houghton, Rogers and other prominent Bath families of Emily's time. In 1894, a fire which started in the Sagadahock House hotel devastated Bath's downtown business district. Much of the world that Emily would have known in her Bath years was destroyed. However, numerous nineteenth-century buildings in excellent states of preservation continue to grace Bath streets, such as the Sewall Mansion (1844), the McClellan House (1845) and First Baptist Church (1852). Affiliated with "Main Street," a program initiated by the U.S. National Trust for Historic Preservation, Bath volunteers are working to restore and revitalize the city's traditional character. Today's Bath is a popular tourist destination, home to the Maine Maritime Museum and a year-round farmer's market. A reconstruction of Maine's first ship, the seventeenth-century pinnace *Virginia*, is taking shape near the Kennebec waterfront.

↳ SAN FRANCISCO

The Great San Francisco Earthquake and Fire of 1906 destroyed most of the docklands and Barbary Coast district of northeast San Francisco, including the Patterson family's former neighbourhood on Pacific Street. Pacific Avenue today includes high-end condominium developments and pedestrian precincts—all within close proximity to San Francisco's central Financial District, where new earthquake-resistant technologies resulted in a flurry of high-rise development from the late 1950s onward. Abbie Jordan's home on Fell Street no longer stands, but many of the trees which captivated Emily in the Panhandle linear park date back to 1871 and continue to thrive. Golden Gate Park's Conservatory of Flowers, opened in 1879, remains one of San Francisco's most beloved heritage structures despite sustaining heavy damage in a 1995 winter storm. Fully restored, it was reopened in 2003. The famed cable car network of San Francisco, inaugurated with the Clay Street Line in 1873, continues to operate both as a tourist attraction and an integral component of the city's public transit network.

↳ ALBERNI

In August of 1866, the vessel HMS *Scout* dropped anchor at the head of Alberni Inlet. Findings were later recorded in the ship's journal:

> It was distressing to see the lately prosperous little settlement of Alberni fast becoming a heap of ruins, only one white man by the name of Drane is there, who takes care of the machinery connected with the sawmill. The pretty little gardens of the settlers are overgrown with weeds and the houses falling to decay.

While sawmilling and related industries have been synonymous with its growth for numerous years, Port Alberni of today, population 17,000+, has steadily reinvented itself as a major mid-Vancouver Island supply, service and transport hub. Thousands of tourists travel Highway 4 through the city in all seasons to access the famed Pacific Rim National Park on Vancouver Island's west coast. Deepwater port facilities at the headwaters of Alberni Inlet provide year-round freight and passenger services to isolated coastal communities. The only remaining vestiges of Captain Edward Stamp's 1860-era sawmill and townsite are a few wooden timbers, carefully preserved in the Alberni Valley Museum. Port Alberni City Hall was officially opened by Alice Crakanthorp on May 20, 1959. The Tseshaht First Nation people continue to live on their traditional territory, one of fourteen nations making up the Nuu-chah-nulth peoples of Vancouver Island's west coast.

→ CHAMPOEG AND BUTTEVILLE

Much history of the Champoeg and Butteville region on Oregon State's Willamette River benchland is preserved in the 615-acre Champoeg State Heritage Area. In partnership with Oregon Parks and Recreation Department, the non-profit Friends of Historic Champoeg maintains and operates park facilities, while offering interpretive programs, historical recreations and guided walks. Built on the site of the Manson home, the Visitor Center includes exhibits, an auditorium, gift shop and the recreation of an 1860's kitchen garden. The adjacent Manson barn, believed to be a relocated survivor of the 1861 Champoeg flood, is regularly used in the Champoeg Promise education program for schoolchildren. Nearby, the 1852 Newell House, fully restored in 1955 by the Daughters of the American Revolution, operates as a museum and venue for weddings and other public gatherings. The 1931 Pioneer Mother's Log Cabin recreates a typical pioneer family dwelling of the mid-nineteenth century.

Downriver at Butteville, accessible via road or the scenic Willamette bikeway, summer visitors can enjoy ice cream and cold drinks in the 1863 Butteville General Store. The bell rescued from the Champoeg flood is displayed outside Butteville Community Church. No monument exists for Emily's son Frank Patterson, although gravestones can still be found for members of the Chenery family in Butteville Cemetery.

→ RAINIER AND THE COWLITZ TRAIL

Rainier, Oregon, of today is a relatively quiet riverside community of approximately two thousand residents, its most notable feature being the 1930 Lewis and Clark Bridge—once the largest cantilever bridge in the United States. Much of the city's "A" Street business district was destroyed by fire on June 28, 1924. In the early 1980s, Rainier's Riverfront Park was built upon dredged volumes of ash and debris that had washed down the Columbia River after the eruption of Mount St. Helens.

During the early years of the twentieth century, the Cowlitz Trail, over which the Patterson family travelled in 1873, was integrated with the Pacific Highway—a coastal road linking the Canadian and Mexican borders through Washington, Oregon and California. In 1913, a four-mile section of the trail was paved, becoming the first paved road in Washington State. Only vestiges of the original wagon trail remain on private property.

↣ HASTINGS MILL

In 1925, Hastings Mill was sold to the Vancouver Harbour Commission for the sum of $2,450,000. Most of the sawmill and townsite structures were demolished in 1928, under the direction of the mill's

Old Hastings Mill Store Museum, c. 1930s.

final owner, Eric Werge Hamber. Bowing to the pleas of a local lodge, the Native Daughters of B.C. Post #1, Hamber agreed to spare Vancouver's oldest building, the 1868 Hastings Mill Store on the condition that it be relocated to a different site. Today, the store that Emily and many others had once regularly visited for groceries, supplies and mail was floated along the inlet and is preserved as a museum at the north foot of Alma Street in Vancouver's Point Grey neighbourhood. The only other surviving mill building is a 1906 prefabricated house, built to provide offices for Hastings Mill managerial staff and showcase the variety of wood products available in British Columbia. It now serves as the Mission to Seafarers and B.C. headquarters of the Flying Angels Club, a society dedicated to the care of seafarers worldwide. Port Metro Vancouver's massive loading cranes, a forest of cargo containers and the facilities of Ballantyne Pier now occupy the location where the old sawmill, its surrounding community and the structures of Kumkumlye once stood.

→ MOODYVILLE

Not a trace remains of the original sawmilling community of Moodyville, with the exception of two chimneys believed to have been salvaged from the site of the Big House. After its 1901 closure, the Moodyville Sawmill was stripped of all equipment and sat vacant for many years, finally burning down in 1916. A few people continued to reside in the community, although most gravitated westward to North Vancouver's commercial and residential hub of Lonsdale Avenue. Moodyville School closed permanently in 1910. The old vessel SS *Senator*, for so many years a fixture in Burrard Inlet waters, sank off Bowen Island in 1925. Between 1927 and 1928, a waterfront road and rail line was built to connect with the newly opened Second Narrows Bridge, during which time the slope leading up Nob Hill was entirely cut away. Bulk terminal facilities and grain elevators now occupy the site of the mill and much of its surrounding townsite. A completed section of the North Shore Spirit Trail, a joint project between government agencies and First Nations to create a fully accessible greenway between Deep Cove and Horseshoe Bay, traverses

Sign in Moodyville Park

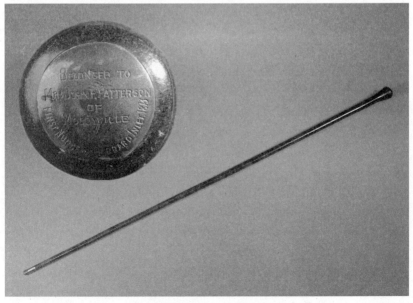

Emily's walking cane

the escarpment above. On 3rd Street East between Moody and Queensbury avenues, Moodyville Park, with its numerous historical plaques, commemorates the activities and people of a bygone era. A small number of Moodyville relics remain in the North Vancouver Museum and Archives collection, including Emily Patterson's walking cane.

→ POINT ATKINSON
Point Atkinson continued to be isolated from Burrard Inlet communities for many years after Emily's heroic 1883 journey. Construction of a coastal wagon trail that would connect Deep Cove and West Vancouver's Eagle Harbour began in 1892. It would take fourteen years to complete, owing to the challenging topography of Burrard Inlet's north shore. Point Atkinson's original 1874 lighthouse and adjoining lightkeeper's residence were demolished to make way for a reinforced concrete hexagonal tower, operational by 1912. A new, fourteen-room duplex for the lightkeeper and assistant lightkeeper and their families, as well as a foghorn building, were constructed on sheltered land behind the tower. During World War II, Point Atkinson, along with a number of light stations up and down the B.C. coast, was used for enemy surveillance and defence. Searchlights were installed and later, following the 1941 attack on Pearl Harbor, an eighteen-pounder Mark 1 gun. Other army facilities included an officer's quarters, kitchen and dining hall, men's barracks and guardhouse. Some of those facilities remain today, including the dining hall, which now serves as the Phyl Munday Nature House run by Girl Guides of Canada and Sk'iwitsut House, the former bunkhouse now operated by West Vancouver Parks and Community Services for recreational programs. Point Atkinson Lighthouse was designated a National Historic Site in 1994. Two years later, the light was automated. Today, the lighthouse is the primary attraction and namesake of seventy-five hectare Lighthouse Park, a popular and scenic West Vancouver locale for hikers and picnickers. Sections of Arbutus and Valley trails lie in the vicinity of the clifftop route that would have been taken by Emily and her First Nation companions to reach the lightkeeper's cottage.

→ GRANITE FALLS

In the aftermath of the Great Vancouver Fire, laws were drawn up requiring new buildings to be constructed of non-flammable materials. In 1887, the *Vancouver Daily News-Advertiser* reported that "the granite quarry on the North Arm of the Inlet is being rapidly developed. Arrangements have been made with the 'Burrard Inlet Towing Company' to deliver two or three large scow loads weekly. . . ." Alice Crakanthorp recollected how family picnicking excursions to Granite Falls stopped in later years—likely as a result of industrialization in the once-pristine area. Quarry operations continued right up until 1961, when the last company owners, McKenzie Barge and Derrick Quarries Co. Limited, put all property and equipment up for sale. In 1965, the Harbour Navigation Company began developing Granite Falls Resort, a high-end vacation retreat with a lodge, marina, dine-and-dance restaurant, roller skating rink, beer garden and children's playground. It was doomed to be a short-lived venture. After the lodge and a staff bunkhouse were destroyed by a fire of unknown cause in October of 1972, the resort closed, never to reopen. Today Granite Falls has reverted to its origins as a peaceful wilderness retreat within the conservation area of Say Nuth Khaw Yum Provincial Park (aka Indian Arm Park). Popular for camping, kayaking, hiking and sport fishing, the park is managed collaboratively between the Tsleil-Waututh First Nation and Province of British Columbia.

→ USTLAWN

Members of the Squamish Nation continue to reside at Ustlawn (Eslha7an), one of several urban First Nation reserves located within the Lower Mainland and the municipality of Squamish. An extensive Squamish Nation administration network coordinates a variety of services for members of the native community. Mosquito Creek Marina, a Squamish-owned business, offers moorage and related amenities on Ustlawn Reserve shoreline to the west of Lonsdale Quay. The Mission church, built in 1884, was extensively remodelled in 1909 and renamed St. Paul's Church in honour of Bishop Paul Durieu. Today it is officially recognized as a Canadian National Historic

Site. St. Paul's Indian Residential School was demolished in 1959. Its former location is now home to the St. Thomas Aquinas Regional Secondary School. On June 11, 2008, Prime Minister Stephen Harper issued a formal apology on behalf of the Government of Canada for the Indian Residential School system.

→ VANCOUVER

Of all the locales that Emily called home throughout her lifetime, Vancouver, despite its twenty-first-century glass towers, trendy restaurants and traffic snarls, is the only place she might have still recognized. Gastown Historic District, home to over 140 buildings dating from post-fire 1886 to 1914, was officially proclaimed a National Historic Site of Canada on April 20, 2009. The Dominion Building, completed in 1910, still stands, as does the 1903 Carnegie Library, the latter serving today as a vibrant neighbourhood gathering place and community centre. Closed as a medical facility in 1906, St. Luke's Hospital was used for a number of years as a women's home and guest house. It continues to serve as a social housing facility. The site of Vancouver's 1888 City Hospital is today a downtown parkade. St. Paul's Hospital, extensively enlarged and renovated over the course of years, still stands at 1081 Burrard Street, although plans are being finalized for a new St. Paul's to be constructed on a 7.5 hectare site near Vancouver's Strathcona and Chinatown neighbourhoods.

The second St. James Anglican Church was demolished in 1935 to make way for the third St. James—a concrete structure which continues to be a venue for worship and community services at 303 East Cordova Street. Oppenheimer Park received an extensive upgrade in 2010 with the addition of a new field house, accessible pathways, a children's playground and other amenities. One mid-summer weekend every year, the park is home to the Powell Street Festival, a celebration of the neighbourhood's Japanese-Canadian heritage.

The North Vancouver ferries ceased operation in 1958 following completion of the Second Narrows crossing now known as the Ironworkers Memorial Bridge. North Vancouver Ferry #1, which Emily would have ridden in her later years, has been preserved as a private home on Strawberry Island near Tofino. The glorious era of the Union Steamships came to a close in 1959. Christ Church Cathedral, dedicated on February 17, 1895, still stands at the northeast corner of Burrard and Georgia streets, having undergone extensive renovations over the years. "The Nurse's Memorial," a stained glass window in the church's Peace Chapel, was designed by Major James Skitt Matthews "in tribute to the nursing profession who have served this city since 1873" and officially unveiled on June 25, 1950.

"The Heroine of Moodyville"

by Nora Duncan

When forests crowned Pacific slopes where Vancouver now stands
The moccasin trod hidden trails through dense unbroken lands
And swift canoes cleft silent seas along the lonely strands.

In Moodyville where sawmill hummed and barques at anchor lay.
Of bravery a tale is told—its glory lives today
And lights historic memories with torch of golden ray.

Around this dauntless deed thoughts weave and burning words unfold
To tell of one who courted death a lonely tryst to hold
When hope waxed dim and dark despair hovered in aspect cold.

From Atkinson's far point had come two Indians with the news:
"The lighthouse keeper's wife is ill—there is no time to lose!
A doctor send or else a nurse, who swiftly cometh, Choose!"

The word goes forth, the jetty throngs with settlers come to hear,
Their weathered faces grave concern in feeling tribute wear—
Alas, no doctor—he has gone on urgent case afar!

The mill grows silent, pike poles lie neglected by the flume;
The peavey waits a practiced hand its cunning to resume
As loggers, caulked and mackinawed, desert the floating boom.

And while they speak the waters heave and thunder's muttering word
Forbids a passenger o'er the Bay, to a sudden frenzy stirred,
While driven gulls seek inland rest, their startled cries unheard.

Now as wild gusts with shrouding winds, the fading landscape veil,
And somber night her mantle casts on dying daylight pale—
The gentle Mistress Patterson hears of the tragic tale.

The wife of sawmill master she, forever by his side,
On horse or foot, in staunch canoe, has travelled far and wide.
And pioneer vicissitudes her presence dignified.

Beloved was she in rancherie and scattered settlement,
Her touch akin to miracle, her life a kindness spent,
A refuge in the wilderness, a foster mother lent!

So thus the people, knowing well her fortitude of yore
Turned hastily with troubled step to knock upon her door,
And of her understanding aid they earnestly implore.

As sadly visions pleading rise of one who suffers there
In isolated rocky keep, far from physician's care,
Her spirit yearns, compassionate, that fight with death to share.

The darkness falls, the wind blows wet, heavy with sheets of rain,
Against the lighthouse on the Point where keeper's wife has lain
In fevered sickness, without hand to soothe the burning pain.

"Oh God," deliriously she prays, "must I in torment be?
Dear God, is no one brave enough to cross through storm to me?"
Laden her weak and wailing cry with mournful misery.

Black is the Inlet, seething seas fling hungry arms on high!
The gale sweeps through the Narrows and lightning rips the sky
While under lee of sawmill wharf the paddle tugboats lie.

Their captains scan the frowning heav'ns, "Tis fools push off tonight!
We cannot face those surging seas that beat in monstrous might
Upon the cliffs and rockbound coast of Atkinson's great light!"

"Oh, pity! pity! Who will go with me on errand blest?"
Ah, daughter of a valiant race, thy life to good confessed!
Wouldst dare the tumult of the winds that suff'ring find rest?

"No! No!" the hoary captains said; but up spake Indian brave:
"With me you go, most merciful, a dying one to save—
Chinalset strong, a Squamish son, fears not the leaping wave!"

And as they pass from foaming crest to foaming crest tossed high,
A tiny speck upon the sea, revealed by fork-ripped sky,
The hours to those upon the shore are slowly creeping by.

The paddles swing and dipping meet the lift of swelling tide,
Then lost to sight, engulfed between black billows brimming wide,
Until it seems no earthly hope their little craft can guide.

Drenched with the clinging salted spray, frozen with icy wind,
Rising and falling in the gloom that swathes of darkness bind,
They bravely battle with the storm the gleaming lamp to find.

On land the watchers, huddled, wait and offer fervent prayer—
But in the dugout, tossed like cork, the woman shows no fear,
And searches strange abysmal dusk to see Skay-witsut near.

Lo, now red Phoebus heralds day across the eastern sky,
And silently the mighty waves in still submission lie—
To sink into the ocean's depth as morning cometh nigh.

And in the birth of rosy dawn, thro' rift of parting cloud,
In sudden white proximity, the lighthouse looming proud
Reveals to nerve-wracked voyagers its noble form unbowed.

And then unfolded through the haze of quickly breaking day
A nestling cove with shining sands in golden welcome lay,
That drew them to its sheltered beach beneath rock bastions grey.

The keeper waits with fearful heart to guide them carefully
O'er roughened trail; by thicket deep, by darkling forest tree—
Until with weary gratefulness the lighthouse door they see.

Thus soon our Mistress Patterson above the sufferer bends
And by her touch and healing grace soft, restful slumber lends,
As from her heart Doxology unto her God ascends!

APPENDIX 4

Emily's Death Certificate

BIRTHS, DEATHS AND MARRIAGES REGISTRATION ACT

SCHEDULE B.—Deaths.

Registration District of _Vancouver_

No.	881
Name and surname of deceased.	Emily Susan Patterson
When died.	Nov 12th 1909
Where died.	Vancouver B.C.
Sex.	Female.
	73 Years.
Rank or profession.	Widow
Where born.	Portland Maine U.S.A.
Certified cause of death, and duration of illness.	Senility 12 weeks
Name of Physician, if any.	Wm C. McKechnie
Signature, description and residence of informant.	J H Clegg Undertaker Van B.C.
When registered.	Nov — 13 — 1909
Religious denomination.	Ch of England
Signature of Registrar.	A B Pottinger, Cmr
REMARKS.	

I hereby certify the foregoing to be the correct Record of the death of
made in pursuance of the provisions of the above-mentioned Act.

As WITNESS my Hand at   Province of British Columbia,

this   day of   , A.D. 19

_____
Registrar.

AUTHOR'S NOTE

From my early days of childhood I decided that I had a horror of nurses. Nurses were people who drew pictures of bunny rabbits on your arm with something bright red called "mercurochrome," brandished a hypodermic needle and cheerfully announced, "Now let's give bunny a drink of water!" I did not fall for it.

What a pity that I had never known a nurse by the name of Emily Susan Patterson.

While gathering research material for my previous book, *Vancouver Is Ashes: The Great Fire of 1886* (Ronsdale Press, 2014), I came across so many long-buried details of early First Nation and pioneering women on Burrard Inlet that further investigation beckoned. A tantalizing title played before my eyes—*Gastown Women: Their Untold Stories*. Realizing that I had set myself a daunting task, I resolved to simplify matters by using the chronological approach. I drew up a list, planning to focus upon one woman at a time. As it happened, Alice Patterson Crakanthorp was the first name on that list.

In the words of her daughter Alice, Emily Patterson was "a very strong-minded woman; she was afraid of nothing, feared nothing, wasn't afraid of anything." The tributes continued to pour in as my research progressed. Emily was "the Heroine of Moodyville," described repeatedly as "a wonderful woman." She had won the admiration and trust of everyone she encountered. Before long, I was so completely immersed with Emily that I decided to make her story my solitary project.

There were roadblocks. While much valuable information on Emily had been recorded by Vancouver City Archivist Major James Skitt Matthews in conversations with members of her family, there were few direct words from Emily herself. The Patterson family had arrived at Hastings Mill in 1873, when amenities like local newspapers and photography studios were nonexistent. Documentation was haphazard and incomplete. If Emily had kept a daily journal, it was not to be found. If she had written newsy letters to family and friends, they were untraceable. A family Bible, said to have been donated to Vancouver City Archives, had inexplicably vanished. It was clear that Emily was a woman of remarkable courage and endurance, yet the *real* Emily, along with her innermost thoughts and feelings, hopes and dreams, lay just beneath the surface—never quite materializing in the way that I had envisioned on paper.

After much deliberation and soul-searching, I decided to employ a smattering of creative licence along with my original plan of writing a biographically correct, true-to-life retelling of Emily's story. While most names, dates and basic details throughout this book are factual, certain embellishments have been added to better show Emily for whom she was and how profoundly she touched the lives of so many individuals. I like to think that she would have approved.

Part proceeds from sales of this book are being donated to the non-profit B.C. History of Nursing Society, for use in their scholarship program. Originally founded by interested registered nurses in 1989 as the B.C. History of Nursing Professional Practice Group, the organization became registered under the Society Act of B.C. in 2008. The B.C. History of Nursing Society's ongoing mission is "to discover, disseminate, and preserve B.C.'s nursing history." Many interesting artifacts and documents related to B.C. nursing are preserved in the Society's archival collection on the UBC campus. Two scholarships are provided each year to nurses and student nurses preparing master's and doctoral theses with a focus on the rich history of nursing in British Columbia. On behalf of the B.C. History of Nursing Society, *thank you for your support*!

ACKNOWLEDGEMENTS

I extend my utmost appreciation to Ronald Hatch of Ronsdale Press for giving me the opportunity to daylight the long-buried story of a very deserving Emily. Special thanks to Julie Cochrane for the beautiful cover design and layout, as well as the ever-efficient Meagan Dyer for streamlining the editing process.

Peter Goodwin and Robin Haynes of the Sagadahoc History and Genealogy Room, Patten Free Library in Bath, Maine, dug deep for many Emily-related items. Marla Davis, Kerry Nelson and Amy Wesson of the West Bath Historical Society were also of assistance. Staff and volunteers at the Alberni Valley Museum and Alberni District Historical Society were most helpful in tracking Emily's Alberni years. Special thanks to Judy Carlson, Shelley Harding and Kirsten Smith for all their assistance. Donna and Mark Hinds, historical interpreters at beautiful Champoeg State Heritage Area, were wonderful with their research assistance and hospitality. Thanks as well to Judy Van Atta of Newell Pioneer Village.

City of Vancouver Archives staff member Chak Yung, among others, was most helpful with my search for Emily-related material. Staff members of Vancouver Public Library Special Collections were also of great assistance. Janet Turner and Karen Dearlove of North Vancouver Museum and Archives were most helpful. The extraordinary amount of research undertaken by Dick Lazenby and Judy Koren was of welcome use. Many thanks as well, Judy, for the wonderful walking tour on the former site of Moodyville. Elaine Graham gave us a fascinating, close-up look at Point Atkinson Lighthouse and surviving remnants from the Erwin years. Many thanks to Rob Godard for helping me to identify the most likely route taken by Emily and her First Nation guides in 1883.

It has been a pleasure to work with members of the B.C. History of Nursing Society—notably Kathleen Murphy, Helen Shore, Sheila Zerr, Nan Martin, Glennis Zilm, Marjory Ralston and Francis Mansbridge. A special "Mahsie" goes to Professor Jay Powell and MLA Sam Sullivan for introducing me to the colourful world of Chinook wawa. I was honoured to liaise with amazing author/historian Jean Barman, who kindly gave me access to her extensive research on John "Gassy Jack" Deighton and Qua-hail-ya. I extend my gratitude to Vanessa Campbell, Lea Edgar, David Gosse, Taryl Guenter, Lorraine Irving, Eve Lazarus, Tiffany Link, Latash Maurice Nahanee, Dale and Archie Miller, Josephine Pegler, Jo Pleshakov, Mary Schaff, James Schmidt, Chelsea Shriver, Reto Tschan, Donald Waite and Native Daughters of B.C. Post #1 for all their assistance.

My intrepid Writers Group—Norma Dixon, Dorothy Macey and Nora Schubert—patiently point me in the right direction while tolerating my egotistical rants and substandard baking. I cannot put into words how much these three ladies mean to me.

To extended members of Emily's family—Michael and Tatiana Swanson, Brooks and Dean Patterson, Rosemary and Andrew Martin, Patricia and Andrew Crakanthorp—I thank you for allowing me the honour of sharing Emily's story. To my own dear family—Doug, Hillary, Bobby, Sunny and Eileen Boberg—I extend much love and gratitude to you all for your support in this latest journey.

Last but not least, I extend my deep appreciation to Jolene Cumming, specialist in B.C. women's history, who laid the groundwork for this project.

NOTES

+ CHAPTER 1: NURSE IN TRAINING

PAGE 8: **Prohibition in the state of Maine:** "The Maine Law." www.state. me.us/legis/general/history/hstry8.htm (accessed January 2015).

+ CHAPTER 2: A CAPTAIN'S WIFE

PAGE 13: **"He hated it":** Canadian Broadcasting Corporation Alice Crakanthorp interview, February 25, 1961. B.C. Archives T1332:0001.

PAGE 18: **Queen Victoria in childbirth:** "The Anaesthetized Queen and the Path to Painless Childbirth." https://thechirurgeonsapprentice.com/2014/08/15/the-anaesthetized-queen-the-path-to-painless-childbirth (accessed March 2015).

PAGE 19: **Orphan Trains:** "The Children's Aid Society: The Orphan Trains." www.childrensaidsociety.org/about/history/orphan-trains (accessed February 2015).

+ CHAPTER 3: TO THE WEST

PAGE 31: **Abraham Lincoln:** "Executive Order—General War Order No. 1," January 27, 1862: Online by Gerhard Peters and John T. Woolley, *The American Presidency Project.* www.presidency.ucsb.edu/ws/?pid=69787 (accessed March 2015).

+ CHAPTER 4: QUARANTINE

PAGE 35: **"As our city is now in almost weekly communication . . .":** "Small Pox," *Daily British Colonist*, March 19, 1862, 3.

PAGE 36: **"... fearful calamity ..."**: "Quarantine," *Daily British Colonist*, March 26, 1862, 2.

↠ CHAPTER 5: ALBERNI

PAGE 40: **Graveyard of the Pacific**: "Graveyard of the Pacific: Shipwrecks on the Washington Coast." www.historylink.org/File/7936 (accessed March 2015).

PAGE 44: **"... the encampment was in commotion"**: Jan Peterson, *The Albernis: 1860–1922* (Lantzville, B.C.: Oolichan Books, 1992), 28.

↠ CHAPTER 6: "NOT KING GEORGE"

PAGE 47: **"It's probably because you're not 'King George'!"**: CBC Alice Crakanthorp interview.

PAGE 49: **"... for the sake of caution ..."**: James Morton, *The Enterprising Mr. Moody, the Bumptious Captain Stamp* (Vancouver, B.C.: J.J. Douglas, 1977), 24.

↠ CHAPTER 7: CHAMPOEG

PAGE 58: **Champoeg flood of 1861**: Mary E. Higley, "Friends of Historic Champoeg: A Personal Account of the 1861 Flood." www.champoeg.org/learn-more/a-personal-account-of-the-1861-flood.html (accessed April 2015).

↠ CHAPTER 8: JOURNEY OF SORROW

PAGE 65: **Origin of name "malaria"**: "Story of Quinine," Interactive Autism Network. https://iancommunity.org/cs/what_do_we_know/story_of_quinine (accessed April 2015).

PAGE 66: **Warburg's Tincture contents**: Warburg's Tincture was a potent concoction of roots, seeds and aloes infused with alcohol and disulphate of quinine. "Warburg's Tincture," Revolvy. www.revolvy.com/topic/Warburg's%20Tincture&item_type=topic (accessed April 2015).

PAGE 67: **Frank Patterson cause of death**: Research would eventually determine that malarial parasites travel to the liver, where they develop and multiply—ultimately rupturing into the circulatory system. Red blood cells are attacked and destroyed, leading to severe anemia. Small blood vessels in the brain and lungs become vulnerable to blockage. If the entire process is not corrected through treatment or the body's natural capability to heal, vital organs like the kidneys begin to shut down due to prolonged shock. A Scottish physician named Ronald Ross, later to be knighted and receive the 1902 Nobel Prize in Medicine, would prove that certain mosquito species were the vectors for transmitting malaria parasites to humans. "The History of Malaria, an Ancient Disease," Centers for Disease Control and Prevention. www.cdc.gov/malaria/about/history (accessed April 2015).

⇢ CHAPTER 10: HASTINGS MILL

PAGE 90: **"I'm a nurse"**: CBC Alice Crakanthorp interview.

⇢ CHAPTER 11: CROSSROADS OF CULTURES

PAGE 96: **"Well, they wouldn't dare lay a hand on you!"**: CBC Alice Crakanthorp interview.

PAGE 96: **"They're human like the rest of us"**: Major James Skitt Matthews, *Early Vancouver*, Vol. 4 (Vancouver: City of Vancouver, 2011), 122.

⇢ CHAPTER 12: "A FUNNY LITTLE PLACE"

PAGE 103: **June 1866 description of Moodyville**: James Morton, *The Enterprising Mr. Moody, the Bumptious Captain Stamp* (Vancouver, B.C.: J.J. Douglas, 1977), 72.

PAGE 103: **"It was a funny little place . . ."**: Moodyville Park signage, City of North Vancouver.

⇢ CHAPTER 13: THE CUSTOM OF THE COUNTRY

PAGE 108: **"Marriages according to . . ."**: Jay Nelson, "A Strange Revolution in the Manners of the Country: Aboriginal–Settler Intermarriage in Nineteenth-Century British Columbia." www.ubcpress.ca/books/pdf/chapters/regulatinglives/chap1.pdf (accessed April 2015).

⇢ CHAPTER 14: THE PASSING OF THE FOUNDERS

PAGE 115: **Gassy Jack's final words**: Raymond Hull, *Gastown's Gassy Jack: The Life and Times of John Deighton of England, California and Early British Columbia* (Vancouver, B.C.: Gordon Soules Economic Research, 1971), 43.

PAGE 116: **"Something sweet and pink in colour!"**: Matthews, *Early Vancouver*, Vol. 3, 309.

PAGE 117: **Report on wreck of SS Pacific**: "Last Night Dispatches: Washington Territory," *Daily British Colonist*, November 9, 1875, 2.

PAGE 118: **"S.P. Moody all lost"**: Vancouver Maritime Museum artifact #Ch2_32.

→ CHAPTER 15: PRESTIGIOUS COMPANY

PAGE 120: **"We will all be grey-haired before it does"**: Matthews, *Early Vancouver*, Vol. 4, 109.

PAGE 123: **"Remind me of the words to 'God Save the Queen'!"**: Matthews, *Early Vancouver*, Vol. 4, 126.

PAGE 124: **". . . I'll hit you over the head with a club!"**: Matthews, *Early Vancouver*, Vol. 4, 105.

PAGE 127: **". . . go right over and see the doctor"**: Matthews, *Early Vancouver*, Vol. 4, 106.

PAGE 128: **"The fracture is not to be of serious character"**: Patterson, John P. fam.doc. North Vancouver Museum and Archives.

PAGE 128: **"Everyone calls him Windy Wymond"**: Matthews, *Early Vancouver*, Vol. 4, 123.

→ CHAPTER 16: DAYS OF PAIN AND SOLACE

PAGE 129: **"She's not well at all, Mama"**: Matthews, *Early Vancouver*, Vol. 4, 132.

PAGE 133: **Addie Patterson obituary**: "New Westminster Items," *Daily British Colonist*, October 26, 1879, 3.

PAGE 136: **". . . the real pioneers on Burrard Inlet"**: Matthews, *Early Vancouver*, Vol. 4, 120.

PAGE 137: **"Why not call it after you, James?"**: Matthews, *Early Vancouver*, Vol. 5, 25.

→ CHAPTER 17: MODERN TIMES

PAGE 140: **"I want you all to put on your best clothes . . ."**: Squire Jones Randall, CVA AM0054.013.03835.

PAGE 145: **"It was horrible!"**: Matthews, *Early Vancouver*, Vol. 4, 119.

→ CHAPTER 18: POINT ATKINSON

PAGE 156: **"I knew you'd come!"**: Major Matthews Incoming Correspondence, *The Epic Story of Mrs. Patterson of Moodyville*. City of Vancouver Archives ADD.MSS No. 54, Vol. 14A, File 30, p. 1851–1854.

→ CHAPTER 20: HISTORIC DAYS

PAGE 169: **"Gastown is burning!"**: CBC Alice Crakanthorp interview.

PAGE 171: **"Mother, I saved my glasses!"**: Matthews, *Early Vancouver*, Vol. 3, 313.

PAGE 171: **"You're all here"**: CBC Alice Crakanthorp interview.

PAGE 171: **"It's so very pitiful, Mama"**: Matthews, *Early Vancouver*, Vol. 3, 313.

→ CHAPTER 21: SISTER FRANCES

PAGE 179: **Signage on the first through CPR train to Vancouver:** "The First Train Reaches Vancouver City on Time Yesterday," *Daily Colonist*, May 24, 1887, 1.

PAGE 187: **Pricing for care at first official City Hospital:** *William's Vancouver and New Westminster Cities Directory 1890*. Hospitals: The City Hospital, 72.

→ CHAPTER 22: OUTBREAK

PAGE 192: **Spread of smallpox in Victoria:** "Precautions Necessary," *Vancouver Daily News-Advertiser*, July 8, 1892, 4.

PAGE 192: **"... very sick and scarcely expected to recover"**: "Precautions Against Small Pox," *Vancouver Daily News-Advertiser*, July 9, 1892, 1.

PAGE 194: **Communications regarding arrival of SS Yosemite in Vancouver:** "The *Yosemite* to Arrive: Her Passengers will be Prevented from Landing by Sheer Force," *Vancouver Daily News-Advertiser*, July 13, 1892, 3.

PAGE 196: **"Notwithstanding clean bills of health . . ."**: "Reinforcing the Quarantine: The *Yosemite* not Allowed to Land her Passengers unless Submitting to Quarantine Rules," *Vancouver Daily News-Advertiser*, July 14, 1892, 5.

✦ CHAPTER 23: LOST SOULS

PAGE 202: **"Now get down on your knees . . .":** Matthews, *Early Vancouver*, Vol. 4, 139.

PAGE 204: **"They tell me he made a good end":** Ian Kennedy, *Sunny Sandy Savary* (Vancouver: Kennell Publishing, 1992), 50.

✦ CHAPTER 24: RETURN TO VANCOUVER

PAGE 205: **Opening of St. Paul's Hospital:** "St. Paul's Hospital," *Vancouver Daily News-Advertiser*, November 24, 1894, 5.

✦ CHAPTER 25: USTLAWN

PAGE 216: **The "Durieu System":** Jacqueline Gresko, "Durieu, Paul," in *Dictionary of Canadian Biography*, Vol. 12 (University of Toronto/Université Laval, 2003). www.biographi.ca/en/bio/durieu_paul_12E.html (accessed September 2015).

PAGE 220: **". . . a soul could not possibly be 'clawed out'":** Matthews, *Early Vancouver*, Vol. 3, 92.

✦ CHAPTER 26: TAKING RESPONSIBILITY

PAGE 227: **"For twenty-five minutes . . .":** "Ambulance Mismanagement Arouses Indignation of the Ladies Committee," *Vancouver Daily Province*, October 9, 1902, 1.

PAGE 228: **"My hands have been tied . . .":** "Verdict of Death by Accident; Rider on the Ambulance Question," *Vancouver Daily Province*, October 11, 1902, 1.

PAGE 229: **"Mayor Thomas Neelands had the final say":** "Take Action on Street Ends: The Ambulance," *Vancouver Daily Province*, October 14, 1902, 9.

✦ CHAPTER 27: TRAGEDY IN TWO CITIES

PAGE 232: **". . . practically a wilderness . . .":** "The Vancouver General Hospital 1902–1923," *Daily Province 25th Anniversary Edition*, March 26, 1923, 6.

PAGE 235: **". . . loss of life was 'incapable as yet of approximation'":** "San Francisco Riven by Earthquake and Swept by Flame," *Vancouver Daily News-Advertiser*, April 19, 1906, 1.

PAGE 240: **"If it had happened many miles away . . ."**: "Passenger-Laden Craft is Sunk in the Narrows; Ten Lives Lost: From the Pulpit," *Vancouver Daily World*, July 23, 1906, 7.

+ CHAPTER 29: THE HEROINE OF MOODYVILLE

PAGE 252: **Official cause of Emily's death**: Province of British Columbia, Births, Deaths and Marriages Registration Act. Schedule B—Deaths. Registration District of Vancouver, Emily Susan Patterson Death Certificate, No. 881, 308.1.

PAGE 252–53: **Emily Patterson obituary**: "Obituary: Mrs. J.P. Patterson," *Vancouver World*, November 13, 1909, 6.

PAGE 254: **Dr. Langis's letter to Muriel Crakanthorp**: CVA Patterson, J.P. AM0054.013.03571.

PAGE 255: **". . . she was afraid of nothing!"**: Matthews, *Early Vancouver*, Vol. 4, 119.

+ APPENDIX 1: EMILY'S FAMILY

PAGE 260: **Alice Crakanthorp's comments on her 95th birthday**: "You Want to Live Longer? 'Live it Up' Says Little Mrs. Crakanthorp," *Daily Colonist*, April 10, 1960, 16.

PAGE 262: **Alice Crakanthorp recalls grand ball at opening of Hotel Vancouver**: CBC Alice Crakanthorp interview.

PAGE 262: **Major Matthews's telegram of condolence to Muriel Crakanthorp**: Canadian Pacific Telegram, Vancouver, B.C., Oct 10—61 410P (Courtesy Michael Swanson).

+ APPENDIX 2: IN EMILY'S FOOTSTEPS

PAGE 264: **Journal record from HMS Scout on Alberni decline**: Jan Peterson, *The Albernis: 1860–1922* (Lantzville, B.C.: Oolichan Books, 1992), 36.

PAGE 270: **Development of granite quarry on North Arm**: Ralph Drew, "Granite Falls History." www.belcarra.ca/reports/Granite_Falls_History.pdf.

PAGE 272: **Nurse's Memorial**: "Nurse's Window," Christ Church Cathedral, Vancouver, B.C. CVA PAM Und. 414.

→ APPENDIX 3: "THE HEROINE OF MOODYVILLE"

PAGE 273–76: **"The Heroine of Moodyville" poem**: Nora Duncan, *"Emily Patterson: The Heroine of Moodyville: An Epic of Burrard Inlet, 1883."* CVA PAM 1936-52.

BIBLIOGRAPHY

PRIMARY SOURCES

⇥ British Columbia Archives

British Columbia Vital Events Indexes.

Canadian Broadcasting Corporation Alice Crakanthorp interview. Item T1332: 0001.

⇥ City of Vancouver Archives

Major Matthews Topical Files, Volumes 1–7.

Matthews, Major. *The Epic Story of Mrs. Patterson of Moodyville.* Vancouver, B.C.: City of Vancouver Archives Incoming Correspondence, Volume 14A File 30, p. 1851–1854, Nov. 23, 1935.

St. James Church Fonds. AM 403.

St. James Parish Paper 1893. PAM 1893-1.

Goad's Fire Insurance Map 1912.

John Peabody Patterson Genealogy as recorded by Muriel Crakanthorp, May 25, 1934.

Microfiche Patterson, J.P. #AM0054.013.03571.

Crakanthorp, Mrs. Alice and Muriel. AM54-S23-2--.

William's Vancouver and New Westminster Cities Directory 1890–1909.

✦ **Patten Free Library, Sagadahoc History and Genealogy Room, Bath, Maine**

Emily Susan Patterson Birth Record. Bath Vital Records: Compiled Records 1757–1892 Microfilm Roll # 10562.

Bath Real Estate Valuations 1847–48.

✦ **North Vancouver Museum and Archives**

Lazenby, A.L. (Dick). *Moody and Moodyville*. Accession number 2010–044.

Lazenby, A.L. (Dick). *The Moodyville Manuscript*. Accession number 2010–044.

Lazenby, A.L. (Dick). Patterson, John P. Fam.doc.

✦ **AncestryLibrary.com**

U.S. Federal Census records, 1850–1930.

U.S. City Directories, 1822–1995.

California, Death Index, 1940–1997.

U.S. Find a Grave Index, 1600s–Current.

✦ **Ancestry.ca**

California, Passenger and Crew Lists, 1882–1959.

Census of Canada Records, 1891, 1901, 1921.

British Columbia, Canada, Death Index, 1972–1990.

Canada, Voters Lists, 1935–1980.

Vancouver, British Columbia, Mountain View Cemetery Index, 1887–2007: Emily Susan Patterson.

✦ **Vancouver Public Library**

British Columbia City Directories 1860–1955. Online at www.vpl.ca/bccd.

✦ **Vancouver Maritime Museum**

Union Steamship Company Collection 1898–2003.

✦ **Newspapers**

Daily British Colonist

Daily Province

Mainland Guardian

San Francisco Call

Sun

Times Colonist

Vancouver Daily News-Advertiser

Vancouver Daily World/Vancouver World

Vancouver News

Vancouver Province

Vancouver Sun

PUBLISHED SOURCES

Alberni Valley Museum and Archives. *Hisheenqu'as, Living Together: Alberni and the Birth of the B.C. Forest Industry*. Port Alberni, B.C.: Alberni Valley Museum and Archives, 2011.

"American Civil War History." Online at www.history.com/topics/american-civil-war/american-civil-war-history (accessed March 2015).

Andrews, M.W. *St. Luke's Home, Vancouver 1888–1936: A Transitional Hospital*. Canadian Church Historical Society Journal, Vol. 24, R 283.705 C21j.

Atkin, John. *Strathcona: Vancouver's First Neighbourhood*. North Vancouver, B.C.: Whitecap Books, 1994.

Barman, Jean. *Stanley Park's Secret*. Madeira Park, B.C.: Harbour Publishing, 2005.

Barnholden, Michael. *Reading the Riot Act: A Brief History of Riots in Vancouver*. Vancouver, B.C.: Anvil Press, 2005.

Bath Historical Society. Online at http://bathhistorical.com (accessed January 2015).

Biography.com: "Florence Nightingale: Nurse (1820–1910)." Online at www.biography.com/people/florence-nightingale-9423539#synopsis (accessed February 2015).

Biography.com: "Louis Pasteur: Chemist, Scientist, Inventor (1822–1895)." Online at www.biography.com/people/louis-pasteur-9434402 (accessed April 2015).

Bogan, Dallas. "The Soap Making Process from the Olden Days." Online at www.tngenweb.org/campbell/hist-bogan/SoapMaking.html (accessed February 2015).

Burrardview Community Association: "History of Our Community." Online at http://burrardview.ca (accessed May 2015).

Capilano Suspension Bridge Park: "Our History." Online at www.capbridge.com/our-story/history (accessed September 2015).

Centers for Disease Control and Prevention: "The History of Malaria, an Ancient Disease." Online at www.cdc.gov/malaria/about/history (accessed April 2015).

Centers for Disease Control and Prevention: "History of Smallpox." Online at www.cdc.gov/smallpox/history/history.html (accessed March 2015).

Chanchal Cabrera: "A Review of Some Medicinal Plants of the Pacific North West." Online at www.chanchalcabrera.com/medicinal-plants-of-pacific-north-west (accessed May 2015).

Changing the Face of Medicine: "Dr. Elizabeth Blackwell." Online at https://cfmedicine.nlm.nih.gov/physicians/biography_35.html (accessed February 2015).

Children's Aid Society, The: "The Orphan Trains." Online at www.childrensaidsociety.org/about/history/orphan-trains (accessed February 2015).

Chirurgeon's Apprentice, The: "The Anaesthetized Queen and the Path to Painless Childbirth." Online at https://thechirurgeonsapprentice.com/2014/08/15/the-anaesthetized-queen-the-path-to-painless-childbirth (accessed February 2015).

Chronicle and SeeSouthwestWa.Com: "Journey on the Cowlitz." Online at http://cowlitz.seesouthwestwa.com/cowlitz-river-gave-birth-to-town-of-toledo (accessed April 2015).

City of Rainier: "Spirited City on the Mighty Columbia." Online at www. cityofrainier.com (accessed April 2015).

Civil War Trust: "Battle of Hampton Roads Monitor vs. Merrimac." Online at www.civilwar.org/learn/civil-war/battles/hampton-roads (accessed March 2015).

Clark, Charles E. *Maine: A History*. New York, NY: W.W. Norton and Company, 1977.

Claydon, Peter S.N. and Valerie Melanson. *Vancouver Voters, 1886: A Biographical Dictionary*. Richmond, B.C.: The B.C. Genealogical Society, 1994.

Cohen, Stan. *The Streets Were Paved With Gold: A Pictorial History of the Klondike Gold Rush 1896–1899*. Missoula, Montana: Pictorial Histories Publishing, 1977.

Crafts, Daniel Stevens. "Barbary Coast Historical Essay." Online at www. foundsf.org/index.php?title=BARBARY_COAST (accessed February 2015).

Dary, David. *Frontier Medicine: From the Atlantic to the Pacific 1492–1941*. Alfred A. Knopf, 2008.

Davis, Marla. "Looking for Granny Lombard—Our First Doctor." *The Middle Ground*, Spring 2003, 5.

Drew, Ralph. "History of Granite Falls." Online at www.belcarra.ca/reports/ Granite_Falls_History.pdf (accessed September 2015).

"England and China: The Opium Wars, 1839–60." Online at: www.victorian-web.org/history/empire/opiumwars/opiumwars1.html (accessed February 2015).

Feldhusen, Adrian E. "The History of Midwifery and Childbirth in America: A Time Line." Online at www.midwiferytoday.com/articles/timeline.asp (accessed February 2015).

Find a Grave: "John C. Branscomb." Online at www.findagrave.com/cgi-bin/ fg.cgi?page=gr&GSln=Branscomb&GSiman=1&GScid=90187&GR id=78652102& (accessed February 2015).

Francis, Daniel. *Where Mountains Meet the Sea: An Illustrated History of the District of North Vancouver*. Madeira Park, B.C.: Harbour Publishing, 2016.

Friends of Historic Champoeg. Online at www.champoeg.org (accessed April 2015).

Gill, Frank B. "Oregon's First Railway: The Oregon Portage Railroad at the Cascades of the Columbia River." Online at www.jstor.org/stable/20610279? seq=1#page_scan_tab_contents (accessed March 2015).

Golden Gate Park: "Views from the Thicket: Trees of the Panhandle." Online at https://fromthethicket.com/2010/09/16/trees-of-the-panhandle (accessed August 2015).

Goodwin, Peter and Robin A.S. Haynes. "Bath's Historic Downtown." Online at http://bath.mainememory.net/page/938/display.html (accessed January 2015).

Goodwin, Peter and Robin A.S. Haynes. "History of Bath Maine." Online at https://visitbath.com/history (accessed January 2015).

Government of Maine: "The Maine Law." Online at www.state.me.us/legis/ general/history/hstry8.htm (accessed January 2015).

Graham, Donald. *Keepers of the Light: A History of British Columbia's Lighthouses and their Keepers*. Madeira Park, B.C.: Harbour Publishing, 1985.

"Graveyard of the Pacific: Shipwrecks on the Washington Coast." Online at www.historylink.org/File/7936 (accessed February 2015).

Gresko, Jacqueline. "Durieu, Paul," in *Dictionary of Canadian Biography*, Vol. 12, University of Toronto/Université Laval, 2003. Online at www.biographi.ca/en/bio/durieu_paul_12E.html (accessed September 2015).

Hamilton, Valerie. *The Schools of Old Vancouver*. Vancouver, B.C.: Renfrew Elementary School, Vancouver School Board, 1986.

Hayes, Derek. *Historical Atlas of British Columbia and the Lower Fraser Valley*. Vancouver, B.C.: Douglas and McIntyre, 2005.

Historica Canada: "Fort Victoria." Online at www.thecanadianencyclopedia. ca/en/article/fort-victoria (accessed March 2015).

Historica Canada: "Lady Aberdeen." Online at www.thecanadianencyclopedia.ca/en/article/ishbel-gordon-lady-aberdeen (accessed August 2015).

History.com: "Brigham Young." Online at www.history.com/topics/brigham-young (accessed April 2015).

History.com: "John Brown's Harper's Ferry." Online at www.history.com/ topics/harpers-ferry (accessed February 2015).

History.com: "Minié Ball." Online at www.history.com/topics/american-civil-war/minie-ball (accessed August 2017).

Holt, Alfred. *Bath Families in the 19th Century*. MS in Patten Free Library.

Hudson's Bay Company History Foundation: "Woodward's." Online at www.hbcheritage.ca/history/acquisitions/woodwards-stores-ltd (accessed September 2015).

Hull, Raymond. *Gastown's Gassy Jack: The Life and Times of John Deighton of England, California and Early British Columbia*. Vancouver, B.C.: Gordon Soules Economic Research, 1971.

Hussey, John A. *Champoeg: Place of Transition: A Disputed History*. Portland: Oregon Historical Society, 1967.

Interactive Autism Network: "Story of Quinine." Online at https://iancommunity.org/cs/what_do_we_know/story_of_quinine (accessed April 2015).

Johnson, Peter. *Voyages of Hope: The Saga of the Bride-Ships*. Victoria, B.C.: TouchWood Editions, 2002.

Kate Chopin: "Childbirth and Birth Control in the 19th Century." Online at www.loyno.edu/~kchopin/new/women/bcabortion.html (accessed February 2015).

Kennedy, Ian. *Sunny Sandy Savary: A History of Savary Island 1792–1992*. Vancouver, B.C.: Kennell Publishing, 1992.

Kirkwood, Charlotte Matheny. *Into the Eye of the Setting Sun: A Story of the West When It Was New*. Hewitt-Matheny-Cooper Family Association, 1991.

Koren, Judith. *Pioneer Families of North Vancouver*. Vancouver, B.C.: North Vancouver Museum and Archives Item 1158, 2016.

Lambert, Tim. "A Brief History of Bath." Online at www.localhistories.org/bath.html (accessed January 2015).

Lane Community College Library: "The Kalapuya: Native Americans of the Willamette Valley, Oregon." Online at http://libraryguides.lanecc.edu/kalapuya (accessed March 2015).

Lee, A. Winifred. *Pioneer Women of Mainland Knew Life in the Raw*. Vancouver, B.C.: *Vancouver Daily Province*, Magazine section, May 20, 1944, 3.

Lighthouse Park Preservation Society: "The History of Lighthouse Park." Online at www.lpps.ca/history-of-lighthouse-park (accessed June 2015).

Maritime Heritage Project, The: "Ships, Captains, Passengers—San Francisco 1846–1899." Online at www.maritimeheritage.org/ships/shippingLines.html (accessed March 2015).

Matthews, Major James Skitt. *Early Vancouver, Volumes 1–7.* Vancouver, B.C.: Vancouver Archives, 1932.

Medical News Today: "Scurvy: Causes, Symptoms and Treatment." Online at www.medicalnewstoday.com/articles/155758.php (accessed August 2017).

Memory BC: "St. Luke's Home (Vancouver, B.C.)." Online at www.memorybc.ca/st-lukes-home-vancouver-b-c (accessed July 2015).

Mental Floss: "The Historical Horror of Childbirth." Online at http://mentalfloss.com/article/50513/historical-horror-childbirth (accessed February 2015).

Metchosin Museum Society: "Quarantine Station." Online at http://metchosinmuseum.ca/heritage-sites/quarantine-station (accessed July 2015).

Morley, Alan. *Vancouver: From Milltown to Metropolis.* Vancouver, B.C.: Mitchell Press, 1961.

Morton, James. *The Enterprising Mr. Moody, the Bumptious Captain Stamp.* Vancouver, B.C.: J.J. Douglas, 1977.

Munro St. John, Rose. "Dauntless Doctors and Horses Served Tiny Vancouver: Emily Patterson Was Doctor, Nurse and Friend to Entire Settlement." *Vancouver Province*, July 18, 1936, Magazine section, 5.

Munro St. John, Rose. "First Shingle Was Hung in Vancouver in 1877." *Vancouver Province*, Sept. 23, 1950, Magazine section, 3.

Museum of Vancouver: "1907 Anti-Asian Riots Teacher's Notes." Online at www.museumofvancouver.ca/sites/default/files/MOVedu%20Anti-Asian%20Riots%20Story.pdf (accessed September 2015).

Mushroom Appreciation: "Oyster Mushrooms: Culinary, Medicinal and Environmental Benefits." Online at www.mushroom-appreciation.com/oyster-mushrooms.html#sthash.F5HK1Drv.dpbs (accessed August 2017).

National Capital Poison Center: "Ipecac." Online at www.poison.org/articles/ipecac (accessed August 2017).

National Marine Sanctuaries: "SS *City of Rio de Janeiro*." Online at http://sanctuaries.noaa.gov/shipwrecks/city-of-rio-de-janeiro (accessed August 2015).

Nelson, Jay. "A Strange Revolution in the Manners of the Country: Aboriginal-Settler Intermarriage in Nineteenth Century British Columbia." Online at www.ubcpress.ca/books/pdf/chapters/regulatinglives/chap1.pdf (accessed April 2015).

Newell Pioneer Village. Online at http://newellpioneervillage.com (accessed March 2015).

New World Encyclopedia: "Florence Nightingale." Online at www.newworldencyclopedia.org/entry/Florence_Nightingale (accessed February 2015).

Nightingale, Florence. *Notes on Nursing: What It Is and What It Is Not.* London, England: Harrison, 1946. (Facsimile of the first edition printed in London, 1859).

Nomura, Kazuko. "They Who Part the Grass: The Japanese Government and Early Nikkei Immigration to Canada, 1877–1908." Online at http://mspace.lib.umanitoba.ca/xmlui/bitstream/handle/1993/5253/Nomura_Kazuko.pdf (accessed August 2017).

Oregon Encyclopedia, The: "Camas." Online at https://oregonencyclopedia.org/articles/camas/#.WTK-Gbigvo4 (accessed March 2015).

Owen, Henry Wilson. *The Edward Clarence Plummer History of Bath, Maine.* Bath, Maine: Bath Area Bicentennial Committee, 1976.

Oxford Medicine Online: "History of Dental Anaesthesia." Online at http://oxfordmedicine.com/view/10.1093/med/9780199564217.001.0001/med-9780199564217-chapter-1 (accessed August 2017).

Panama Railroad, The. Online at www.panamarailroad.org/history1.html (accessed February 2015).

Peña, Devon. "GoodFood World: Salal: Food, Medicine and Culture of the Coast Salish Peoples." Online at www.goodfoodworld.com/2013/01/salal-food-medicine-and-culture-of-the-coast-salish-peoples (accessed May 2015).

Peterson, Jan. *The Albernis, 1860–1922.* Lantzville, B.C.: Oolichan Books, 1992.

Powell, Jay. *Chinook Jargon: The Language of Northwest Coast History.* Vancouver, B.C.: UBC Museum of Anthropology Archives, Jensen-Powell fonds (unpub. ms), 1973.

"Project of Heart: Illuminating the Hidden History of Indian Residential Schools in B.C." Online at www.bctf.ca/HiddenHistory/eBook.pdf (accessed June 2017).

Public Health Agency of Canada: "Scarlet Fever Fact Sheet." Online at www. phac-aspc.gc.ca/id-mi/scarl-eng.php (accessed June 2015).

Revolvy: "Warburg's Tincture." Online at www.revolvy.com/topic/Warburg's%20Tincture&item_type=topic (accessed April 2015).

RocketSwag.com: "Treatment for Scarlet Fever in the 1800s." Online at www. rocketswag.com/medicine/disease-prevention/infectious-diseases/bacteria/ scarlet-fever/Treatment-For-Scarlet-Fever-In-1800s.html (accessed June 2015).

Rushton, Gerald A. *Whistle up the Inlet: The Union Steamship Story*. Vancouver, B.C.: J.J. Douglas, 1974.

Shore, Helen L. "Emily Susan Patterson: Vancouver's First Nurse." *B.C. Historical News*, Summer 1993, 20.

Sleigh, Daphne. *The Man Who Saved Vancouver: Major James Skitt Matthews*. Surrey, B.C.: Heritage House Publishing, 2008.

Smedman, Lisa. *Vancouver: Stories of a City*. Vancouver, B.C.: Vancouver Courier, 2008.

Smith, Yolanda. "News Medical Life Sciences: Typhoid Fever History." Online at www.news-medical.net/health/Typhoid-Fever-History.aspx (accessed June 2015).

Sommer, Warren F. *The Ambitious City: A History of the City of North Vancouver*. Madeira Park, B.C.: Harbour Publishing, 2007.

Sullivan, Eleanor. "Midwifery in the 19th Century." Online at www.eleanorsullivan.com/2012/02/06/midwifery-in-the-19th-century (accessed February 2015).

"Telegraph Hill Historic District." Online at www.foundsf.org/index. php?title=Telegraph_Hill_Historic_District (accessed February 2015).

"Timeline of San Francisco History." Online at www.zpub.com/sf/history/ sfh2.html (accessed February 2015).

Underwood, Todd. "The Oregon Trail." Online at www.frontiertrails.com/ oldwest/oregontrail.htm (accessed February 2015).

Victorian Order of Nurses Canada. Online at www.von.ca (accessed August 2015).

Waite, Donald. *Vancouver Exposed: A History in Photographs*. Maple Ridge, B.C.: Waite Bird Photos Incorporated.

Webster, Henry Sewall. *Vital Records of Pittston, Maine, to the Year 1892*. Gardiner, Maine: The Reporter-Journal Press, 1911.

Woodward-Reynolds, Marjorie. "A History of the City and District of North Vancouver." Online at https://open.library.ubc.ca/cIRcle/collections/ubctheses/831/items/1.0098663 (accessed August 2017).

ABOUT THE AUTHOR

Lisa Anne Smith was born in Burnaby, B.C., and has been at work on the study of B.C. history for much of her life. She is a longtime education docent at the Museum of Vancouver and is a member of Native Daughters of B.C. Post #1, owners/operators of Old Hastings Mill Store Museum, Vancouver's oldest building. Her published books include *Our Friend Joe: The Joe Fortes Story* (Ronsdale Press, 2012), *Vancouver Is Ashes: The Great Fire of 1886* (Ronsdale Press, 2014) and *Travels with St. Roch: A Book for Kids* (2001). Lisa lives in Vancouver with her husband, occasionally-resident grown children and Sunny, the world's least intelligent but most lovable golden retriever.

INDEX

MARQUIS

Québec, Canada